FINANCIAL TIMES

PERSONAL FINANCE LIBRARY

Understanding

Mutual Funds

Your No-Nonsense Everyday Guide

By Steven G. Kelman

Penguin Books

PENGUIN BOOKS
Published by the Penguin Group
Penguin Books Canada Ltd., 10 Alcorn Avenue, Suite 300, Toronto, Canada, M4V 3B2
Penguin Books Ltd., 27 Wrights Lane, London W8 5TZ, England
Viking Penguin Inc., 40 West 23rd Street, New York, New York 10010, USA
Penguin Books Australia Ltd., Ringwood, Victoria, Australia
Penguin Books (NZ) Ltd., 182-190 Wairau Road, Auckland 10, New Zealand
Penguin Books Ltd., Registered Offices: Harmondsworth, Middlesex, England

Published in Penguin Books, 1991

10 9 8 7 6 5 4 3 2 1

The information in chapters fourteen, fifteen, and sixteen and in appendices one and two
was compiled by Southam Business Communications Inc. from data contained in its
Mutual Fund Sourcebook, Sourcedisk and mutual fund data bank. *Financial Times of
Canada* would like to express its appreciation to David Groskind and Allan Lou for their
cooperation.

Canadian Cataloguing in Publication Data
Kelman, Steven G. (Steve Gershon), 1945 –
Understanding mutual funds
(Financial times personal finance library)
Rev. and updated.
ISBN 0-14-016861-3

1. Mutual funds – Canada.   I. Title.   II. Series
HG5154.5.K45 1991   332.63'27   C91-095596-6

Cover design by: Creative Network
Cover illustration by: Thomas Dannenberg

CONTENTS

Tables and Illustrations

Introduction

INVESTOR INTEREST IN MUTUAL funds has soared in recent years as more Canadians have discovered the potential for profit in funds. Between the summer of 1982 and October 1987, the value of funds held by Canadians jumped seven-fold, from about $5 billion to about $35 billion, and the number of Canadians investing in funds had climbed from a few hundred thousand to close to 1.5 million. The October stock-market crash cooled investor ardor somewhat and, indeed, the value of mutual fund sales in the eight months following the crash ran at less than half its pre-crash level with sales barely exceeding redemptions. At the end of June 1988, the value of funds held by Canadians was about $30 billion. The trend soon reversed and by June 1990 the value of funds held by Canadians exceeded $41 billion, rising to $50 billion by June 1991.

The industry itself is going through a period of consolidation. In the year following the October 1987 crash, the number of funds offered climbed from about 390 to more than 483. Although the past three years has seen some consolidation with several smaller fund groups being taken over by larger organizations, investors could choose among more than 600 funds by mid-1991.

More financial service companies, including banks and trust companies, have entered the fund business. People who have never considered anything other than bank or trust company guaranteed investments are looking at funds.

The reasons are simple. Mutual funds offer professional investment management at an affordable price. They offer safety through diversified portfolios. There is a broad choice of funds to meet virtually every investment objective. Finally, funds have given investors excellent returns, better than most individuals would have been able to achieve on their own.

But choosing the right fund or funds from the hundreds offered by fund dealers, stockbrokers, banks, trust companies, insurance companies or fund managers directly can be confusing. First, buyers must consider the objectives of a fund and whether those objectives are compatible with their own investment goals. Second, they must determine how a fund has performed in recent years.

Understanding Mutual Funds explains in detail the aspects of the fund business that you need to understand to make a wise buying decision. *Understanding Mutual Funds*, for instance, shows you how fund managers manage their funds, how you can match funds to your specific investment objectives and your age, even how to evaluate a fund salesperson.

It also contains essential information on the largest 100 mutual funds in Canada to help you determine exactly which funds might best meet your personal investment objectives. A lot has happened in the world of Canadian mutual funds since *Mutual Fund Advisor*, the predecessor to *Understanding Mutual Funds*, was published in September 1986.

First and foremost in the minds of investors is the October 1987 stock-market crash. During that month, the Toronto Stock Exchange total return index, which is a broad measure of stock market performance, fell more than 22 percent. (From the August peak to the October trough the decline was 31 percent.) However, many funds which invest in Canadian stocks did a lot better than the general market. Indeed, some funds which held bonds made gains during October as interest rates fell. And even after the biggest market drop in a generation, most funds invested in stocks could still report positive returns for the year. What the October crash did was put the market back to where it had been less than a year earlier. The October disruption also gave some investors a buying opportunity. Those investors who bought at the October bottom – there were a few who had the courage – were up about 20 percent by the end of June 1988, if the performance of their investments matched that of the stock market itself.

Nevertheless, the October crash had some major negative effects on the mutual fund industry. Many people selling funds had never experienced a market decline and had difficulty comprehending it, never mind explaining it to clients. As well, the drop made many investors rethink their strategy of investing everything they own for growth.

It also cooled mutual fund sales drastically, to the point where many people who sold funds left the industry rather than face incomes which were at least 50 percent lower than pre-crash levels. Indeed, several fund distributors went out of business because of the decline in sales volume. Most notable was British Columbia-based Stenner Financial Services Ltd. A key point, however, was that except for some inconvenience, clients did not suffer. Money paid to firms for purchase of funds is held in trust and is not part of a distributor's assets. In the case of Stenner, clients' accounts generally moved with their brokers.

Western Canadian investors had more than their share of crises in 1987. The collapse of Principal Group Ltd. was a disaster for investors in British Columbia, Alberta, Saskatchewan and the Atlantic provinces. Some 67,000 people who bought investment contracts issued by two Principal subsidiaries, First Investors Corp. Ltd. and Associate Investors of Canada Ltd., faced losses of more than $100 million.

Principal also had a mutual fund subsidiary, Principal Securities Management Ltd. It was sold to Metropolitan Life Holdings Ltd. Investors in Principal mutual funds suffered inconvenience. But the assets in the funds, like the assets in all mutual funds, belonged to the investors in the funds and were not at risk.

More recently, several other fund distributors, including Toronto-based Tillcan Financial Corporation and Montreal-based National Financial Business Centre, closed their doors. Sales representatives' registrations were quickly transferred to other firms and clients suffered no inconvenience.

About the author

Steven G. Kelman is an investment counselor and one of Canada's foremost experts on registered retirement savings plans and other aspects of personal financial planning. He has acted as a financial planner for individuals and as a consultant in the mutual fund industry. Mr. Kelman is a vice-president of Dynamic Fund Management Ltd., a subsidiary of Dundee Capital Inc. He is consulting editor with the *Mutual Fund Sourcebook,* the mutual fund information guide used by fund professionals in Canada and is an advisor on the Mutual Fund Sourcedisk, both published by Southam Business Communications Inc.

Mr. Kelman is the author of *RRSPs 1992* and co-author of *Investment Strategies* – both produced by the *Financial Times of Canada*. His articles have appeared in the *Financial Times*, in magazines and on the business pages of daily newspapers from coast to coast. He has lectured on financial planning, RRSPs and mutual funds across the country. For several years, Mr. Kelman taught a course on applied investments to MBA students at the Faculty of Administrative Studies at Toronto's York University.

Mr. Kelman is a chartered financial analyst and a member of the Toronto Society of Financial Analysts. After graduating in 1969 from York University with his MBA, Mr. Kelman worked as an analyst, then portfolio manager, for a major insurance company before becoming a senior analyst with an investment dealer. In 1975 he joined the *Financial Times* as a staff writer; he became investment editor in 1977. In April 1985 he joined the Dundee Group of Companies.

Acknowledgements

As I noted in previous editions, there are literally dozens of people whose views and advice are reflected in *Understanding Mutual Funds*. I would like to thank my colleagues at Dynamic Fund Management Ltd. and Dundee Capital Inc. for their support and advice, especially my assistant Leslie Murray for keeping track of my research notes. I would like to thank David Groskind and Allan Lou of Southam Business Communications Inc. for their efforts in preparing the data on the 100 largest funds, the directory of fund management companies and the fund performance tables. The source of that material is Southam's sourcedisk, *Mutual Fund Sourcebook* and mutual fund databank.

I would also like to thank Elaine Wyatt at the *Financial Times of Canada* who is responsible for producing this book and the others in the series.

Steven Kelman
October 1991

CHAPTER 1

How It Started

NINETEEN-THIRTY-TWO WAS an unlikely time to establish Canada's first open-end mutual fund. Unemployment in the depression-ravaged economy was running at about 40 percent. Canadian share prices as measured by the *Financial Times of Canada* were off about 80 percent from their 1929 highs.

Yet it was in 1932 that thirty-one-year-old Alan Chippindale of the New York-based Calvin Bullock organization travelled to Montreal. His assignment: to start and manage Canada's first open-end mutual fund, the Canadian Investment Fund (CIF).

It was not an easy task. First, tax regulations had to be changed to accommodate the mutual fund corporation concept. Second, he faced the problem of selling a new investment concept to a public that was gun-shy, to say the least.

The only experience most people had with funds of any type involved investment trust shares. These were closed-end funds whose shares were bought and sold on stock exchanges. Most had leveraged, unpublished portfolios and there were few restrictions on what they could buy and hold in their portfolios. Chippindale's open-end fund was different in that the fund issued and redeemed shares on an ongoing basis at a price reflecting the full value of the assets the fund held.

The closed-end investment pools had performed exceedingly well during the Roaring Twenties. But when the market crashed, the value of their underlying assets plunged as well. Those investors who wanted to sell couldn't as the market for the shares had dried up.

CIF offered shares through dealers and brokers in the United States and Britain as well as in Canada. Chippindale spent $50,000 on newspaper advertising in Canada in the three months after launching the fund in December 1932. Gross sales during that period were disappointing – only about $50,000. It was years before the fund turned a profit.

But Chippindale had pioneered the concepts that mutual fund investors today take for granted: regular reports to investors, redemptions at net asset value, diversification, no borrowing, and no conflicts of interest.

The concept of open-end funds caught on slowly. In 1934, Commonwealth International (now Viking Commonwealth Fund Ltd.) changed to an open-end fund from a closed-end fund. In the same year, a new fund, United Gold Equities, was established. (It later was wound up as investor interest in gold declined.) In 1938, Corporate Investors Ltd. converted to an open-end fund from a closed-end fund.

But funds really didn't take off until the 1950s. It was at this time that Investors Syndicate of Canada formed Investors Mutual of Canada. This group, with an expanding sales force, increased investor awareness in funds by selling through instalment accumulation plans.

Statistics on mutual funds covering that period are sketchy. The Investment Funds Institute of Canada (IFIC) – the umbrella organization of the Canadian mutual fund industry – estimates that the market value of funds offered by its members in 1951 was about $57 million held in 22,000 accounts.

But through the 1950s the industry grew quickly. By 1960 IFIC members had assets of about $540 million in 179,000 accounts. In 1963 the figure broke $1 billion in 324,000 accounts.

It was during 1962 that IFIC's predecessor organization, the Canadian Mutual Fund Association, was founded, with the objective of becoming a self-governing and self-disciplining association of mutual fund companies. The name was changed to the Investment Funds Institute of Canada in 1976.

IFIC membership includes funds representing about three-quarters of fund assets held by Canadians. Its Canadian Investment Funds Course is recognized by provincial regulators as a requirement for registration of mutual fund salespeople. Its views are sought by provincial securities commissions. Its various committees – which consider everything from advertising ethics to education – have a major influence on the funds business in Canada.

As the stock market soared in the 1960s, the industry expanded. A number of "private" funds were established during this period.

Tradex Investment Fund Ltd. was set up for federal government employees posted overseas. MD Growth Investments was established by the Canadian Medical Association for its members.

At the end of 1968, IFIC-member funds controlled $2.8 billion in assets in 702,000 shareholder accounts. Sales continued at a hefty pace until 1969. But the stock market peaked in May and prices began to fall. By year-end total assets for the industry were down marginally. More importantly, redemptions began to exceed sales.

For the next nine years, the industry's shareholder base shrunk as redemptions outpaced sales. Several U.S.-based fund companies left Canada because of declining sales as well as new regulations that required Canadian ownership of investment companies. Many fund salespeople who jumped in during the boom years also left the industry, leaving their clients to fend for themselves.

Most importantly, it was in the early 1970s that the mutual fund business suffered through a scandal that shattered investor confidence.

In the late 1950s, Bernard Cornfeld, an American, established Investors Overseas Services (IOS) to manage and distribute mutual funds. By the late 1960s he was the undisputed king of the fund business with more than one million investors and more than $2 billion in assets under management. His organization, which was registered in Panama, operated primarily in Europe, Central and South America and the Middle East. It was not registered with the U.S. Securities and Exchange Commission (SEC) so it could not operate in the U.S. Similarly, these offshore funds were not cleared in Canada. IOS, however, did purchase a Canadian group of funds. These were operated under Canadian law and were not involved in the subsequent IOS offshore funds scandal and the collapse of IOS.

Cornfeld and his colleagues, as controlling shareholders of IOS, were paper multi-millionaires. To convert some of this paper wealth to cash they decided to go public. Their first step was to change IOS from a Panamanian company to a Canadian one, registering the head office in Saint John, N.B. Its base of operations, however, was Switzerland. The share issue in 1969 was a roaring success, with the opening price more than double the $10 issue price.

But when IOS released its annual report in April 1970, its financial results were dismal. Moreover, its auditors questioned the value of some of the company's assets, including 22 million acres of Arctic oil leases. By the summer, IOS shares were trading at $2.

Concerns about IOS caused massive redemptions of its fund shares and, as a result, bailout proposals were made by a number of parties. In the summer of 1970 control of IOS passed to Robert Vesco, an American financier. Vesco obtained control as part of a deal that included a $5 million rescue loan to IOS. He then allegedly diverted assets of the offshore IOS funds into investments which provided indirect benefits to him. In November 1972, the SEC and other regulators in Canada, Luxembourg, the Netherlands Antilles and the United Kingdom forced IOS and its related funds into liquidation.

When the Canadian operations of IOS were liquidated by a trustee, the Eaton group of funds bought the contracts to manage the Canadian IOS funds and integrated them into the Eaton group – now the Viking group.

It took a long time for the industry to recover. By 1978 fund sales began to exceed redemptions once again and the industry began its major growth from a base of about 150 funds and an asset base of about $2 billion. By 1985 there were about 200 funds with assets exceeding $10 billion. Two years later there were more than 350 funds with assets exceeding $35 billion.

The surge reflected the growing recognition by both investors and the investment industry that funds are the best way for many people to participate in the stock and bond markets. Billions of dollars of RRSP money flows into mutual funds each year from people seeking better long-term returns than are available from guaranteed plans. And many stockbrokers who previously ignored funds or discouraged their clients from investing in funds now see them as an important source of business. Indeed, a number of investment dealers offer their own families of funds or funds managed by their chartered bank parents. Similarly, many insurance companies are offering mutual funds to their clients. Banks and trust companies have also expanded their fund operations. These newcomers have increased general investor awareness about mutual funds.

As well, the industry has expanded its product line to include a wider range of funds. Besides the traditional stock and bond funds, investors have a choice of ethical funds, precious metals funds, and funds that specialize in foreign government bonds, health-care product companies and investments in the food industry.

The October 1987 crash had a short-term negative impact on fund sales, which plunged in the months following the crash. However, sales growth returned, reflecting the variety of funds available to meet investor needs and expectations of high returns.

Companies continue to introduce new funds to meet investor needs, real or perceived. The banking and trust industries have trained individuals to sell funds through their branch networks. Fund companies are offering more funds that have a declining redemption fee instead of a commission – funds that are designed to compete with bank and trust company funds that are sold without commissions.

The fund industry will continue to grow as more and more Canadians discover how funds can be used to meet virtually any type of investment objective and bring returns that are superior to the guaranteed investments that they traditionally have chosen.

CHAPTER 2

What Is a Mutual Fund?

A MUTUAL FUND IS A POOL of savings that belongs to many investors. This pool is invested by a professional manager or a team of managers in a broad portfolio of investments. Depending on the objectives of the fund, these can be Canadian common stocks, foreign common stocks, bonds, mortgages, preferred shares, precious metals, specialty investments, treasury bills or combinations of several groups. Some funds are designed for specific purposes, such as RRSPs, others are multi-purpose.

Funds that issue and redeem shares or units on a continuous basis are called open-end funds. There are more than 600 open-end funds offered in Canada. The value of their shares or units changes with the underlying value of the securities in the fund. But each share or unit represents a portion of the underlying portfolio. Most funds are valued daily, although some are valued weekly and a few monthly or quarterly. The fund company determines the value of the underlying portfolio at the close of the stock and bond markets, then divides that value by the number of shares or units outstanding to determine the net asset value of each share or unit. The number of shares or units outstanding varies on a day-to-day basis, depending on sales and redemptions.

Bolton Tremblay Canada Cumulative Fund is a typical open-end fund that invests primarily in foreign common stocks. Its portfolio, as of June 30, 1991, was valued at $66.5 million. At that date it had about 4.65 million units outstanding. So the value per unit was $14.31. That is the amount you would pay for a share on June 30, adjusted for acquisition fees. It is also the price you would have received for your shares if you redeemed them on that date.

In addition to open-end funds, there are a handful of closed-end funds. Unlike open-end funds, closed-end funds have a fixed number of shares. These are traded on stock exchanges. The market value of their shares may be greater or less than the underlying value of their securities. For example, BGR Precious Metals shares trade on the Toronto Stock Exchange. On June 21, 1991, BGR shares closed at $7.75. But the underlying value was $9.00 a share. Closed-end funds can be useful for some investors and will be discussed in detail in chapter six.

At least one fund, Global Strategy Corp., is a hybrid. It was originally offered to the public as a unique fund that invested its assets entirely in foreign property but at the same time was eligible for RRSPs. The fund was able to do this because its managers discovered a way around the law that limits RRSP-eligible funds to 10 percent foreign property. The federal government soon plugged that loophole but allowed the fund to continue to operate, provided no new shares were issued. Shareholders can redeem their shares at net asset value, just like every other open-end fund. However, the shares trade on the Vancouver Stock Exchange and investors who want to sell their shares find they are better off doing so on the exchange where their price exceeds the net asset value. Apparently, some investors are willing to pay a premium for the fund's shares so they can hold an RRSP investment in which the assets are not tied to the Canadian market.

The majority of investors in funds hold open-end funds. With the exception of the chapter on closed-end funds, all examples and comments in this book refer to open-end funds.

The advantages of funds

A mutual fund offers several important advantages to you as an investor which you might have difficulty achieving on your own:

1. Diversification

Funds generally hold a large number of securities. It is common for a fund invested in Canadian common stocks to hold shares of forty or more companies. By holding such a large number of securities your risk is spread – if one company flounders, it will have little impact on the performance of the overall portfolio. Few individuals have enough assets to build a diversified portfolio on their own. With a mutual fund you can get diversification with a small amount of money.

How small? The minimum contribution allowed to most funds is between $500 and $1,000. However, most funds also have monthly contribution plans that allow you to start with as little as $100 a month. According to the Investment Funds Institute of Canada, the average investment by individuals in a fund at June 30, 1990 was $11,138. But many investors hold several funds and the holdings of mutual fund investors range from a few hundred dollars to $1 million or more.

2. Liquidity

A key benefit of mutual funds is that they are liquid. You can purchase or redeem shares and units on short notice, generally locking in a purchase or sale price on the day you make your decision to buy or redeem (in the case of funds valued daily). This is an advantage to individuals who want to be able to cash in their investments at any time. In this way, holding a mutual fund can be more advantageous than holding stocks, particularly if the stocks held rarely trade in large volumes and may be harder to sell at any one time at a good price.

Orders to buy mutual fund shares or units received by the fund before the close of business on a day when shares are valued will be purchased at that price, less any sales fee if applicable. Orders received to redeem shares will be redeemed at that price, less any redemption fee if applicable, and your money will be available within a few days, generally in five. The trend in the industry is toward daily pricing and virtually all major fund groups now price daily. (In the U.S., some funds are priced hourly.)

A handful of funds, mainly real estate funds, are valued monthly or quarterly and as a result are somewhat less liquid.

3. Professional management

Mutual fund investors benefit from having investment professionals decide what securities should be held and at what prices they should be bought or sold. Most fund managers have substantial experience in the investment field and have taken specialized investment courses leading to the designation of chartered financial analyst. The cost of professional management is low to mutual fund holders because the cost is spread so widely. Generally, you can expect to pay about 2 percent a year for portfolio management and other fund expenses, excluding the costs of trading the underlying securities. This management fee is generally charged to the fund rather than to your account.

Mutual funds are the only cost-effective way for individuals with limited funds to get a diversified, professionally managed portfolio. No stockbroker or other investment professional can afford to service a small account, except through mutual funds. Unless you are able to generate several thousands of dollars of trading commissions a year, you are unlikely to get timely advice and top-quality service on a stock portfolio from a stockbroker.

But small investors aren't the only investors who use mutual funds. Many wealthy individuals who don't want to be bothered making decisions about the stock market also use funds. Similarly, some people use funds for specific purposes in their investment portfolios. For instance, if you decide you want to invest part of your assets in Japanese securities, the easiest way is through a fund that specializes in this market.

The funds in Canada can be divided into two broad categories: those that invest in growth securities such as common stocks and whose objective is to provide long-term growth, and those that invest in income securities and whose objective is to provide current income or stable growth.

Types of funds

Growth funds historically give the highest rates of return measured over a long period of time, say ten years. While the returns of all mutual funds are a combination of capital gain and income, the major portion of return from growth funds is from capital appreciation. It is impossible to predict what a growth fund's future rate of return will be. The assumption is that it will be higher than the rate of return of a fund that invests for income. That has been the case historically. But annual rates of return for growth funds vary widely. In some years, the returns will be large; in other years, the returns will be mediocre. There will be years when fund values drop.

Fixed income funds give somewhat lower long-term rates of return than growth funds. However, their annual returns are more stable because the major portion is income. This income comes in the form of interest in the case of bond and mortgage funds, and dividends in the case of preferred-dividend income funds.

Growth funds

Growth funds include common stock and real estate funds as well as balanced funds whose portfolios may include both stocks and bonds to provide more stable growth than pure growth funds.

The largest group of growth funds – about 150 funds at June 30, 1991 – is Canadian common stock funds. Because they concentrate in the Canadian market, holding no more than 14 percent of their assets in foreign securities, they can be registered as RRSPs. Ottawa proposed changing the foreign property limit from 10 per cent to 12 percent for 1990, 14 percent for 1991, 16 percent for 1992, 18 percent for 1993 and 20 percent in subsequent years. Even though the legislation has not been passed, fund companies have generally been operating on the premise that the legislation will be passed retroactively.

Most Canadian common stock funds invest across the spectrum of the market, generally sticking to issues traded on the Toronto Stock Exchange and the Montreal Exchange. A few funds, however, specialize in specific segments of the market. For example, Royal Trust Energy Fund invests in Canadian energy issues; Dynamic Precious Metals Fund invests in shares of precious metals producers and precious metals.

There are almost fifty growth funds that invest in American stock markets. While most of these funds stick to senior blue-chip issues, others concentrate on specific areas. For example, the Putnam Health Sciences Trust invests primarily in the U.S. health-sciences industry. Still others focus on junior stock issues or resources.

If international diversification interests you, there are about fifty-six funds that invest outside North America. Some, such as AGF Japan Fund or Dynamic Europe 1992 Fund, concentrate on specific markets. Others, such as Bolton Tremblay International Fund, invest in a variety of overseas markets. A few funds, such as Trimark Fund, will invest in whatever markets, including Canada and the U.S., are perceived to offer the best values. There are also about a half-dozen international bond funds which may provide growth through changes in currency values as well as shifts in interest rates.

Mutual funds that invest primarily outside Canada are considered "foreign property" by the federal government for purposes of the Income Tax Act and cannot be registered as RRSPs. However, they can be held in self-directed RRSPs as part of the foreign property component, provided the total foreign property holding does not exceed 14 percent of the plan. (As already mentioned, Ottawa has proposed raising the foreign property limit.)

Balanced funds

More than 100 funds call themselves balanced or asset-allocation funds. Historically, a balanced fund was one that invested a portion of its assets in bonds and a portion in stocks. Such funds aimed to have long-term rates of return that were larger than those offered by pure bond funds and more stable than pure stock funds.

Lately, however, the term balanced has been used by a number of new funds which have the traditional balanced fund objectives but whose portfolios are primarily equities. Depending on their holdings, some balanced funds are eligible for RRSPs, while others are not. As a group balanced funds are significantly less volatile than pure equity funds.

Real estate funds

There are a handful of funds that invest in real estate. These differ from other mutual funds in several major respects. First, they use borrowed capital in addition to shareholder capital; virtually all other funds use just shareholder capital.

Second, their unit or share values are based on appraisals rather than actual market transactions. The net asset value per unit or share in an equity fund is determined by the value of the portfolio as measured by the closing trades in each stock divided by the number of shares outstanding. With a real estate fund, the value of the fund is based on annual appraisals of each property the fund owns. An appraisal is simply the opinion of a real estate expert of the market value of a particular property.

Third, real estate funds are less liquid than other funds. Although the trend is toward monthly valuations, a few are valued quarterly which means you can buy or sell only four times a year.

Income funds

The second major category of funds is income funds which aim to produce a predictable and relatively stable flow of income. Also, the rates of return on income funds are less uncertain than the rates of return from growth funds, albeit slightly lower.

Income funds can be divided into two broad categories: those that invest in bonds, mortgages or both and those that invest primarily in preferred shares of Canadian corporations. At the end of June, 1991 there were ninety funds which invested in Canadian bonds, nineteen mortgage funds, nine funds which invested in both bonds and mortgages and sixteen funds which invested primarily in preferred shares of Canadian companies. In addition there were eighty-six money market funds or short-term yield funds which invested primarily in treasury bills, top quality commercial paper and bank deposits.

To understand the differences between the two broad categories you have to consider how the federal government taxes individuals on the interest and dividends they receive from Canadian corporations. Interest is taxable at the marginal tax rate – the rate of tax paid on an individual's last dollar of income earned. A person with taxable income of $40,000 could have a marginal tax rate of about 39 percent, depending on the province and ignoring surtaxes. So, on $1,000 in interest income, this person would have to pay $390 in taxes.

To encourage Canadians to invest in dividend-producing shares, the government devised the federal dividend tax credit. It works like this: instead of simply adding dividend income to other sources of income, dividends are grossed up by 125 percent. Then, after you have determined how much tax you owe, you can subtract a tax credit equal to 13.33 percent of 125 percent of your dividends. In the end, you pay less tax than if you'd simply added the dividends to income in the normal way.

For example, let's say you have $1,000 of dividend income. For tax-calculation purposes this would be grossed up to $1,250. Assuming your federal tax rate is 26 percent, the federal tax payable on the dividend would be $362.50. From this, subtract the dividend tax credit of 13.33 percent of $1,250, or $167. The net federal tax payable on the dividend would be $196. Add the provincial tax at 50 percent of federal tax ($98) and the total tax bill on $1,000 in dividends ends up being $294, or about 29 percent of the actual dividend received. That would compare with $390, or 39 percent, on interest received by the same person. The rule of thumb is that on an after-tax basis, $1 of dividend income has the same after-tax value as $1.26 of interest income. So an 8 percent dividend yield is about equal to a 10 per cent interest yield.

Now, back to the two categories of income funds. Funds that invest primarily in preferred shares are usually called preferred-dividend income funds. Their purpose is to maximize after-tax income. They are popular with people who want current income and the highest after-tax return possible without taking significant risk.

Bond and mortgage funds may have slightly lower after-tax rates of return than preferred-dividend income funds. But many people prefer the security of having debt instruments and are willing to give up some income as a trade-off for more security.

When an income fund is to be registered as an RRSP, bond and mortgage funds make more sense. All income is untaxed inside an RRSP and RRSP investors cannot take advantage of the tax break that comes with the preferred-dividend income.

There are several different types of non-dividend fixed income funds. There are funds that invest only in bonds, those that invest only in mortgages, funds that mix bonds and mortgages, and, finally, there are money market funds and savings funds.

Bond funds generally invest in government or government-guaranteed bonds and bonds and debentures issued by the strongest banks and corporations. Besides quality of underlying bonds and general interest rate levels there are other factors that can affect performance, such as the maturities of the various bonds held and whether a major portion of the fund is invested in bonds that are denominated in currencies other than the Canadian dollar.

Mortgage funds are designed to provide maximum current income to investors by investing in mortgages. Mortgage rates are generally at least a point higher than bond yields. They are less likely to provide capital appreciation than bond funds because mortgage funds rarely trade their mortgages.

Money market and savings funds – also known as short-term yield funds – have similar objectives: to provide current income with no fluctuation in the value of an investor's capital. Money market funds invest in short-term debt securities with maturities of less than a year. Typically, a money market fund's portfolio will be concentrated in treasury bills, bank-guaranteed debt and short-term issues of strong corporations.

The unit value of most money market funds is fixed at either $10 or $1, so the unit value of the fund is always constant. Income earned on capital accrues to your account daily, weekly or monthly, depending on how often the fund is valued, and is generally used to purchase additional units of the fund. Money market funds are by far the least risky of mutual funds.

A savings fund has the same objective as a money market fund. But rather than investing in a portfolio of short-term securities, it keeps the fund's assets on deposit with major financial institutions earning wholesale deposit rates which can be a couple of percentage points more than the rate paid to individuals on premium savings accounts. In mid-1991 no major fund group was offering a savings fund.

How funds can be used

Mutual funds can be used for virtually any type of savings or investment program. The fund or funds you use should be matched to your specific investment objective. You should also develop an understanding of what is called fund volatility or rate-of-return variability.

Unlike a guaranteed investment, you do not know what your rate of return will be from a mutual fund because the rate you earn will depend on the rates of return of the underlying investments. You expect to get back substantially more than you put in – that's the reason you would buy a fund rather than purchase a guaranteed investment certificate or hold money in the bank. However, the rates of return from some types of mutual funds are a lot more stable than rates of return of some other types of funds.

Stocks Versus Treasury Bills

TOTAL RETURNS
FOR PERIODS ENDING JUNE 30

Year	TSE Total Return	T-Bills
1973	7.0%	4.1%
1974	-9.1	6.8
1975	10.0	7.5
1976	4.8	8.5
1977	3.1	8.2
1978	14.7	7.5
1979	50.4	10.2
1980	33.0	12.9
1981	19.0	14.8
1982	-39.2	16.5
1983	86.9	10.7
1984	-5.7	10.0
1985	26.7	10.7
1986	17.4	9.3
1987	24.6	8.0
1988	-5.2	8.7
1989	13.5	11.1
1990	-2.4	12.8
1991	1.9	10.9

TABLE I

Since money market and savings funds invest only in short-term securities, you can predict fairly accurately your rate of return over a relatively short period of time.

In contrast, there are some funds whose rates of return over short periods are virtually impossible to predict. These funds may give very high rates of return over long periods but over the short-term their rates will vary widely.

For example, funds that invest in the Japanese stock market are very volatile. Much of this volatility is caused by the exchange rate of the Canadian dollar against the Japanese yen. Exchange rate fluctuations can be as much as several percentage points up or down in a month. Similarly, funds that invest in gold and other precious metals have historically been volatile.

Money market funds as a group are the least volatile, followed by mortgage funds, bond funds and preferred-dividend income funds. Common stock funds are more volatile than fixed income funds. Equity funds that invest in senior stocks and balanced funds are generally much less volatile than equity funds that concentrate on specific groups of stocks such as energy shares, junior companies or gold.

So if your savings objective is rather short term, like saving for a vacation or a down payment on a home, the fund that would best suit your needs is a money market fund. Your money would not be at risk and you would likely earn a rate of return that is a couple of points above what you would get in a bank account.

If you don't need your money for a couple of years, a mortgage or bond fund might suffice. Similarly, you could consider a preferred-dividend income fund. In this case you would have to consider the individual portfolios of the funds and your tax situation. Fixed income funds that have securities maturing in a few years are likely to be less volatile than fixed income funds whose portfolios have securities that mature in fifteen to twenty years. This will be discussed in more detail later in the book.

If you are saving for the long term, you would likely consider funds invested primarily in equities. You would expect to do better with these funds than you would with income funds. But on a month-to-month or year-to-year basis such growth funds would have more volatile rates of return than fixed income funds.

Historically, investors who are willing to accept some fluctuation in their rates of return have done better over the long haul than investors who want guaranteed returns.

The *Financial Times of Canada* has been publishing its comprehensive mutual fund surveys for more than a decade. On a ten-year basis to June 30, 1991, funds that invested primarily in equities had annual average returns about 13 percent. Fixed income funds had returns averaging just over 11 percent, while money market funds had returns averaging 11 percent.

In Table I you can see the dramatic difference between the year-by-year performance of the Toronto Stock Exchange total return index and the rate of return you would have earned if you held treasury bills. The TSE index is a good representation of what you would have earned holding an "average" mutual fund investing in Canadian stocks. Its one-, three-, five- and ten-year compound returns to June 30, 1989 are 13.5 percent, 10.3 percent, 14.8 percent and 13.0 percent, respectively. The treasury bill returns parallel the returns you would have earned holding a money market fund before management fees of about one percentage point. One-, three-, five- and ten-year rates for bills are 11.1 percent, 9.3 percent, 9.5 percent and 11.2 percent. On average, you can reasonably expect to earn several percentage points more a year investing in equities. But year-to-year differences vary dramatically.

Indeed, if you look at periods ended June 30, 1991 the one-, three-, five- and ten-year rates for the TSE are 1.9 percent, 4.1 percent, 5.9 percent and 7.8 percent respectively, while the rates for treasury bills are 10.9 percent, 11.6 percent, 10.3 percent and 10.8 percent. This does not mean that T-bills are better than equity funds as long-term investments. Rather it means that for this one specific ending date, short- and medium-term rates of return for equities were below expectations. Markets move in cycles and recent returns for equity funds reflect the recession. The disappointing ten-year returns to June 30, 1991 reflect the dismal performance of equities in 1982 and 1990, even though there were years of successive gains in between the two recessions.

CHAPTER 3

The Impact of October 1987, Meech Lake and Iraq

TWO MARKET DEVELOPMENTS dramatically influenced the mutual fund industry over the past decade. First was the stock market surge between July 1982 and August 1987. Over that sixty-one month period, the Toronto Stock Exchange 300 composite index gained 202 per cent. It was during those months that the asset base of the Canadian mutual fund industry climbed from a few billion dollars to $35 billion as high rates of return – in many cases greater than 18 percent a year – attracted investors who had previously kept the bulk of their assets in guaranteed investments. The second influence was the October 1987 stock market crash which demonstrated the obvious – that markets move in cycles, and from time to time prices will drop substantially.

The fact that the stock market fell sharply in October 1987 was no surprise to most professional investors. In fact most fund managers had been building cash positions in the months prior to the decline because they felt that stocks were expensive or that the market was ahead of itself. As well, the markets had become exceptionally volatile, with the major indexes moving sharply up and down on a day-to-day basis as investor confidence rose and fell.

What caught virtually every manager off-guard was the magnitude of the decline. In the six sessions to October 23, the Toronto Stock Exchange 300 composite index – a widely used measure of stock market performance – fell about 16 percent.

The biggest drop was on Black Monday, October 19, when the TSE 300 fell 407 points, losing 11 percent of its value. However, the bloodbath really began on the previous Friday when the TSE 300, taking its lead from the New York market, fell 76 points, or 2 per cent. By the time the month ended, the TSE was more than 22 percent below its September closing level. Investors who bought near the top of the market in August saw the value of their investment, assuming they had a broadly based portfolio, plunge by one-quarter. If they bought the day the market peaked and sold the day the market bottomed, they would have lost about 31 per cent of their capital before commissions.

While some investors bought at the peak, hundreds of thousands of investors had been in funds for years, holding them as long-term investments. These investors saw the crash eliminate most of the gains they had made over the previous twelve months. Even then, many funds tied to the stock market showed significant gains in 1987 despite October. Several funds tied to natural resource stocks had gains of more than 25 percent. Some funds with substantial cash positions and broadly based portfolios showed small but positive returns.

Surprisingly, the industry was not hit with a flood of redemptions. While there was a substantial amount of switching from growth funds to more stable bond and money market funds, few fund companies reported a mass exodus from funds. In total, about 2 percent of mutual fund assets were redeemed the week of the crash.

There are several explanations for this. Many fund salespeople claim that most of their clients are long-term investors and decided to continue holding. Indeed, with ten-year rates of return for many funds in excess of 16 percent, long-term investors could still smile. But the lack of redemptions might also reflect the fact that many investors got busy signals when they tried to call their brokers to redeem. By the time they got through, the market had levelled and they decided to hold, particularly when they realized that the damage wasn't as great as they thought.

There was concern in the industry that some investors who bought their holdings partly with borrowed money would be forced to sell by banks and trust companies which had financed the purchases. However, this did not become a major problem because the crash only trimmed profits and did not eliminate them, at least for investors who had held funds for some time.

As to the cause of the crash, a simple explanation is that the number of people who wanted to sell exceeded the number of people who wanted to buy. There are many more complex explanations. One points to sales of stocks by major U.S. fund companies. Mutual fund investors can redeem at any time. Apparently, on Friday, October 16, fund companies were hit by an extraordinary number of redemptions when the New York Stock Exchange fell 108 points as measured by the Dow Jones industrial average. To raise cash to meet these redemptions, some funds became major sellers of stocks on October 19. This helped drive the market down further because many potential buyers were on the sidelines.

Those investors who bought stocks or funds which invest in stocks on October 19 did quite well. By the end of June 1989, they were showing gains of about 40 percent, using the Toronto index as a bench-mark. In the subsequent twelve months the market slipped about 2.4 percent.

The crash has had some major effects on fund investing. For one thing, many investors started taking a more cautious approach. Rather than putting everything in funds that invest in growth stocks, more and more investors are taking a balanced approach, spreading their money among different classes of assets such as bond funds, precious metals funds and money market funds.

However, new sales dried up and the incomes of people who sold funds plunged. At least one company which had planned to enter the fund business, New York Life Insurance Co., changed its mind. As well, a number of Canadian fund companies or fund-management contracts were sold to other management companies. Fund groups absorbed by larger companies included the Sentinel group of funds, the Walwyn funds, the Rabin-Budden funds and the Hume funds.

The drop in sales hurt fund sales organizations, which quickly discovered that revenues were not enough to cover overheads. In the West, Canadian Equity Planners, a major distributor, decided to close its doors. Two other firms – Stenner Financial Services Ltd. and the Herman Group – had their doors closed for them by regulatory bodies. In Eastern Canada, several firms talked merger. Salespeople at various firms jockeyed for position within their own firms or with other firms that offered them a better deal.

Clients of the firms that ceased operations suffered inconvenience but no financial losses. Money held by a fund company on behalf of a client is kept in a trust account that is separate from company funds. Also, any securities held by the firm are held in trust.

Other economic and political developments have influenced the markets and fund investors more recently. The slowing economy led many investors to consider bond funds instead of equity funds from late 1989 to mid-1991. Indeed, investors who chose bond and mortgage funds were rewarded as interest rates fell in late 1990 and early 1991.

Similarly, confusion about the impact of the failure of the Meech Lake accord pushed many investors to the sidelines and helped explain the growth of money market funds during early 1990.

The Persian Gulf Crisis had a mixed impact. It initially benefited energy funds, but hurt the value of most other equity funds, in particular funds invested in overseas stocks. The equity markets, however, started to improve in late 1990 as investors learned to live with the Gulf Crisis and started to look beyond the recession at recovery.

CHAPTER 4

All About Growth Funds

IF YOUR INVESTMENT OBJECTIVE is long-term capital growth, consider equity funds, which invest primarily in common stocks. These are the most popular type of fund. About 300 are included in the *Financial Times of Canada* monthly survey of investment funds.

There are several major groups of equity funds that are designed to meet particular objectives by investing in specific markets or certain areas of specific markets.

Regardless of their type, all equity funds have the common thread of a diversified portfolio of shares, and performance that reflects individual funds' objectives and the skills of their managers.

Many people buy equity funds the same way they buy GICs. They look at rates of return and buy the one with the highest rate. This is a mistake. An equity fund's long-term rate of return indicates how that fund has performed in the past. It is not a guarantee, or even a strong indicator, of future performance. Performance is a single indicator which is best used combined with another indicator, volatility.

In fact, it is very important to consider a fund's volatility, or the stability, of its monthly rate of return when choosing an equity fund. The *Financial Times* ranks mutual funds by variations in its monthly rate of return using a statistical measure called standard deviation. It indicates the amount a return is likely to diverge from its average monthly rate of return. Sixty months of data is used where available, or a minimum of thirty-six months, to determine standard deviation.

Volatility is useful in comparing two funds with similar rates of return. For investors who buy and hold for the long term, a fund with a high historical return and a low volatility ranking would be preferable to a fund with the same return but a high volatility rating.

Conversely, if you're trying to catch the swings in a market cycle, you might want to choose a fund with a high volatility rating over one with a low ranking.

For example, AGF American Growth Fund and AGF Money Market Account had identical average annual returns over the past ten years of 10.9 percent. However, the equity fund is much more volatile than the money market fund. A fund's volatility will change from time to time. But usually the changes are not significant because the fund objectives and investment philosophy are generally stable.

Certain groups of funds tend to be more volatile than others. Gold funds, for instance, are among the most volatile, reflecting the volatility of precious metals prices and gold mining stocks. Similarly, Japanese funds are fairly volatile as a result of swings in the exchange rates of the Japanese yen and Canadian dollar. Generally, funds that invest in a narrow segment of the market are more volatile than funds that draw their portfolios from a broad spectrum of industries. Equity funds that have relatively low volatility tend to invest in securities that are more stable in price than the general market. For example, a fund holding stocks with substantial dividend yields would have below-average volatility. One such fund is Corporate Investors Ltd., which invests in shares that pay, or are expected to pay, above-average dividends. Here is a summary of the major types of growth funds:

1. Canadian equity funds
The largest group of investment funds are those that invest primarily in Canadian stocks and are eligible for RRSPs. Most invest in a broad spectrum of industries and have rates of return that are similar to that of the Toronto Stock Exchange total return index. Others, however, have somewhat different objectives. For instance, several invest primarily in dividend-paying common shares of mature companies giving rates of return that are somewhat more stable than the market. Others specialize in specific areas of the market such as natural resources.

2. U.S. equity funds
Funds that invest in the U.S. are also very popular among Canadian investors. These funds appeal to individuals who expect the U.S. markets to outperform their Canadian counterparts or who want a

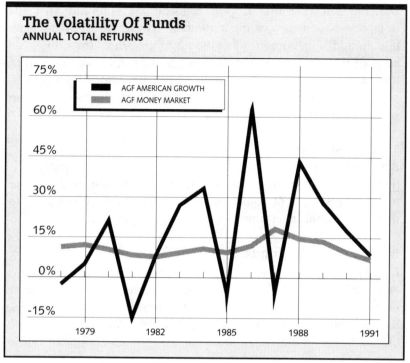

The Volatility Of Funds
ANNUAL TOTAL RETURNS

- AGF AMERICAN GROWTH
- AGF MONEY MARKET

CHART I

hedge against the Canadian dollar. Within this group there is a wide variety of choices. Some invest primarily in blue chips. Others base their portfolios on companies that offer above-average growth potential or in specialty areas of the marketplace.

3. International funds
International funds take advantage of investment opportunities in different countries. Some will invest in any country, including Canada. Others will exclude Canada or concentrate on overseas markets. International funds performed quite well until recently as the Canadian dollar fell against overseas currencies. In the past year or so Canadian funds had the performance edge as the Canadian dollar moved higher against most other currencies.

4. Specialty equity funds
A number of funds specialize in specific industries, specific markets or follow hedged investment strategies. For instance, AGF Hitech Fund Ltd. invests in high-technology stocks in Canada, the

U.S., Japan and certain European countries. Several funds specialize in Japanese securities, while a number concentrate on precious metals. In addition, some funds attempt to give their investors stable rates of return through hedging strategies such as writing call options against positions. This involves buying a stock then selling a call option which gives the buyer the right to buy that stock at a preset price up until a specific date.

5. Balanced funds
Balanced funds try to stabilize returns by combining equities with fixed income securities. A few, however, have rates-of-return patterns more typical of equity funds in that they have concentrated their investment in equities.

Canadian equity funds
Lured by promises of returns far above those available from guaranteed investments, individuals poured billions of dollars in recent years into mutual funds that invest primarily in Canadian equities. Indeed, many funds have given their holders rates of return far in excess of the rates that could be earned by holding guaranteed investments.

But it's important to realize that year-to-year rates vary widely. Over the ten years ended June 1991, the annual returns of the Toronto Stock Exchange total return index ranged from a low of -39.1 percent to a high of 86.6 percent.

And because stock markets move in cycles, annual rates don't tell the whole story. The returns depend on when stocks are bought and when they are sold. Over the past sixty years, the Toronto market has gone through eleven cycles consisting of declining markets followed by rising markets.

Toronto statistician Richard Anstett has compiled some of the most comprehensive statistics available on the performance of the TSE. Looking at some of the more recent cycles, Anstett notes that the Toronto market rose 193 percent in the seventy-two months ended November 1980, then proceeded to slide 44 percent over the next twenty months to June 1982. Between June 1982 and August 1987 the market rose 202 percent. Then it started its slide, which ended in late October, down 31 percent from its peak. From October 1987 to October 1989 it rose about 42 percent before pulling back 25 percent over the following twelve months. In each of these cycles,

Market Cycles Since 1921
on the Toronto Stock Exchange

Bull Markets	No. of Months	% Gain	Bear Markets	No. of Months	% Loss
August 1921 to			September 1929 to		
September 1929	97	300	June 1932	33	80
June 1932 to			March 1937 to		
March 1937	57	201	April 1942	61	56
April 1942 to			May 1946 to		
May 1946	49	159	February 1948	21	25
February 1948 to			July 1956 to		
July 1956	101	273	December 1957	17	30
December 1957 to			May 1969 to		
May 1969	137	162	June 1970	13	28
June 1970 to			October 1973 to		
October 1973	40	64	December 1974	14	38
December 1974 to			November 1980 to		
November 1980	72	193	July 1982	20	44
July 1982 to			August 1987 to		
August 1987	61	202	October 1987	2	31
October 1987 to			October 1989 to		
October 1989	24	42	October 1990	12	25

Note: Changes in market sentiment reflect gains or declines of 20 percent or more. The stock market began climbing in October 1990, gaining more than 15 percent in the nine months to June 1991.

TABLE II

day-to-day swings varied widely. For example, the June 30, 1990 level of the TSE index was about 12 percent below its best level of the previous twelve months.

The return that a broadly-based fund earns in any period or cycle depends on what happens in the market and on the skills of the fund's investment advisor. But it is difficult for a fund manager to consistently outperform the market. Superior returns do occur but usually only for short periods of time or with smaller funds. Such performance is generally due to the decisions of a single manager or a handful of individuals working together. But most managers parrot the general market or follow the crowd. As a result, on a long-term basis it is unrealistic to expect mutual funds as a whole to generate returns significantly greater than the general market.

To understand why, you have to look at the environment in which managers of broadly based Canadian equity funds have to work. You also have to consider a fund manager's objectives and management style.

Most fund managers try to outperform the market. So a manager of a broadly based Canadian equity fund would gauge his or her performance against the TSE 300 composite index, the index which includes the 300 stocks with the largest market capitalizations traded on the exchange, or against the TSE total return index, which includes dividends paid by the stocks included in the TSE 300.

There are several ways fund managers can construct portfolios. One way is to structure portfolios along the lines of the general index, overweighting or underweighting specific industry groups. In fact, there are funds such as First Canadian Equity Index Fund which invest in each industry group in the same proportion as the index.

As Table III shows, the index is divided into thirteen major industry groups: metals and minerals, gold and silver, oil and gas, paper and forest, consumer products, industrial products, real estate and construction, transportation, pipelines, utilities, communications, merchandising, financial services and management companies. At the end of June 1991, metals and minerals were about 8.6 percent of the index, while financial services were 19.5 percent. A portfolio manager who is positive on the outlook for metals and minerals but negative on banks might put a heavier weighting than 8.6 percent in metals shares and a lower weighting in financial services.

A variation of this is to adjust the cash component of the portfolio. All mutual funds hold cash. But the percentage held in cash reflects the fund manager's view on the direction of the market. A manager who expects a sharp rise in the market soon might hold only enough cash to cover normal redemptions. A manager who expects the market to pull back or who believes that prices of individual stocks are expensive might have 30 percent or more of the fund's assets in cash.

Alternatively, fund managers can build portfolios choosing individual securities while ignoring what is in the general index. Many fund managers, however, end up with portfolios that are similar to the general index.

TSE Subindex Weights

AS A PERCENTAGE OF THE TSE 300

Metals & Minerals	8.56	**Real Estate & Construction**	1.13
Integrated Mines	7.75	Developers & Contractors	0.21
Metal Mines	0.41	Property Management	0.92
Non Base Metal Mining	0.30		
		Pipelines	2.11
Gold & Silver	8.12	Oil Pipelines	0.29
Gold and Silver Mines	8.00	Gas Pipelines	1.82
Precious Metals Funds	0.11		
		Utilities	11.18
Oil & Gas	7.80	Gas Utilities	0.31
Integrated Oils	2.69	Electrical Utilities	1.69
Oil & Gas Producers	5.11	Telephone Utilities	9.18
Paper & Forest	2.42	**Communications**	4.56
		Broadcasting	0.33
Consumer Products	8.92	Cable & Entertainment	0.61
Food Processing	0.71	Publishing/Printing	3.61
Tobacco	1.37		
Distilleries	4.30	**Merchandising**	5.81
Breweries and Beverages	1.60	Wholesale Distributors	0.43
Household Goods	0.31	Food Stores	1.84
Autos & Parts	0.33	Department Stores	0.61
Packaging Products	0.25	Clothing Stores	0.20
		Specialty Stores	1.63
Industrial Products	10.94	Health & Hospitality	1.09
Steels	1.41		
Metal Fabricators	0.25	**Financial Services**	19.53
Machinery	0.50	Banks	16.25
Transportation Equipment	0.77	Trust, Savings & Loan	0.81
Electrical/Electronic	3.70	Investment Companies	0.61
Cement/Concrete	0.32	Insurance	0.52
Chemicals	1.96	Financial Management	1.34
Business Forms &			
Equipment	2.10	**Management Companies**	6.46
Transportation	2.46		

JUNE 30, 1991

TABLE III

The major problem they face is finding stocks that can be bought and sold in volume. There are several thousand public companies listed on Canadian exchanges. But only a relatively small number trade in large enough volume or have enough shares outstanding to be considered by fund managers. A fund with assets of $5 million could have a portfolio of smaller companies. But a fund of $500 million would have to have the bulk of its assets in larger companies. Otherwise its manager would be faced with a portfolio containing too many companies to be manageable.

You can figure out a stock's capitalization by multiplying its share price by the number of shares outstanding. A company with ten million shares outstanding and a stock price of $25 would have a market capitalization of $250 million.

The heaviest weighting among the 300 stocks in the TSE composite index belongs to BCE Inc., with 7.8 percent of the index at June 30, 1991. Next is Royal Bank with 4.3 percent followed by Seagram Ltd. with 4.2 then Canadian Pacific Ltd. with 3.7 percent. These four stocks represent 20 percent of the total value of the TSE 300. The top ten stocks in the index represent almost 38 percent of the index; the top 100 represent almost 87 percent of the index; the top 200 represent more than 96 percent of the index. In contrast, the smallest fifty stocks in the index represent 1 percent of the index; the largest of the fifty is 0.03 percent of the total.

Virtually all funds have rules that limit their holdings of individual stocks. For example, concerns about liquidity would prevent a fund, along with any other funds managed by the same advisor, from holding more than 5 percent of the outstanding shares of a specific stock.

Consequently, Canadian equity funds, particularly medium and larger funds, end up having larger companies as a major portion of their portfolios, and these are generally the stocks that are found in the TSE 300.

Since the federal government allows RRSP-eligible mutual funds to hold up to 14 percent of their assets in foreign stocks, many Canadian equity funds have a U.S. or overseas component that may contribute to results that differ from the Canadian market.

Some managers try to beat the market by catching the swings. They build up cash when they believe the market is near the top and they spend their cash when the market is near the bottom. These managers are called market timers and they often base their decisions on technical analysis – the analysis of market cycles and graphs. Market timers face some major difficulties.

First, it is very difficult to call a market top or bottom. Second, it is even more difficult to move out of or into a stock if you have a large portfolio. The manager will simply be unable to sell as much as he or she wants at peak prices, or buy at the bottom. The third problem faced by market timers is that if they are wrong in their timing, they will drastically underperform their competitors.

The funds that do seem to outperform the market have three things in common: the decisions are made by a single person or a small group of individuals, the decisions are made quickly, and the decision-makers are not afraid to act differently from the crowd.

Moreover, their methods of choosing stocks are based on finding undervalued situations. They seek out companies whose shares trade in the market at levels below the values of the assets, less liabilities, and which offer good potential for earnings growth. Such managers will spend cash when they find plenty of stocks that meet their criteria and will build cash when shares become overvalued and they cannot find undervalued stocks to purchase.

In most cases the stocks held may not represent the largest companies. Moreover, such funds' monthly performance may differ from the general market's performance.

In contrast, many funds have their decisions made by ponderous committees that are unable to act quickly. By the time they act on the data available – which is most likely the same information available to other institutional investors – the information has been fully reflected in share prices. Consequently, such funds are unlikely to do better than the market, nor much worse.

U.S. equity funds

If you're interested in investing in U.S. markets, you can choose from among about forty-seven U.S. equity funds. These are very popular among investors who believe that the U.S. market offers investment opportunities not available in Canada and who expect the U.S. economy to outperform Canada's.

Since most U.S. funds accept subscriptions in either Canadian or U.S. dollars, these funds also appeal to people who have U.S. dollar savings and want to keep this money in U.S. dollar-denominated growth securities. Similarly, individuals who plan to retire in the U.S. often invest a portion of their assets in U.S. securities.

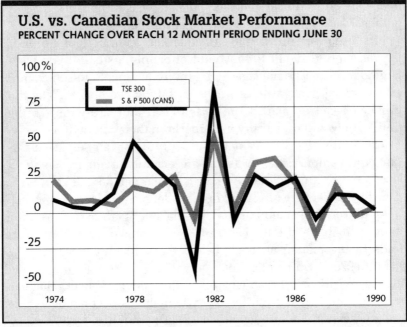

U.S. vs. Canadian Stock Market Performance
PERCENT CHANGE OVER EACH 12 MONTH PERIOD ENDING JUNE 30

CHART II

U.S. equity funds should be considered as an alternative to U.S. stock portfolios in estate planning. If you own substantial U.S. assets, such as stocks, and you die, your estate could be subject to U.S. probate. However, holding mutual funds invested in U.S. assets avoids this potential problem because the funds are a Canadian asset.

Like Canadian equity funds, there is a wide variety of funds that invest in the U.S. Many try to parrot the major U.S. stock market indexes. For example, Jarislowsky Finsco American Equity Fund invests primarily in companies included in the Standard & Poor's 500 composite stock index and which "best represent the investment characteristics of blue-chip securities." Similarly, Green Line U.S. Index Fund tracks the performance of the S&P 500.

Other funds have investment policies that are a variation of this theme. Century DJ Fund seeks above-average rates of return by investing in major blue-chip companies with above-average earnings and dividend records.

Others attempt to beat the averages by choosing investments from a broader range of stocks. AGF Special Fund Ltd. looks for com-

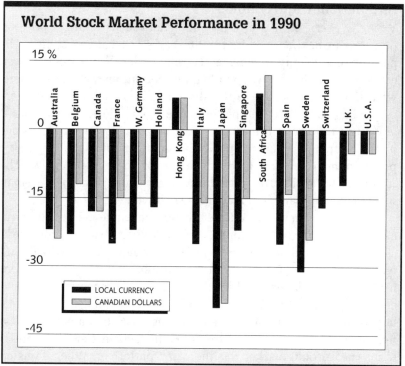

World Stock Market Performance in 1990

CHART III

panies that are expected to grow at above-average rates of return. AGF American Growth Fund Ltd. has a similar objective but puts the greatest portion of its assets in stocks listed on the New York Stock Exchange.

United American Fund seeks long-term capital growth by investing its assets in U.S. common stocks that its managers consider undervalued in relation to earnings, dividends and assets.

When the performance of U.S. funds is looked at in Canadian dollars, as a group they have not fared better than Canadian funds, particularly in periods when the Canadian dollar has risen against its U.S. counterpart. A comparison of the top ten performers for one year and ten years reveals a significant overlap; over a three- or five-year basis, Canadian funds are the winners. Different measurement dates, however, will provide different results.

International equity funds

Virtually every industrialized country and many Third World nations have stock markets that trade shares of local companies. The performance of any given market reflects local and international economic conditions. And while all important markets move somewhat in concert because of the shrinking global marketplace, there can be large differences in performance. This reflects the fact that at any given time certain markets might be in an earlier or later stage of the economic cycle than North American markets. A nimble portfolio manager can take advantage of these differences. The result is that an international fund might show gains in a year in which U.S. and Canadian markets head lower.

The performance also reflects the fact that some markets perform better than others. For example, in 1986 virtually all major world stock markets had positive returns. These ranged from Switzerland, with an increase of 0.1 percent in Swiss franc terms, to 108 per cent for Spain. Canada was at the bottom end of the range with a 5 percent gain for the TSE 300. The Tokyo Stock Exchange, the world's largest market, was up 44 percent. During 1986 the Canadian dollar fell against most overseas currencies. In fact, in Canadian dollar terms the Toronto market was the worst performer. When adjusted for exchange rates, the Swiss market was up 25 percent, the Spanish market was up 138 percent, and the Tokyo market was up 79 percent. In 1990 most markets were down. Still, as Chart III shows, some performed better than others.

While there are several dozen countries with stock markets, most international funds stick with the major European, Far East and Australian markets as well as Canadian and U.S. markets. A typical fund might restrict the bulk of its portfolio to shares traded in the United Kingdom, Germany, France, Switzerland, Australia, Japan, Canada and the U.S.

Occasionally, it will invest in shares traded in other markets such as Italy, Austria, Singapore, Hong Kong or the Scandinavian countries. But equity investments in these markets usually reflect a view of the outlook for a specific company rather than an economy or currency. Trading volumes in many overseas markets are simply too light to allow a portfolio manager to invest with reasonable diversification. So while a specific overseas market may rise 138 percent, as Spain's did in 1986, it is unrealistic to expect a fund manager to have a heavy position of Spanish stocks in a portfolio.

Managers of international funds must consider the relative values of assets in different countries, currency trends and, of course, stock market movements.

Managing an international fund can be more complicated than managing a single-market fund. Some firms have developed the expertise and have Canadian managers who base their decisions on their own research or on information supplied from abroad. Others retain overseas advisors to make recommendations. For instance, Global Strategy Fund uses N. M. Rothschild International Asset Management Ltd. of London; National Trust Global Fund uses Hill Samuel Investment Management Ltd., also of London; Dynamic Europe 1992 Fund has La Compagnie Financière Edmond de Rothschild Banque of Paris as its advisor.

The rates of return of the top-performing international funds suggest that location of the manager should not be a concern for investors.

Specialty funds

For investors who want a hefty weighting in a specific market or industry there are a number of specialty funds. These can be useful for investors who want to speculate on one industry or who want a heavier weighting in their portfolio of a specific type of investment than they can get by holding a broadly based fund.

Specialty funds can be divided into several categories: Japan funds, energy funds, gold funds, technology funds, small-company funds, health funds and natural resource funds.

Specialty funds include some of the best performers in some periods. For example, the four top-performing mutual funds in Canada in 1986 were Japanese funds: Universal Sector Pacific, formerly Universal Savings Japan (up 68 percent); Royal Trust Japanese Stock Fund (up 63.5 percent); Investors Japanese Growth Fund (up 61.2 percent); and AGF Japan Fund Ltd. (up 54.7 percent).

But often this kind of performance goes hand in hand with volatility. Three of the four Japanese funds have been in existence long enough to be ranked by volatility. They are among the 20 percent most volatile funds. Indeed, in the twelve months ending June 30, 1991, their returns in Canadian dollars were dismal. Universal Sector Pacific was down 1.8 percent, Royal Trust Japanese Stock Fund was down 8.5 percent, Investors Japanese Growth Fund down 9.5 percent and AGF Japan Fund Ltd. down 16.3 percent. During the twelve-month period ended June 30, 1990, their performance was once again very good compared with Canadian equity funds as a group.

The ten-year average annual compound rates of return for Japanese funds are superior to the rates for Canadian funds over the same period. However, to understand these rates you have to look at year-by-year performance. An investment made in the Japanese market in 1976 and held until 1983 or 1984 would have performed about the same as an investment in the Canadian market, although year-by-year performance would have varied widely. But 1985 and 1986 were banner years for Japanese funds because stock prices and the yen soared.

Gold funds are the most volatile mutual funds, reflecting the volatility of bullion prices and gold mining shares. In 1979, Goldfund jumped 161.5 percent; in 1980 it added 89.7 percent. The following year it was off 38.7 percent.

Energy funds have also had their ups and downs. They rose spectacularly during the late 1970s as world energy prices soared. But the federal government's national energy program and the oil glut made them dismal performers from 1981 to 1986, underperforming the general market. In 1987 they did well because of rising energy prices and increased investor interest in energy-related stocks. Their fortunes reversed again in 1988 but during the first part of 1989 they had mixed results. In August 1990 when Iraq invaded Kuwait energy funds were indeed the market leaders.

The specialty group includes what are called "small-cap" funds. These invest in companies with smaller capitalizations. Small can mean capitalizations of less than $150 million or less than $50 million, depending on the fund.

Several studies of market performance suggest that small-cap companies outperform the general market during bull markets and don't fall as much as the general market during bear markets. The theory is that smaller companies have a better growth rate than large, mature companies. Consequently, portfolios holding small-cap companies would have, over time, superior performance. In fact, the performance of small-cap funds reflects this.

Balanced funds

Balanced, or variable asset mix, funds have as their objective maximizing growth and income while preserving capital. They do this by changing the asset mix ratio of stocks to bonds to reflect anticipated market conditions. Some funds restrict their investments to Canadian stocks and debt securities. Others will include a wider range of instruments.

The funds that are truly balanced should be less volatile than pure equity funds because of the revenue from the fixed income portion of the portfolio or because of the types of stocks held, and indeed, the majority of balanced funds are less volatile than equity funds. Some balanced funds, however, have investment policies that allow them to hold any proportion of fixed income securities and equities so from time to time the fund could be 100 percent equities. Because they do not have to be diversified among asset classes, they may prove more volatile than funds that always have some stocks and some bonds.

While equity funds are the largest group, balanced funds have been attracting new investors at a faster pace. The toughest investment decision for many people centres upon asset mix – the percentage they should hold in Canadian stocks, bonds, short-term deposits, foreign securities and gold. For investors who don't want to get involved in this type of investment decision, a good balanced fund might make the most sense.

Real estate funds

Real estate funds invest primarily in income-producing commercial real estate properties. The return from a real estate fund includes income as well as capital gains from the change in value of the underlying properties.

Real estate funds differ in three important ways from other mutual funds. First, real estate funds use borrowed capital as well as investors' capital to purchase properties. Virtually every equity, bond, mortgage and money market fund has a prohibition against borrowing to invest. Second, real estate funds are much less liquid than other funds. Where most other funds are valued daily or weekly, real estate funds are generally valued quarterly, and in some cases monthly. Investors can only redeem on specific dates and may have to give prior notice. Over the past five years two real estate funds have suspended redemptions while their portfolios were reappraised. Don't buy a real estate fund if you need liquidity.

Finally, real estate mutual funds are valued differently. Their values are based on appraisals. The net asset values per share of equity, bond and mortgage funds are based on market values of underlying assets. These reflect actual prices of trades that took place in the market at the close of trading on the day when the fund shares or units were valued.

But a real estate holding is very different from a position in BCE common shares. While BCE shares held in a mutual fund are identical to shares traded on the TSE, no two pieces of real estate are exactly alike. They may be similar to other properties. But there are likely to be significant differences that will affect the value of one compared with the other.

The value of a real estate fund is based on appraisals of the properties held by a fund. And appraisals are only educated guesses or estimates – what a qualified appraiser believes the market value of a specific property to be on a given date.

In January 1987, the Ontario Securities Commission introduced new regulations for real estate mutual funds, including guidelines for appraisals. The new rules removed a cloud hanging over real estate funds as a group. During 1985, Real Property Trust of Canada suspended redemptions after its trustees changed managers and the appraised values of its properties were questioned. In 1986, Halifax-based Canadian Property Investors Trust suspended redemptions after the OSC expressed concerns about appraisals on two of its properties.

The new regulations set general investment standards as well as standards for appraisals and valuation of shares. Appraisals of each property in a real estate fund are generally performed annually. So in a rising real estate market the selling and buying price of a fund unit might be less than the actual value of the underlying assets.

As well, an appraisal is an estimate. There is no way of knowing whether the appraisal accurately reflects the amount that would be received if the property were sold. Moreover, if the fund were liquidated, the amount shareholders receive might be less than the net asset value of the fund. If the assets of a real estate fund were put on the block, some of its holdings might go at fire-sale prices.

While the minimum capital for an equity fund is $100,000 and for a mortgage fund $350,000, the OSC sets minimum capital requirements for a real estate mutual fund at $10 million. Any new fund must raise that amount before it can invest in real estate.

These subscriptions have to be in cash. The fund cannot issue shares in return for a property or on the condition that the seller of the property buy units of the fund. The purpose of this rule is to avoid a potential conflict of interest.

The appraiser cannot be affiliated with the fund, its manager or the property being appraised. The fee charged can't be based on the valuation or on the appraisal reaching a specified value. The OSC requires that the independent appraiser, whose name must be included in the prospectus, be a member of the Appraisal Institute of Canada and have the Accredited Appraiser Canadian Institute designation. The appraiser must also have five years' experience appraising the type of property being appraised in the province where the property is located.

Each property in the fund must be reappraised annually on the anniversary of its acquisition or last appraisal. However, the trustees of the fund are required to obtain an appraisal more frequently if, in their opinion, there is a development that may materially change the value of the property. For instance, an arm's-length bid for the property could be made at a price substantially different from the appraised value.

Equity-based mutual funds can have sharp jumps or declines in value reflecting changes in the marketplace. Values of real estate funds, however, are less volatile because their values are "managed." To prevent sharp fluctuations in a fund's unit value, no more than 50 percent of the fund's properties can be reappraised in the same calendar quarter.

Not only may values be out of date and too high or too low, but real estate funds will be shown as having relatively low volatility on the *Financial Times* monthly fund survey. As a result, comparing the volatility of real estate funds with other mutual funds is not valid.

Because real estate funds appraise their properties so infrequently, they cannot price their shares more than once every quarter. The exceptions are funds that update their annual appraisals monthly on the basis of the income stream generated by those properties.

Real estate isn't as liquid as a stock portfolio so a fund may require thirty days' notice to redeem shares. A fund must pay for the shares it redeems within fifteen days of the day on which the net asset value is calculated. If it doesn't have the cash to redeem all shares submitted, it must redeem on a pro rata, or proportional, basis.

No delay in payment can exceed six months unless approved˙by a two-thirds vote of investors. The suspension can't exceed twelve months unless 80 percent of investors agree. A defeat of such a motion would likely mean a fund would be forced to sell off all or part of its property portfolio to raise funds to meet redemptions.

Commodity funds

It's even possible to have a mutual fund that speculates in the futures markets. Futures are contracts calling for the delivery of a specified commodity, security or currency at a specific price on a specific date. Futures contracts cover major food commodities, precious metals, trading currencies, bonds and even the stock market. Trading in futures is very risky because investors have to put up only a fraction of the value of the underlying contract as a "down payment." Because of this enormous leverage, investors either make a lot or lose a lot.

Because of the risks involved in futures trading, anyone who wants to offer a mutual fund that invests in commodity futures must meet some stringent criteria. And while commodity funds have been brought to market from time to time in Canada, they have failed to generate lasting investor interest. Currently, it appears that none is being offered nationally, although one, Mustard Seed Fund, is available in British Columbia. This fund is especially unique since its manager earns an incentive fee based on profits.

The lack of interest in commodity funds largely reflects the regulatory environment. First, the OSC, whose rules must be followed by anyone who wants to sell securities to the public in Ontario (most other provinces have regulations borrowed from or patterned after those of the OSC), must be satisfied that an investor's liability is limited to the amount invested. If you speculate in commodities on your own, your liability is unlimited.

Second, the people selling such a fund generally have to be registered under the Commodity Futures Act as well as the Securities Act. This dual registration reflects the OSC's recognition that someone selling a commodities fund should have expertise both in trading commodities futures and mutual funds.

Third, to be a potential investor, you have to be wealthier and more experienced in investing than the average person. The OSC demands that dealers offering such an investment must determine that the potential investor understands the nature of the investment through work experience, education, independent advice or prior experience.

As well, the OSC sets minimum suitability standards based on income and assets:

• Investors must have a minimum annual gross income of $30,000 and a net worth of $30,000. Alternatively, a net worth of $75,000 is required.

• The maximum annual management fee can't exceed 6 percent of net assets of the fund. Incentive fees can't exceed 25 percent of the profits calculated no more frequently than quarterly.

• The minimum capital for a commodity fund is $500,000.

• The prospectus must state on the front page that a participant in the fund must be able and prepared to lose his or her entire investment, that the fund is highly speculative, and that there are substantial management and advisory fees and brokerage commissions before an investor is entitled to a return on investment.

• Investors in a commodity fund must be notified within seven days of any decline in net asset value of 50 percent or more from the beginning of the year or the last valuation date.

• Potential investors must be informed in the prospectus whether the fund will wind up automatically if the fund's net asset value per share falls below a certain level. As well, the manager of the fund must disclose his or her track record in managing comparable pools.

Because of the volatile nature of commodities futures, disclosure requirements are more stringent than for other mutual funds. Investors get monthly reports on performance, commissions paid, and the like.

CHAPTER 5

All About Income Funds

FIXED INCOME MUTUAL FUNDS are primarily designed to provide maximum income rather than growth, while preserving capital. These types of funds invest in income-producing securities – bonds, mortgages, treasury bills, and in some cases common stocks and preferred shares that have high yields. By investing for income rather than growth, fixed income fund returns are more stable than equity fund returns.

Managers of fixed income funds are concerned primarily with the quality of the issuers of the securities they purchase, interest-rate trends and, depending on the fund, currency exchange rates.

Because preservation of capital is a primary objective, most fixed income funds have similar policies regarding the quality of the investments they make. All mortgage funds invest primarily in first mortgages, the most secure type of mortgage. If a borrower defaults, the holder of the first mortgage has first call on the assets. Similarly, most bond funds have a major portion of their assets in government bonds and government guaranteed obligations. Any debentures in fixed income portfolios are usually of large companies whose assets are significantly greater than their debt loads and whose earnings have historically exceeded interest expense by a broad margin.

Preferred income funds generally have the vast majority of their assets invested in preferred shares of blue-chip Canadian companies whose securities are rated highly by the widely used rating services, Canadian Bond Rating Service Ltd. and Dominion Bond Rating Service or in securities which the manager's analysis indicates are secure. In order to assign ratings, the rating services examine the income statements and balance sheets of major companies that issue preferred shares, and consider industry trends. Most preferred income funds have some common shares but the portion is generally limited to a maximum of 20 percent to 25 percent.

Returns from fixed income funds have two components. First, of course, there is the income which reflects interest and dividends paid by the underlying securities. Second is capital appreciation, which reflects the impact of the market on the value of the underlying securities. Although it is a secondary objective for most bond, mortgage and preferred dividend funds, capital appreciation or depreciation can be a significant portion of total return, particularly during periods of volatile interest rates.

In periods of rising interest rates, the market values of fixed income securities decline. For example, in December 1980 Government of Canada bonds with 13 percent coupons maturing May 1, 2001 were trading at about $1,000. Seven months later, interest rates were at record levels and long-term Government of Canada bonds were yielding about 17.5 per cent. At that point the bonds with 13 percent coupons were changing hands at about $750. The decline from $1,000 reflects the price that investors were willing to pay for that bond when new bonds were available at substantially higher yields.

This is an extreme example because the shift in interest rates over that time was exceptional. The volatility of a specific bond depends on the number of years to maturity – the date when the issuer will redeem the bond at face value. Bonds with only a few years to maturity are much less volatile than bonds that won't mature for decades. A small change in rates will mean a significant change in price for a long-term bond. For example, a Government of Canada 8.5 percent bond maturing June 30, 2011 traded at $795 per $1,000 face value in September 1987 when its yield was just under 11 percent. Five months later, yields had dropped to about 9.4 percent and it was trading at just over $917, a gain of more than 15 percent.

Bond fund and preferred share fund managers can control the performance of their funds through the structure of their portfolios. Managers who expect a jump in rates sell their longer-term securities and move into shorter-term securities. Mortgage fund managers have less control because they have few, if any, opportunities to trade their portfolio to shorten or lengthen the terms of mortgages they hold. Also, the terms of the mortgages which they hold largely reflect what was available in the marketplace at the time they made their purchases. More on this later.

Taxation of Interest and Dividends

	Interest	Dividend
Interest received	$100.00	–
Dividend received	–	$100.00
Dividend "gross up"	–	$25.00
Taxable dividend	–	$125.00
Federal tax (29%)	$29.00	$36.25
Less dividend tax credit	–	$16.67
Net federal tax + surtax	$29.87	$20.17
Add provincial tax*	$14.50	$9.79
Total tax paid	$44.37	$29.96
NET RETURN	$55.63	$70.04

NOTE: *50% of basic federal tax. Provincial tax rates vary from province to province.

TABLE IV

Some fixed income fund managers try to increase their returns by holding debt instruments issued in foreign currencies. Several provinces, some Crown corporations and many major banks and corporations borrow abroad by issuing bonds and debentures denominated in U.S. dollars, Japanese yen, Australian dollars and some European currencies. Funds that hold these securities will benefit if the foreign currencies appreciate against the Canadian dollar. However, performance suffers if the Canadian dollar does better.

Preferred-dividend income funds

If your investment objective is current income, and the capital you want to invest is outside your RRSP, consider a preferred-dividend income fund. Your after-tax rate of return will generally be higher than the after-tax return from an interest-income mutual fund.

The federal government taxes various types of investment income differently. Interest income is fully taxed. In contrast, the first $100,000 of capital gains is tax free, as a lifetime exemption, subject to certain adjustments. Dividend income from Canadian corporations is treated in yet another way. To encourage Canadians to invest in shares and to help companies raise capital, the government invented the federal dividend tax credit to reduce the effective tax rate on dividend income from Canadian corporations. Your after-tax rate of return from investing for dividends should exceed the after-tax return from interest vehicles. Table IV compares the taxation of interest and dividends and shows that you would pay just under $30 tax on $100 of dividend income compared with just over $44 tax on $100 of interest income. However, pre-tax yields on dividends are generally lower than interest yields. But market spreads on an after-tax basis generally mean you get a higher return from dividends.

The impact of the dividend tax credit is to reduce the tax you pay on dividends from Canadian corporations so that on a pre-tax basis $1 of dividends is equal to about $1.26 of interest. On an after-tax basis a 6.4 percent dividend yield is equal to an 8 percent interest yield, an 8 percent dividend yield is equal to a 10 percent interest yield, and a 12 percent dividend yield is equal to a 15 percent interest yield.

Quebec sets its own tax rates independent of federal rates. A Quebec resident paying the top federal and provincial tax rates would net about $49 after tax on $100 of interest income and about $62 on $100 of dividend income.

Managing a preferred share fund is a complicated task. First, there are several different types of preferred shares. Straight preferred shares pay a fixed dividend in perpetuity. They can be very volatile in periods of rapidly changing interest rates and, as a result, many investors are reluctant to buy them. So the investment community has developed other types of preferred shares in response to changing market conditions.

Floating-rate preferred shares, for instance, offer a dividend rate that is a certain percentage of the prime rate, say 70 percent. And there are floating-rate preferreds that have a fixed-minimum dividend rate. Retractable preferreds give investors the right to return their shares to the issuer at full face value at a specific date. Sinking-fund preferreds require the issuer to purchase or redeem a specific number of shares each year so that the total issue is retired after a certain number of years. Convertible preferred shares give the holder the right to convert the shares into common stock. Investors buy convertible preferred shares because they provide more income than common shares. If the common dividend grows to a point where it exceeds the preferred they can convert the preferred share to a common.

A few companies have issued preferred shares denominated in U.S. dollars. A fund manager might also hold some common shares in a preferred fund if the yield on the shares was attractive.

Most fund managers use a similar universe of preferred shares, basing their investment decisions on quality, yield, liquidity and specific features of a preferred share, such as whether it is floating or retractable.

Quality considerations don't vary much from fund to fund. All invest the majority of their assets in high-quality preferred shares. By high quality, most Canadian fund managers mean preferred shares that carry P1 and P2 ratings issued by the Canadian Bond Rating Service and Dominion Bond Rating Service. A portion of a fund may be invested in preferred shares that aren't rated or that have a lower rating if the expected returns are superior, provided the manager is satisfied with the safety of the dividend and the return is superior. Similarly, a portion of the portfolio may be invested in high-yielding common shares.

Depending on interest rate spreads, a portion of the fund might also be invested in treasury bills. Because fund expenses, such as the management fee, can be charged against interest income, a fund manager will include some interest-paying investments such as treasury bills if the interest rate is higher than the rate available from preferreds.

Interest income funds

If interest income or a stable return is your major investment objective, as it is for many investors in RRSPs or registered retirement income funds, you have your choice of four different types of mutual funds: bond funds, mortgage funds, funds that invest in both bonds and mortgages, and money market and savings funds. Savings funds, which hold wholesale bank deposits, have virtually disappeared from the marketplace.

All four are backed by assets that carry little or no risk. Bond funds, for example, include bonds and debentures that are guaranteed by governments, Crown corporations, major banks or the credit-worthiness of major corporations. Mortgage funds have as their underlying securities mortgages that are secured by specific properties. In some cases these mortgages are insured against default, guaranteed by a government agency or guaranteed by the manager of the fund. Money market funds generally hold treasury bills that are guaranteed by the federal government, provincial treasury bills that are guaranteed by the issuing province, securities issued or guaranteed by major financial institutions and sometimes top-quality short-term notes issued by major corporations.

As a result, with an interest income mutual fund you don't have to worry much about losing your money. On rare occasions, bond funds suffer defaults, but the quality of the overall portfolios as well as the various guarantees make the impact of any losses insignificant to the value of an interest income fund.

There are, however, some differences among the four different types of income interest funds, and these affect the returns you may receive. These differences reflect the types of securities they hold. To understand how this works you have to look at the underlying securities in which such funds invest.

Let's assume you have a choice of three funds. The first invests only in Government of Canada treasury bills, the second in Government of Canada bonds and the third in mortgages guaranteed by the federal government under the National Housing Act. In all three cases we have Ottawa guaranteeing the underlying securities.

Even so, the returns you can earn from these funds may differ widely. For instance, during the twelve months ended June 30, 1991, the top ten bond funds gave rates of return that ranged from 16.3 percent to 14.2 percent; the top ten mortgage funds gave returns between 19.2 percent and 15.4 percent; and money market and savings funds had returns clustered around 10.8 percent.

The high returns of bond and mortgage funds during the year reflect the sharp declines in bond yields and mortgage rates during that year.

Money market and savings funds have the most stable rates of return. That's because the securities they hold are very short term and will be redeemed at full face value by the issuer within one year. So the rates of return on money market funds are almost entirely income, with little that can be attributed to changing market values of the underlying securities.

A mortgage fund is more volatile than a money market fund. A mortgage fund holds securities that may mature in as little as six months or as long as five years. Its rate of return includes the interest paid on the mortgages it holds, plus or minus an adjustment to the market value of the mortgages in its portfolio. The market values change with changes in mortgage rates. If rates go up, the values of mortgages in the portfolio decline, with longer-term mortgages declining more than shorter-term mortgages.

A $50,000 five-year mortgage issued at 12.5 percent, for example, would have a market value of about $40,000 if new five-year mortgages were available at 19 percent. But mortgage funds are not as volatile as this example seems to indicate because fund holdings include both short- and long-term mortgages. Also, new money coming into the fund or mortgages coming up for renewal will enter at prevailing rates. This serves to stabilize returns.

Bond funds are generally more volatile than mortgage funds because they hold securities that may not mature for twenty years or more. A manager expecting rates to fall will trade the portfolio to increase the percentage of bonds which mature in, say, twenty years. This way the portfolio locks in a high rate of return. Conversely, a manager expecting higher rates will move into the shorter end of the market.

To sum up, money market and savings funds have the most stable rates of return. But over the long haul that stability has a cost. The cost comes in the lower rates of return that money market funds earn over the longer term compared with bond or mortgage funds. Bond funds have given higher long-term total returns than mortgage funds. But they have been more volatile and in some years have underperformed mortgage funds. For current income, however, mortgage funds often have an edge over bond funds because mortgage rates are generally higher than bond yields. Funds that invest in bonds and mortgages combine the characteristics of both types of funds.

Bond funds

The primary objective of most bond funds is to earn the maximum interest income possible without taking significant risk. But an important part of a bond fund's total return can include capital gains that stem from trading. Still, earning income is more important. The fund manager meets this objective by investing in quality bonds. Virtually all bond funds offered in Canada hold a major portion of their assets in government and government-guaranteed bonds, issues guaranteed by the major chartered banks and high-quality corporate debt. Some, such as AGF Canadian Bond Fund, restrict their holdings to Government of Canada bonds.

The investment policies of bond funds generally reflect the investment objectives of the conservative investors who use them for their RRSPs, RRIFs and for income.

But even though virtually all funds invest in the same quality of issuers, performance can vary widely. These variations reflect the expertise of the fund manager as well as the fund's investment policy.

There are many ways that bond fund managers can increase returns. Most involve structuring a portfolio to reflect anticipated moves in interest rates. A fund manager who expects long-term rates to fall might increase the fund's holdings of long-term bonds. This would lock in high-yielding coupons of bonds which mature in, say, twenty years. Conversely, a manager who expects interest rates to rise will move into shorter-term bonds. A manager who expects rates to rise then decline might hold a mixture of long and short bonds with few medium-term holdings.

The actual management of the bond portfolio can be quite complicated. Not only does the manager have to consider the direction of interest rates, but also the relative yields of short-term and long-term bonds. In some periods long-term bonds yield significantly more than short-term bonds. At other times their yields will be about the same. There have been some occasions, such as 1989 and the first half of 1990, when short-term rates have actually been higher than long-term rates.

Managers will trade bonds to improve yields. Each trade may improve the yield of a small portion of the portfolio by only a fraction of a percentage point. But done often enough, this can have a significant impact on overall performance.

Bond funds can also generate significant capital gains. This can happen when a manager sells bonds at a profit. For instance, a fund manager expecting an imminent drop in rates might buy discount bonds – bonds that sell at a discount to their face value because their coupons offer lower yields than new bonds.

Fund managers can also boost yields by increasing the portion of their portfolios invested in corporate bonds. Corporate bonds generally have higher coupon rates than government bonds of the same maturity. The higher yields, of course, reflect the fact that corporate bonds don't have the backing of a government. In addition, corporate bonds aren't as liquid as government bonds so the spread between the buy and sell prices can be significantly wider. As a result, the trading costs of a fund that has a heavy corporate component may be higher.

Another way of potentially boosting return is to invest in bonds denominated in foreign currencies. Crown corporations, provinces, banks and companies sometimes raise money outside Canada by issuing bonds and debentures in foreign currencies. The U.S. dollar is the most common currency used but Canadian governments and companies also commonly raise money in Australian dollars, New Zealand dollars, Japanese yen, Swiss francs and German marks.

Even though these bonds are denominated in foreign currencies, their issuers are Canadian so they are eligible for inclusion in RRSPs and pension funds.

A fund manager might hold foreign currency bonds if the interest rate paid were substantially higher than the rate paid on Canadian dollar bonds of the same issuer and same maturity and there appeared to be no foreign exchange risk. Or, the manager might want to hold foreign currency bonds because he or she expected a sharp decline in the value of the Canadian dollar.

Specialty bond funds

Most of the bond funds offered by investment counsellors, investment dealers, banks and trust and insurance companies are designed to appeal to investors seeking income rather than capital appreciation. These funds are eligible for RRSPs and pension funds.

There are several exceptions, such as AGF Global Government Bond Fund. It invests in bonds issued by central governments of countries with developed capital markets. Its objective is high income and capital appreciation.

Another exception is Dynamic Strip Bond Fund. It invests in coupons of bonds issued or guaranteed by government. Investors therefore know years in advance what their investment will be worth. This fund is suitable for people who want to lock in a set return for part of their RRSP or who want to speculate on interest rates falling.

Some years ago, one company launched a "junk-bond" fund that invested in lower-quality bonds of U.S. corporate issuers. The fund provided a yield much higher than other bond funds offered in Canada. The fund failed to attract investor attention and was dropped. Apparently, few investors understood how the manager selected securities for the portfolio.

One equity fund that has done well with lower-quality bonds is Vancouver-based Cundill Value Fund. Its manager, Peter Cundill, looks for debentures of companies in financial difficulty. He purchases these at a fraction of face value, anticipating corporate reorganizations that will make the debentures much more valuable.

Mortgage funds

Mortgage funds are designed to provide maximum interest income for investors. Because mortgage rates are generally at least a point higher than bond yields, mortgage funds pay more current income per dollar invested than bond funds.

Unlike bond funds, mortgage funds rarely trade what they buy. Consequently, capital gains are unlikely to be part of a mortgage fund investor's income – unless he or she redeems fund units when interest rates are relatively low at a value in excess of average cost. And because few mortgages are available with interest rates fixed beyond five years, mortgage funds as a group are less volatile than bond funds.

A mortgage is a loan secured by property. A residential mortgage is on a home; a commercial or industrial loan is on a commercial or industrial property. Commercial and industrial loans often have longer terms than residential mortgages and higher yields. A property can have several mortgages on it representing several loans. A second mortgage is less secure than a first mortgage; a third mortgage is less secure than a second mortgage. Virtually all the major bank, trust company, investment counsellor and insurance company mortgage funds hold first mortgages only. The amount of the loan is generally no more than 75 percent of the value of the property. Lenders can go higher than the 75 percent ceiling but in these cases they usually insure the mortgage against default.

Some funds, such as London Life Mortgage Fund, invest in residential, commercial and industrial mortgages. But most restrict their investments to residential mortgages.

Because the funds invest in first mortgages, investors needn't worry much about losses. For example, First Canadian Mortgage Fund, offered by the Bank of Montreal, invests only in mortgages that amount to no more than 75 percent of the value of the property or are guaranteed under the National Housing Act or insured by the Mortgage Insurance Co. of Canada. If a mortgage goes into default, the bank guarantees to buy it at no penalty to the fund.

As part of its marketing strategy, the bank has had its fund reviewed by the Canadian Bond Rating Service and Dominion Bond Rating Service, the first fund to be rated by the two agencies. Both gave it an "AAA" rating, which demonstrates minimum risk and good returns. Generally, ratings are used for institutional investment products rather than investments aimed primarily at smaller investors.

Unlike bonds, mortgages – especially residential mortgages – are not traded actively. Consequently, mortgage fund managers are somewhat restricted in their ability to change the structure of their portfolios in anticipation of changes in interest rates.

Mortgage fund managers, particularly of bank and trust company funds, have little choice in the terms of mortgages purchased by the funds. The mix of six-month, one-year, three-year and five-year mortgages is dependent largely on market conditions rather than on what the managers want. For instance, if most mortgage customers of the sponsoring bank or trust company choose four- and five-year terms – as happens in periods of rising interest rates – then that's where new money in the fund will be invested. Conversely, in periods of falling rates, when managers would like to increase the portion of four- and five-year mortgages, more borrowers will opt for shorter-term mortgages.

How this affects a fund depends on the portion of mortgages up for renewal in a given period and the growth rate of fund sales. Of course, if demand for longer-term mortgages drops drastically, then the spread between longer-term and shorter-term mortgages will narrow, shifting some of the demand.

The difference in the rate of return between two mortgage funds reflects the manager's ability to keep the portfolio balanced to minimize interest rate risk and keep the unit value relatively steady. Funds offered by the larger financial institutions probably have more flexibility because the funds are often a small fraction of the total mortgage portfolio offered by the institution, in some cases less than 1 percent of the total. This gives fund managers some discretion over mortgages that will be acquired by the fund.

Bond and mortgage funds

There are a number of funds that invest in both bonds and mortgages. Some have rigid asset-mix ratios. For example, Canada Life Fixed Income S-19 fund invests 75 percent of its assets in liquid, fixed income securities and the balance in securities "which provide a premium return in exchange for a lower level of liquidity." Others don't follow fixed ratios. Several, such as Mackenzie Mortgage and Income Fund, may include common and preferred shares with attractive yields and the opportunity for capital appreciation.

Rates of return of these funds, as a group, are more volatile than simple mortgage funds but less volatile than pure bond funds.

Money market funds

Money market funds, or short-term yield funds, provide interest income with virtually no risk to capital. In fact, most money market and savings funds price their units at a constant value – $1 and $10 are the most common. Yields on these funds move in concert with short-term yields such as on treasury bills. Interest earned on the fund is used to purchase additional units on investors' behalf. Income is credited to clients' accounts daily in the case of funds that price their units daily and weekly in the case of funds that price weekly. Depending on the fund, interest compounds weekly or monthly.

Money market funds invest in a portfolio of highly liquid short-term debt instruments which generally mature within one year. These include federal and provincial government treasury bills, chartered bank certificates of deposit and instruments guaranteed by chartered banks, such as bankers' acceptances, and short-term notes issued by the most credit-worthy major corporations. Changes in the yields on money market funds may lag or precede changes in the prime rate, depending on the holdings of the portfolio and the moves in the "short end" of the market, say T-bills maturing in less than thirty days. Therefore, in periods of volatile interest rates, the yield a buyer gets on a fund reflects the yield generated by the portfolio and may not match current yields.

Most fund management companies disclose two rates of return or yields for their money market funds in their advertisements. The first is the indicated yield; the second is the effective yield. The indicated yield is more accurate. Generally, it is the yield earned by the fund in the latest seven-day period and calculated on income accrued or paid during the seven days. It's shown on an annualized basis. The effective yield is based on the compounding of the indicated yield; it assumes that the fund will continue to yield this amount every week – which is not likely.

Fund companies are required to show the indicated yield in any advertising that includes yields. They have the option of showing the effective yield but do not have to do so. The effective yield, however, could mislead an investor into expecting a higher return than will actually be earned, especially if rates are declining.

It would be more accurate for a fund company to show its indicated yield and the period or average term to maturity over which investors could expect to continue to earn that yield. Both the indicated yield and average term to maturity will change as new units are sold or investors redeem.

Returns vary moderately among money market funds, with the differences reflecting the aggressiveness of the manager. Some funds will restrict their holdings to instruments that mature within ninety days and keep them until maturity. Even a sharp jump in interest rates would have only a moderate impact on such funds' performance. Other funds might hold instruments with longer maturities to pick up a slightly higher return or because they expect rates to fall. Managers of these funds would trade their holdings to increase yields, too. Rates will also reflect management fees which vary from 0 percent to 1 percent or more (a company charging no management fee uses its money market fund as a loss leader to attract business to its other funds).

Income payments

Before buying an income fund, find out how often you will receive your income payments. Bond funds usually distribute income quarterly or monthly, mortgage funds distribute income quarterly, preferred share funds distribute income monthly, and money market funds usually distribute income weekly, or monthly. Realized capital gains for bond funds and preferred share funds are generally distributed at year end.

Knowing the payment dates may have a bearing on the timing of your purchase. For instance, don't buy a bond fund the day before the dividend date because you'll be responsible for paying taxes on the interest paid, if the holding is outside your RRSP, even though you held the fund for only a day before the payment date. You will receive the interest but you will have converted a portion of your capital into taxable income.

Make sure you're aware of any restrictions on interest payments. For example, you are only entitled to a specific month's interest in the AGF Canadian Bond Fund, formerly Canadian Trusteed Income Fund, if you hold the units for a full calendar month. In this case, you would buy on the last day of the month and redeem on the first.

CHAPTER 6

All About Closed-End Funds

NOT ALL FUNDS ISSUE NEW shares automatically when investors want to buy. A handful of funds called closed-end funds have a fixed number of shares or units. These are traded on a stock exchange such as the Toronto Stock Exchange. Closed-end precious metals funds even have their own TSE subindex. If you want to own shares of a closed-end fund, you have to buy them from someone who already owns them by placing an order with your stockbroker.

Closed-end funds, like other funds, invest in a portfolio of investments. Most closed-end funds are specialty funds that invest in particular areas such as precious metals, global investments or bonds. These funds are closed-end investment holding companies.

There is also a small group of funds called income trusts. These use investors' and borrowed capital to invest in a portfolio of fixed income investments that pass on the interest income to investors.

The closed-end investment holding companies that invest in gold and in international portfolios are corporations, just like other companies listed on stock exchanges. But instead of making or selling something, they invest capital. They have the same powers and responsibilities as other corporations. In fact, they can have much more leeway in their investment policies than open-end funds.

In addition, their profits are taxable like those of other corporations. Any income earned or capital gains realized by a closed-end fund are taxable at corporate rates. This differs from open-end funds where income and gains generally flow through to the individual investor. Since corporations aren't eligible for the lifetime capital gains exemption, the rate of return to an investor holding a closed end fund might be lower than the rate of return earned on an open-end fund with a similar investment program.

Closed-end funds have been around for more than half a century, but their numbers increased in the early 1980s. The surge in

A Survey of Closed-End Funds

Fund	TSE Share Price	Net Asset Value
BGR Precious Metals Inc.	$7.75	$9.00
Canada Income Plus	8.63	9.90
Central Fund of Canada Ltd.	4.75	5.30
First Australia Prime Income	11.75	12.44
First Mercantile Currency	7.00	8.13
Germany Fund of Canada	9.25	10.34

June 27, 1991

TABLE V

popularity of closed-end funds coincided with the push by brokerage houses to promote self-directed RRSPs. At the time, shares listed on Canadian stock exchanges could be held in self-directed RRSPs without any restrictions. Closed-end funds qualified, even if their portfolios held investments, such as gold bullion, that would be ineligible if held directly in an RRSP or if their portfolios exceeded the 10 percent limit on foreign property in RRSPs.

Therefore, closed-end funds were promoted by investment dealers as a way of getting around the intent of the rules restricting RRSP investments. During this period Central Fund of Canada Ltd., one of the older closed-end funds, became a gold fund and had a share issue. Three new closed-end gold funds – Goldcorp Investments Ltd., Guardian-Morton Shulman Precious Metals Inc. and BGR Precious Metals Inc. – were also established. Shortly after, several global funds were underwritten – Guardian Pacific Rim, Guardian International Income and Worldwide Equities.

Ottawa revised its rules in 1986 so that closed-end funds that were primarily invested in foreign securities would be considered foreign property and limited to 10 percent of an RRSP. Closed-end funds that were already primarily invested in foreign property were "grandfathered" provided they did not arrange to issue additional shares after December 4, 1985, the date when Ottawa proposed the change.

Closed-end funds have a limited following compared with open-end funds. That's largely because closed-end funds have tended to trade at a significant discount to the value of their underlying assets. The discounts apparently reflect the relative lack of liquidity of closed-end funds. Shareholders of open-end funds can redeem their shares at full net asset value on any valuation day. But holders of closed-end funds can sell their investments only if other investors are buyers. In a falling market, potential buyers of a closed-end fund might be scarce. The discount from underlying asset value will increase accordingly, reducing the market value of the fund units.

In a rising market the discount may shrink or even disappear. If, for instance, foreign investors become heavy buyers of closed-end gold funds as a way of buying a portfolio of Canadian gold shares, their prices might rise sharply.

The discount might also shrink on speculation that a closed-end fund might convert to an open-end fund. In mid-1987, Guardian Pacific Rim announced it was asking shareholders to approve a proposal to convert the closed-end fund to an open-end fund. Its shares were trading at a 17 percent discount to asset value before the announcement. Two months later the discount had shrunk to about 12 percent. Similarly, Privatization Investment Fund became an open-end fund at the end of 1987. The fund's units traded for as little as $3 in October 1987 but at the end of the year, when redemptions were allowed, their value was just over $10 per unit.

Although there can be disadvantages to the fact that the shares of a closed-end fund cannot be redeemed on demand, there are also advantages. For instance, managers have more leeway in making investments. Because shareholders can't redeem shares on demand, the manager of a closed-end fund might decide to invest more heavily in shares with restricted marketability than would the manager of an open-end fund. About 90 percent of the portfolio of open-end funds must be in liquid investments.

Also, a closed-end fund might invest in part with borrowed funds. For investment income trusts, the Ontario Securities Commission restricts debt to a maximum of 25 percent of the assets of the fund. In contrast, open-end funds may not borrow other than temporarily to meet redemptions – even then only up to 5 percent of assets.

The minimum equity capital for an investment income trust closed-end fund is $1 million. The minimum for an equity mutual fund is $100,000. The investment policies of closed-ends funds are generally included in their annual reports.

There are also several closed-end funds that were originally issued as flow-through limited partnership tax shelters. These funds purchased flow-through shares from mining companies and obtained certain writeoffs which the tax shelter investors were able to use to reduce their personal taxes. After the minimum holding period required by regulatory authorities, these closed-end funds could roll their holdings tax free into open-end funds in exchange for shares in the open-end funds. At this point the limited partnerships would dissolve and the holdings of open-end fund shares would be distributed to their investors.

Among the better known flow-through limited partnerships that follow this route are the CMP partnerships, which roll into funds in the Dynamic Group and the NIM partnerships.

CHAPTER 7

What to Do
First

MUTUAL FUNDS CAN BE USED
successfully to meet both your short-term and long-term objectives,
either inside RRSPs or outside of them. The trick, of course, is to
make sure the funds you choose meet your objectives and are compatible with your financial picture.

Assuming you've taken care of the basics, such as making sure
you have adequate life and disability insurance, an up-to-date will
and a cash cushion equivalent to several months' salary, the first
thing you should do is make a list of your investments, including
your home, and your debts.

Interest paid on personal debts such as outstanding credit card
balances and mortgages is generally not deductible from income for
tax purposes. The cardinal rule to follow is to pay off all personal
debt before starting any long-term investment program outside your
RRSP.

Look at it this way. Paying off your debt is like making a risk-free
investment that pays premium rates of return. Bank credit card
charges are around 18 percent, higher in some cases. And while
many mutual funds have given moderately higher long-term rates of
return, you wouldn't run out to borrow money at 18 percent in the
hope of earning 20 percent, particularly if the 20 percent rate wasn't
guaranteed and the 18 percent wasn't deductible from tax. Yet that
is exactly what you would be doing if you invested in mutual funds
while carrying unpaid balances on your credit cards.

Paying off your mortgage isn't as cut-and-dried as paying off your
credit card debts because mortgage rates are generally a lot lower
than the historical rates earned on equity-based mutual funds. Even
so, you should still pay off your mortgage as quickly as possible.
You always have the option of borrowing against the equity in your
home and using the proceeds to buy mutual funds. You'll still owe
money on your home. But this way the interest on the loan will be

tax deductible. Whether you should borrow against your home is another story. More on this later.

Once you've got your balance sheet in order, you should develop a basic understanding of how the federal government taxes different types of investment income. Knowing this will help you structure your portfolio so that you'll pay the least amount of income tax possible on your investment income.

There are four basic types of investment income to consider: interest from Canadian sources, dividends from Canadian corporations, interest and dividends from foreign sources and capital gains.

Interest income from Canadian sources, such as interest earned on bank and trust company deposits, Canada Savings Bonds and mortgages, is fully taxable at marginal tax rates. (Remember, your marginal tax rate is the rate of tax you pay on the last dollar you earn. As income increases, so does your tax rate in most cases. So your marginal rate is the highest rate of tax you pay.)

Interest income and dividends from foreign corporations are fully taxable at your marginal tax rate. This includes interest earned on foreign bank deposits, such as a trust company account in Florida, income from a U.S.-based money market fund or from one of several Canadian money market funds which hold U.S. dollar short-term investments. It also includes dividends from U.S. corporations such as General Motors Corp. and International Business Machines Corp., even if the shares are listed on Canadian exchanges or flowed through to you through a Canadian mutual fund.

Dividends from Canadian corporations, whether paid directly or flowed to you through a mutual fund, are eligible for the dividend tax credit which effectively reduces the rate of tax paid.

Capital gains are the gains made on the sale of capital property. This includes real estate, stocks, mutual funds and precious metals. The property can be Canadian or foreign. Gains on the sale of your principal residence are tax free and excluded from capital gains, but gains on the sale of a second property, such as a cottage, are considered capital gains for tax purposes.

The Mulroney government originally allowed each individual a lifetime capital gains exemption of $500,000. Under tax reform this has been capped at $100,000, except for farms and small business corporations, where the $500,000 limit still applies.

In 1987, half of any capital gains you earned beyond the exempt $100,000 were taxable. So if you realized $100,000 of capital gains in 1987 and had not previously claimed any of your exemption you would have paid no tax. If you realized $150,000 in capital gains and had not yet claimed any of your exemption, the first $100,000 would have been tax-free and one-half of the remaining $50,000 would have been taxed.

The rules changed dramatically for 1988 and beyond. First, the portion of capital gains that are taxable increased from 50 per cent in 1987 to 66.7 percent in 1988 and to 75 percent in 1990.

Moreover, you can apply capital gains to your lifetime exemption only after subtracting any cumulative net investment losses. For 1987, you were able to claim a capital gains exemption on cumulative capital gains less cumulative capital losses and cumulative allowable business losses. Simply put, if you have realized gains of $60,000 and realized losses of $20,000, you could have claimed only $40,000 against your exemption.

For 1988 and beyond it became more complicated: only those gains that exceed your cumulative net investment losses (investment losses less investment income) can be applied against the lifetime exemption.

In 1989, 66.7 percent of your capital gains were taxable. If you realized capital gains of $150,000, had no cumulative net investment losses and have not previously claimed any of your lifetime deduction, the first $100,000 was tax-free and you paid tax on two-thirds of the remainder, or on $33,333. If, however, you had $10,000 of interest expense net of dividends and interest received, you paid tax on $43,333. You'll be able to claim the remaining $10,000 of your exemption in a subsequent year.

For 1990 and beyond, 75 percent of capital gains will be taxable. Using our example of $150,000 realized capital gains, 75 percent of the amount exceeding the lifetime exemption will be taxable, in this case $37,500.

It is important to note that inside RRSPs – the largest if not the only major savings program for many people – investment income compounds untaxed. However, when money is withdrawn from an RRSP either directly or in payments from an annuity or registered retirement income fund, the money is fully taxable whether it reflects interest income, dividends or capital gains.

Consequently, you should structure your total savings and investment package to reflect this tax treatment of investment income. In fact, many people don't do this and end up paying more tax than they should. Many people hold interest-paying investments such as CSBs and guaranteed investment certificates outside their RRSPs and growth mutual funds inside their plans. They pay tax on the interest earned outside their RRSPs. The capital gains inside their RRSPs grow untaxed but they will eventually be fully taxed when withdrawn from the RRSP.

If these people restructured their holdings so that their growth assets were outside their RRSPs and their interest-paying assets were inside their RRSPs they would reduce their taxes. They would still own the same assets, but the interest would compound untaxed inside their RRSPs while any capital gains earned would be eligible for the lifetime capital gains exemption.

If you currently hold interest-paying assets outside your RRSP and growth assets inside your RRSP you can switch them around dollar-for-dollar using a self-directed RRSP available through virtually all investment dealers and most trust companies.

CHAPTER 8

How to
Meet Your
Objectives

ONCE YOU HAVE STRUCTURED
your savings and investments, the next step is to list your specific
investment objectives. They could include saving for the down payment on a house, saving for retirement, saving for your children's
education, investing for current income or simply investing for
long-term growth.

Investment objectives can generally be categorized as short term,
medium term or long term. For our purposes, short term means up
to a couple of years, medium term means three to ten years, and
long term is anything longer than that.

Generally, short-term savings objectives are best met with money
market funds simply because they are virtually risk-free. If you
know that you will need the money fairly soon for a specific purpose, then a money market fund is for you.

If you won't need the money for three years or more, you have far
more leeway. You can use fixed income funds without too much
worry. Even in years with sharp increases in interest rates, most
fixed income funds show positive returns. Over a three-year period,
virtually all fixed income funds show positive returns.

Whether you use equity funds really depends on how much risk
you are willing to take. There is nothing wrong with using equity
funds for medium-term investment objectives, provided you can accept the risk. It depends largely on whether you might find yourself
forced to sell your holdings in a period when prices are down.

For long-term objectives, consider equity funds, which have
traditionally outperformed fixed income and money market funds
over most periods of a decade or more.

Your investment objectives should be considered as flexible
guidelines. There will be times when even long-term investors may
want a heavy portion of assets invested in income and money
market funds because of nervousness about the stock market. There

will be other times when stocks seem very inexpensive and conservative investors who would normally invest for income may move into growth funds. Saving for the down payment on a home is usually considered a short-term objective; your strategy for saving for children's education will depend on the children's ages. If you start the program when your child is born it's a long-term program. If you wait until the child is in his or her teens, it's a short- to medium-term program. Similarly, a twenty-year-old's RRSP is a long-term savings program while a sixty-three-year-old's RRSP is a short-term program.

The rule of thumb is that the shorter the term of the savings program, the more conservative you should be and the less risk you should take.

Meeting short-term objectives

If you're going to need your money soon, perhaps within a year or so, it is probably best to play it safe and invest in a money market fund. You'll earn, at least in most periods, a relatively low return and pay tax on the interest earned but you'll know that you are not taking any risk and you'll get all your money back, plus interest.

Alternatively, you may want to look closely at preferred dividend funds. Many have had relatively stable returns. Depending on your income and tax bracket, the difference in rate of return between a money market fund and dividend fund can be significant. But remember: dividend funds, while relatively stable, are still more volatile than money market funds.

Generally, equity funds, and to a lesser extent bond funds, are too volatile to meet short-term savings objectives, particularly if a decline in capital will affect your lifestyle. If you're saving for the down payment on a home, don't invest in equity funds if a decline in the value of your investment will keep you out of that home. If you do invest in equity funds, particularly a specialty fund, in the hope of significant short-term performance, realize that you are a speculator – possibly even a gambler – betting that the market will perform as you expect.

Meeting medium-term objectives

If you are a conservative investor your best bet is probably a fixed income fund, either a bond or mortgage fund for an RRSP, or a preferred dividend fund if you are trying to maximize your after-tax return.

You can, of course, go into growth funds, too. It all depends on where the market is. A lot can happen in relatively short periods of time. During the first three months of 1987 the Toronto Stock Exchange 300 total return index gained 22.8 percent. But the stock market doesn't always move up, as many investors learned when the index plunged 31 percent between its August peak and October trough. Unless you've got a crystal ball, or more than enough financial assets to meet your medium-term objectives, you should look at fixed income funds rather than equities.

Meeting long-term objectives

If you won't need the money for more than a decade, go for growth using equity-based funds. Even if you measure performance using a market bottom as an ending date, such as the summer of 1982, almost all equity funds show positive returns over a ten-year period.

Of course, it makes little sense to jump into equity funds at a market top. So if you are a bit nervous about the near-term direction of the market, take a conservative stance by putting only part of your money into equity funds and place the rest in money market funds.

Alternatively, look for funds that have heavy cash components, indicating that the manager has the same concerns as you. You should also consider balanced funds because managers of these funds change asset mixes to reflect market conditions, increasing or decreasing equities according to market outlook.

Meeting personal objectives

The following pages outline six common savings and investment objectives and how mutual funds can be used to meet them.

1. Saving for the down payment on a home

If you're saving for a home, you are probably hoping to buy within a couple of years. This makes your savings program relatively short term and you can't risk having to redeem your holdings when the market is down. Consequently, your investments should be confined to low-risk funds – funds in which the investment policies virtually guarantee your principal and interest.

Money market funds are the only funds that meet these requirements. They should be used exclusively if you expect to need your money within a year or so.

If you don't intend to buy a house for several years, you can accept more risk in the expectation of earning a higher rate of return. Look at dividend income funds or bond funds. While more volatile than money market funds, both are substantially less volatile than equity funds. Over most one-year periods, bond funds have done better than money market funds. In periods of sharply rising interest rates, a bond fund could do worse than a money market fund, even declining in value. Nevertheless, over a three-year period or longer you will almost certainly do better in dividend income or bond funds than in money market funds, if history holds true for the future.

Again, there are always exceptions and three-year returns from bond or dividend income funds for the three years ended June 30, 1990 were below rates from money market funds. Still, an investor who had started a medium-term program in the summer of 1987 using fixed income funds might have switched into a money market fund part-way during the three years locking in high rates of return.

You may be tempted to use equity funds to save for the down payment on a home. Indeed, long-term returns and some recent gains may make this a tempting option. Just remember that equity funds are volatile and that there will be some periods when prices will drop dramatically. If you can't afford to see the value of your savings drop, then don't go near equity funds.

2. Paying down your mortgage

Most banks and trust companies allow you to prepay the principal outstanding on your mortgage. The limit is generally 10 percent of the principal annually on the anniversary of the mortgage, although some institutions allow 15 percent. As well, you can pay off any or all of your mortgage at the renewal date.

Paying off your mortgage should be a priority before starting any long-term savings program other than your RRSP. You pay interest on your mortgage using after-tax dollars. This means that you have to earn $1.63 to pay off every $1 of interest, if your taxable income is between $28,276 and $56,550 in 1990. If it's higher, you have to earn at least $1.78 to pay $1 of interest after tax, more if you must pay surtaxes.

Therefore, if your mortgage rate is 12 percent, you would have to earn more than 19 percent on your investments before tax to break even. And remember, paying down your mortgage is a risk-free investment.

You can, of course, have your cake and eat it too by paying down your mortgage, borrowing against the equity in your home, then investing the capital. That way your mortgage interest is deductible. This strategy will be covered in detail in the next chapter.

3. Saving for your children's education

Since for most families, saving for children's education is a medium- to long-term objective, mutual funds fit the bill. What you must remember is that any interest or dividends earned on the money you invest for your children, even if it is invested in their names, is taxable in your hands. However, any capital gains earned are attributed to the child. And interest or dividends earned on interest or dividends on which you paid tax is deemed to be your child's.

You should also keep in mind that if you invest family allowance cheques directly in your children's names, any interest or dividends earned are taxable in their hands, not yours. Each child can earn several thousand dollars of interest and dividends tax free, so it makes sense to use family allowance as the cornerstone of any education savings program.

If you prefer to be on the conservative side when it comes to investing your children's money, use a bond or a mortgage fund. Alternatively, choose a balanced fund. If university or college is a decade or more away, consider growth funds to give you a higher expected rate of return.

Many families use a combination of income and growth funds. Family allowance cheques are invested in bond and mortgage funds while other capital is invested for growth. Just remember, when the children are a few years away from university, educational savings become a short-term objective. You may want to lock in your profits from growth funds and move into income or money market funds.

You can also consider a mutual fund registered education savings plan, a RESP. The capital contributed to a RESP (limited to $1,500 a year for each child under new rules effective after February 20, 1990) is not deductible for tax purposes. However, any income earned within the RESP grows untaxed. The income is taxable in the child's hands when withdrawn to finance post-secondary education but the capital you invested originally is withdrawn tax-free. However, the child's total income will probably be low and many of the expenses of education can be deducted by the student, so little or no tax will likely be paid. There is one potential problem; the money must be used to finance post-secondary education. However, if the child who is named as beneficiary does not continue his or her education, you can name another beneficiary.

A number of mutual fund companies, including Bolton Tremblay Funds Inc. and Mackenzie Financial Corp., offer RESPs through mutual fund dealers and brokers.

4. Saving for retirement through RRSPs

By far, the largest single use of mutual funds is in RRSPs. Some estimates indicate that more than half the $50 billion that Canadians have invested in mutual funds is in RRSPs. Because of the federal government's requirement that limits the foreign component of RRSP assets, RRSPs are concentrated in Canadian equity and balanced funds, bond funds and mortgage funds.

However, as noted previously, investors are allowed 14 per cent foreign content in their RRSPs and this percentage will rise by 2 percent a year to a maximum of 20 percent in 1994. To maximize foreign content, many people have mutual funds in their RRSPs that invest outside Canada. This can be done by holding your mutual funds in a self-directed RRSP. These are available from virtually every organization involved in marketing mutual funds.

An RRSP is an extremely tax-efficient way of saving for retirement. Your contribution is deductible from income for tax purposes and you are saving untaxed dollars. Also, income within an RRSP grows untaxed. It is not until you withdraw money from an RRSP, either by cashing in your plan or by using one of the retirement options, such as a registered retirement income fund (RRIF) or annuity, that the proceeds are taxed.

Your contribution limit is 18 percent of the previous year's earned income up to a maximum contribution of $11,500 for 1991, $12,500 for 1992, $13,500 for 1993, $14,500 for 1994, and $15,500 for 1995. From these contribution limits you must subtract any contributions made to a pension plan by you or by your employer on your behalf.

Contributions must be made in the taxation year or within sixty days of year end to get a deduction for the tax year. It is possible to build a hefty cache of savings in your RRSP. When investing these savings in mutual funds, there are two important questions you should ask yourself: how does your RRSP fit in with your other savings? How much risk are you willing to take?

Remember, when you withdraw money from an RRSP, it will be fully taxable whether your gains are interest, dividends or capital gains. If you are saving both inside and outside an RRSP and you have both growth and interest-paying investments, you should structure your holdings so that as much of the interest-paying portion as possible is inside your RRSP. Keeping the growth portion outside your RRSP allows you to take advantage of the $100,000 capital gains exemption. Even if you have already exhausted your exemption, your capital gains will only be partially taxed.

As far as risk is concerned, you have two basic strategies from which to choose, one that is active and one that is passive. The active strategy is to constantly change the mix of mutual funds within your RRSP, moving into growth funds when they offer the best values and into income funds and money market funds when the outlook for equities is cloudy. This strategy, if successful, will give you the best returns from growth and income while preserving capital.

The passive strategy reflects the view that your age dictates the type of mutual funds you hold – the younger you are the more risk you can afford to take, the closer you are to retirement the more conservative you should be. The following are some guidelines based on age for structuring your retirement savings between interest-paying and growth investments. They apply to your total retirement savings, including those outside your RRSP.

If you are in your twenties, you have at least three decades before retirement. You can accept volatility in your RRSP and should invest the bulk of your RRSP for growth. Over the years you'll experience some ups and downs. But over the long haul you will probably come out significantly ahead of what you would have by playing it safe.

If you're in your thirties, you still have many years to go before retirement, so you can still put the bulk of your assets into equity funds, as much as 80 percent, and invest the remaining 20 percent for income.

If you're in your forties, you should become a bit more conservative and move to around 60 percent in growth funds and 40 percent in bond funds, mortgage funds or both.

Once you're in your fifties, retirement is in sight. Consider moving to 40 percent growth and 60 percent income.

When you're within a decade of retirement, your main objective should be preservation of capital rather than growth. Move to 80 per cent income and 20 percent growth funds as a longer-term hedge against inflation.

But remember, these are only guidelines. People who are approaching retirement with substantial investment assets – more than enough to comfortably finance their retirements – may decide to keep most of their assets invested for growth. Indeed, someone who started investing in his or her twenties might well decide to remain in equities because of the wealth he or she would likely accumulate. Similarly, if you have an adequate pension plan you might opt to keep the bulk of your RRSP invested for growth.

You also have to consider market conditions. It doesn't make much sense to plunge into equity funds if it looks like the markets are due for a sharp correction, even if you won't be retiring for thirty years or more. Similarly, people approaching retirement may want to put more of their money in growth funds if the market has been declining and prices seem relatively cheap.

You should also consider the portfolio components of the funds you hold. For example, balanced funds hold a blend of growth and income investments. You may want to consider this in structuring your RRSP. A fifty-year-old man or woman might hold 50 percent to 60 percent of his or her RRSP in a balanced fund and the remainder in bond funds, rather than 40 percent in growth funds.

Just remember that the objective of retirement savings is to finance retirement. Therefore, it should be the most conservative portion of your portfolio.

5. Registered retirement income funds

You can't have an RRSP beyond December 31 of the year in which you turn seventy-one. You have to roll your RRSP into an annuity or registered retirement income fund (RRIF) or cash it in and pay tax on the proceeds.

The RRIF option meets the needs of most investors. With a RRIF you can hold the same investments as in an RRSP. Moving from an

RRSP to a RRIF is a simple matter which involves filling out a form provided by your fund broker or the mutual fund company with which you have your RRSP.

You can withdraw as much from your RRIF each year as you want. The least you are allowed to withdraw is determined by this formula: divide the dollar value of your plan by ninety minus your age. For example, a seventy-year-old with $100,000 in a RRIF must withdraw a minimum of $5,000 a year (100,000 divided by twenty.) Beyond this minimum, the income you draw from a RRIF is very flexible.

You can convert your RRSP to a RRIF at any age. But because you have to withdraw some capital from a RRIF each year, you should postpone rolling your RRSP into a RRIF until you retire and need income from your plan. The first payment may be received in the year in which you open your plan, but you have the option of starting payments in the following year. In fact, you can postpone receiving your first payment, if you want annual payments, to December 31 of the year you turn seventy-two.

Your RRIF should be invested conservatively with the objective of providing income rather than growth. Consequently, it should be invested primarily in bond and mortgage funds. A portion, however, can be invested in equity or balanced funds to give you a longer-term hedge against inflation.

Overall preservation of capital is of the utmost importance because you will be withdrawing money from your plan each year. If you had a significant portion invested in growth funds and the market turned down, you could find yourself redeeming fund units after prices have fallen. You could seriously erode your financial security.

Again, this is a general guideline. If you retire with substantial assets you may decide you can afford to accept the volatility associated with growth funds and keep a major portion of your assets in growth funds.

6. Financing retirement outside a RRIF

Circumstances sometimes offer the option of a unique solution. Someone with limited assets and income would generally opt for a safe solution such as investing in bond mutual funds. However, sometimes the safe solution isn't always the best. Take, for instance, a widow with $50,000 in capital and no income other than government benefits. If she invested for interest income she would get her basic government benefit. But if she invested for growth and cashed in a portion of her units each month her income would largely be a return of her own capital and she might qualify for the guaranteed income supplement because her "income" doesn't fit the government definition. Such strategies aren't for everyone and they should be examined against an individual's circumstances.

CHAPTER 9

Strategies and Gimmicks

MAKING $1 MILLION THROUGH mutual funds isn't difficult. All it takes is the ability to set aside money each year and a long time to do it. If you can set aside $4,000 a year and earn an average annual return of 12 percent you'll have $1 million in less than thirty years. If you could earn an average of 16 percent, you would have $1 million in less than twenty-five years.

Saving can be difficult because of the temptations to spend. So virtually every mutual fund company has a program to make saving less painful. Depending on the fund company or the salesperson, such plans are called dollar-cost averaging plans, automatic-purchase plans or pre-authorized purchase plans. You decide how much you want to invest each month or every three months and in which funds, fill out a bank authorization form and supply a sample cheque marked "void." The fund company will do the rest. Each month on the same date, the amount you chose will come out of your bank or trust company account and be invested in the fund or funds you pick. The plans are available for RRSPs and non-sheltered savings.

A key advantage of such plans is that if the market declines, your purchases will buy more mutual fund units, lowering your average cost. Conversely, you'll raise your average cost in rising markets. But with these programs you're in funds for the long term and in the end you'll do well.

You can establish a savings plan with as little as $100 a month. However, such a modest plan would be a money loser for the fund company and the salesperson for the first few years if the fund carries an acquisition fee. As a result, some funds have introduced a contractual monthly accumulation plan. Under these plans, an investor puts up a lump sum, often around three months' contributions, which is used to pay the sales fee. However, the investor is repaid a bit of this each month he or she remains in the plan. The total fee is repaid after a few years, usually five.

As an alternative, many funds offer their monthly accumulation plans with a declining redemption fee. This is the option to choose because long term investors don't pay redemption fees.

Chart IV shows how your investment would have grown if you had contributed $100 a month to a typical equity fund invested in the Canadian market during the ten years ended June 30, 1991. It assumes you purchased the fund either on a no-load basis or with a declining deferred redemption fee so that all your money is invested. The chart is based on monthly returns of a Canadian equity fund and assumes contributions are made at the end of the month. Different funds use different dates for investing contributions.

Withdrawal plans

A second type of plan offered by mutual fund companies is the withdrawal plan. These plans allow you to invest a lump sum and withdraw a constant amount each month. For example, you might invest $100,000 in a typical equity fund with monthly withdrawals of $1,000. Only a small portion of the $1,000 is regarded as realized capital gain by the federal government in the early years of the plan – most is seen as a return of capital.

The table in appendix one simulates the results over ten years of a $1,000 monthly withdrawal plan from a Canadian equity fund started with $100,000 on June 30, 1981. Acquisition and redemption fees are ignored because many funds now allow such a plan to be set up with no acquisition fees and ignore or reduce substantially any redemption fees which might be applicable.

The value of the plan declined during the bear market that lasted from November 1980 to July 1982 but then rose in value until August 1987, declined again in the late 1987 market crash. The value of the plan has continued to decline, reflecting the fact that withdrawals have exceeded earnings. In fact, users of such plans should be prepared to cut their withdrawals if the value of their capital falls significantly. Although you will pay little if any tax in the early years of such a plan, an increasing portion of your withdrawals will be seen as taxable capital gains and your after-tax income could be less than $1,000. Nevertheless, a withdrawal plan is an excellent alternative to investing in fixed-income securities which generate fully taxable interest income.

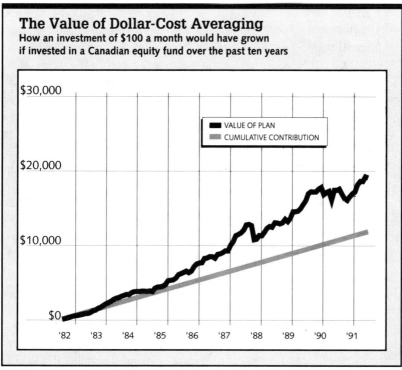

The Value of Dollar-Cost Averaging
How an investment of $100 a month would have grown
if invested in a Canadian equity fund over the past ten years

CHART IV

Leverage programs

Be very cautious about borrowing money to buy mutual funds. Changes under tax reform make leverage – as the use of borrowed money to invest is called – a marginally profitable exercise in some cases and unprofitable in others. It can, however, be very profitable if used wisely. The key is to examine any proposal thoroughly and work out your projections on an after-tax basis. You must compare how you would fare with leverage and without.

Investing in growth funds with borrowed money is big business. In fact, it has been estimated in the industry that as much as a third of all mutual fund purchases are made with borrowed money.

Of course, the reason for using borrowed money to invest is to make more money more quickly. If you can put $100,000 of the bank's money to work along with your own $100,000 you'll double your profit before interest expense and tax. Your interest is deductible. If the bank charges you 12 percent and your marginal tax rate is 39 per cent, your after-tax cost of borrowing is 7.3 percent. (In fact, loan rates were running at about 16 percent during the first half of 1990). If you have $7,300 a year available for investment, instead of investing the money you could use it to finance a loan of $100,000.

Leverage has been extremely popular in the fund industry as a means of building business. Several major fund groups made arrangements with trust companies to finance leverage programs. Many individual salespeople made their own arrangements to bring clients to banks. Several years ago, one trust company, First City Trust, even produced a video on leverage designed to encourage investors to use borrowed money to buy mutual funds.

Leverage sounds like a good idea but tax reform has made it far less attractive. Lower marginal tax rates have reduced the benefits of deducting interest, the taxes on capital gains have increased and the new CNIL rules have made it difficult for investors who leverage to use their lifetime capital gains exemption. It is still profitable in some situations, but in many cases it is unlikely you will be compensated for the risk involved.

Even before the white paper on tax reform, many people involved in the fund industry issued warnings about the dangers of borrowing to invest in the event of a market decline. In 1986, the Investment Funds Institute of Canada and the Ontario Securities Commission issued a joint statement cautioning investors about leverage. The OSC added the requirement that mutual fund dealers who recommend leverage programs give clients a written statement warning them of the risks.

The following six examples look at the results of leverage under certain circumstances and under specific assumptions. In each case the amount borrowed is $100,000. The annual interest expense is $12,000, which has an after-tax cost of $7,320. The key assumption is that if the investor does not borrow $100,000, the $12,000 that would otherwise be available to pay interest will be taxable and its after-tax value of $7,320 will be available for investment.

The first two examples look at the results of leverage in which an investor with $100,000 borrows an additional $100,000, a relatively common strategy. Table VI covers a holding period of one year; Table VII covers the more realistic holding period of five years. Table VII also assumes that the investment profits would increase the investor's marginal tax rate from 39 percent to 43.5 percent. All six examples ignore federal and provincial surtaxes.

Borrowing to Invest

A ONE-YEAR HOLDING PERIOD AND 15% RETURN

	Without Leverage	With Leverage
Investment	$100,000	$200,000
Loan	–	100,000
Cash savings over year	7,320	–
Interest expense	–	12,000
CAPITAL GAIN (15%)	$15,000	$30,000
WITH LIFETIME EXEMPTION		
Equity after one year	122,320	130,000
Capital gain	15,000	30,000
Taxable gain (75%)	11,250	22,500
Interest expense	–	12,000
Tax (39% of $12,000)	–	4,680
After-tax profit	15,000	25,320
Cash savings	7,320	–
INCREASE IN NET WORTH	$22,320	$25,320
WITHOUT LIFETIME EXEMPTION		
Equity after one year	122,320	130,000
Capital gain	15,000	30,000
Taxable gain (75%)	11,250	22,500
Tax (39%)	4,387	8,775
After-tax profit	10,613	21,225
Cash savings	7,320	–
INCREASE IN NET WORTH	$17,933	$21,225

TABLE VI

The first two examples clearly show that on an after-tax basis, the benefit of using leverage is, at best, marginal, and, at worst, negative. Moreover, the additional profit stemming from leverage doesn't appear to compensate for the increased risk.

Borrowing to invest for one year

Consider two scenarios. In the first you invest $100,000 of your own capital and get a 15 percent return over twelve months. You also have $7,320 available for saving or paying the interest on a loan, enough to cover your after-tax cost of borrowing $100,000 (assuming your marginal tax rate is 39 percent).

Depending on your own situation and whether you have unused lifetime capital gains exemption, your after-tax profit from investing just your own $100,000 can be as much as $15,000. If your capital gains are taxable and your marginal tax rate is 39 percent, the maximum tax is $4,387. Thus, your after-tax profit is $10,613.

If you cash in at the end of one year, you'll have your $100,000 principal, your profit of up to $15,000 and your cash flow of $7,320 – for a total of $122,320 if your capital gains are tax free or $117,933 if your gains are taxable.

Now let's look at the same time period and returns but assume that you invest $100,000 of your own money and $100,000 borrowed from your bank at a rate of 12 percent. Your interest expense of $12,000 is deductible from income. Using your 39 percent marginal tax rate, your after-tax cost of borrowing is $7,320. After twelve months you cash in with a gross profit of $30,000. But there will be taxes to be paid – even if you haven't used any of your lifetime exemption.

The federal government requires you to pay tax on that portion of your taxable gain equal to your "investment loss", which in this case is your $12,000 interest expense.

It works like this: your taxable capital gain is 75 percent of $30,000, or $22,500. From this, you must subtract your interest expense of $12,000. Therefore, only $10,500 ($14,000 gross) may be applied to your lifetime exemption from the $22,500 taxable capital gain ($30,000 gross) earned on your $200,000 investment.

The tax paid on your capital gain will be $4,680. Your profit will be $30,000, less $4,680 tax. This leaves you with $25,320. If you've already used your lifetime exemption you'll pay $7,800 tax, leaving you with $22,200.

Hardly worth the risk

Comparing the two cases, if you haven't used your lifetime exemption, you'll have earned $22,320 without leverage and $25,320 with leverage. If you have used your lifetime exemption, you'll be ahead $17,933 without leverage and $21,225 with leverage.

By leveraging you double your risk in order to increase your profit by 13 percent, if you haven't used your lifetime exemption, or by 18 percent, if you have used your exemption.

Let's look at what happens if the market declines 15 percent. If you're using your own capital, you'll be down $15,000 on paper at

Borrowing to Invest

A FIVE-YEAR HOLDING PERIOD AND 15% RETURN

	Without Leverage	With Leverage
Investment	$100,000	$200,000
Loan	–	100,000
Annual cash savings	7,320	–
Annual interest expense	–	12,000
Total cash savings	36,600	–
Future value of savings	49,354	–
Gain on cash	12,754	–
Capital gain on investment	101,136	101,136
Capital gain on borrowed funds	–	101,136
TOTAL CAPITAL GAIN	$113,890	$202,271
WITH LIFETIME EXEMPTION		
Taxable capital gain (75%)	85,418	151,703
Interest expense	–	60,000
Exemption	75,000	15,000
Taxable portion of gains	10,418	136,703
Tax (43.5%)	4,532	59,466
After-tax profit	109,358	142,805
Cash savings	36,600	–
INCREASE IN NET WORTH	$145,958	$142,805
WITHOUT LIFETIME EXEMPTION		
Taxable capital gain (75%)	85,418	151,703
Interest expense	–	n/a
Exemption	–	–
Taxable portion of gains	85,418	151,703
Tax (43.5%)	37,157	65,991
After-tax profit	76,733	136,280
Add back cash savings	36,600	–
INCREASE IN NET WORTH	$113,333	$136,280

TABLE VII

the end of the year. So your equity will have dropped to $85,000 – $92,320 if we add back the cash you have available for savings. Using leverage you'll be down $30,000 on paper, leaving you with $70,000.

Borrowing to Invest
A FIVE-YEAR HOLDING PERIOD AND 12% RETURN

	Without Leverage	With Leverage
Investment	$100,000	$200,000
Loan	–	100,000
Annual cash savings	7,320	–
Annual interest expense	–	12,000
Total cash savings	36,600	–
Future value of savings	46,503	–
Gain on cash	9,903	–
Capital gain on investment	76,234	76,234
Capital gain on borrowed funds	–	76,234
TOTAL CAPITAL GAIN	$86,137	$152,468
WITH LIFETIME EXEMPTION		
Taxable capital gain (75%)	64,603	114,351
Interest expense	–	60,000
Exemption	75,000	15,000
Taxable portion of gains	–	99,351
Tax (43.5%)	0	43,218
After-tax profit	86,137	109,251
Cash savings	36,600	–
INCREASE IN NET WORTH	$122,737	$109,251
WITHOUT LIFETIME EXEMPTION		
Taxable capital gain (75%)	86,137	152,468
Interest expense	–	n/a
Exemption	–	–
Taxable portion of gains	86,137	152,468
Tax (43.5%)	37,470	66,324
After-tax profit	48,667	86,145
Cash savings	36,600	–
INCREASE IN NET WORTH	$85,267	$ 86,145

TABLE VIII

You'll likely make the money back and more in subsequent years. But tax reform makes leverage a marginal proposition in this case.

Borrowing to invest for five years

Consider two other scenarios. In the first, we'll consider the impact of borrowing at 12 percent to invest for a 15 percent return. In the second, we'll look at what happens if your investment returns just match your interest costs.

In the first scenario, you invest $100,000 and get an average annual appreciation of 15 percent over five years. At the end of five years you gain $101,135. In addition, you have an annual cash flow of $7,320 available for investing. We'll assume it is invested at the end of each year. Therefore, at the end of five years you have an additional $49,354, assuming a 15 percent annual earnings rate.

Depending on your situation and whether you have unused lifetime capital gains exemption, your after-tax profit can be as much as $100,000 tax free plus another $13,890, of which 75 percent will be subject to tax. Your tax on $13,990 would be $4,532 using a 43.5 percent tax rate, so your profit would be $109,358. Adding back your $100,000 capital plus $36,600 additional investment ($7,320 times five years) you would have $245,958 for an increase in net worth of $145,958.

If your capital gains are taxable, your maximum tax will be $37,157. So your after-tax profit is $76,733. At the end of five years you'll have $213,333, for an increase of $113,333.

In contrast, if you decide to leverage, you would have $100,000 of your own money to invest plus $100,000 borrowed at 12 percent. After five years of 15 percent returns you would cash in with a gross profit of $202,271.

Your annual interest expense of $12,000 is deductible from income. Using your 39 percent marginal tax rate, you can see that your after-tax cost of borrowing is $7,320 each year.

Again, you won't escape paying tax on a portion of your capital gains. You would still have to pay tax on any taxable gain equal to your investment loss, which in this case is your $60,000 interest expense. Working through the example, your taxable capital gain is 75 percent of $202,271, or $151,703. From this, you must subtract your interest expense of $12,000 a year, or $60,000. Your lifetime exemption is $100,000, or $75,000 of taxable gains. So of the taxable gain, only $15,000 ($20,000 gross) may be applied to your lifetime exemption from the $151,703 taxable capital gain ($202,271 gross) earned on your $200,000 investment.

Borrowing to Invest
A ONE YEAR HOLDING PERIOD AND 30% RETURN

	Without Leverage	With Leverage
Investment	$100,000	$200,000
Loan	–	100,000
Cash savings over year	7,320	–
Interest expense	–	12,000
CAPITAL GAIN (30%)	$30,000	$60,000
WITH LIFETIME EXEMPTION		
Equity after one year	137,320	160,000
Capital gain	30,000	60,000
Taxable gain (75%)	22,500	45,000
Taxable portion of gains (equal to interest expense)	–	12,000
Tax (39% of $12,000)	–	4,680
After-tax profit	30,000	55,320
Cash savings	7,320	–
INCREASE IN NET WORTH	$37,320	$55,320
WITHOUT LIFETIME EXEMPTION		
Equity after one year	137,320	160,000
Capital gain	30,000	60,000
Taxable gain (75%)	22,500	45,000
Tax (39%)	8,775	17,550
After-tax profit	21,225	42,450
Cash savings	7,320	–
INCREASE IN NET WORTH	$28,545	$42,450

TABLE IX

Your profit will be $142,805 – $202,271 capital gain less $59,466 tax. So at the end of five years you'll have capital of $242,805. If you've already used your lifetime exemption you'll pay $65,990 tax. In that case, at the end of five years your profit would be $136,281, leaving you capital of $236,281.

The figures speak for themselves. If you haven't used your lifetime exemption you may be worse off using leverage in some circumstances. In others the gains may prove marginal.

Let's look at our second scenario. In all the previous examples we have assumed a rate of return of 15 percent, which is three percentage points higher than the assumed interest costs. But what hap-

Borrowing Against Your Home
A FIVE YEAR HOLDING PERIOD AND 15% RETURN

	Without Leverage	With Leverage
Investment		$100,000
Loan	–	100,000
Annual cash savings	$7,320	–
Annual interest expense	–	12,000
Total cash savings	36,600	–
Future value of savings	49,354	–
Gain on cash savings	12,754	–
Capital gain on investment	–	101,136
TOTAL CAPITAL GAIN	$12,754	$101,136
WITH LIFETIME EXEMPTION		
Taxable capital gain (75%)	9,566	75,852
Interest expense	–	60,000
Exemption	9,566	75,000
Taxable portion of gains	–	60,852
Tax (43.5%)	–	26,471
After-tax profit	12,754	74,665
Cash savings	36,600	–
INCREASE IN NET WORTH	$49,354	$ 74,665
WITHOUT LIFETIME EXEMPTION		
Taxable capital gain (75%)	9,566	75,852
Interest expense	–	n/a
Exemption	–	–
Tax (43.5%)	4,161	32,996
After-tax profit	8,593	68,140
Cash savings	36,600	–
INCREASE IN NET WORTH	$45,193	$68,140

TABLE X

pens if the rate of return earned over five years only matches the interest rate. Table VIII assumes a compound annual return of 12 percent over five years and an interest expense of 12 percent. It demonstrates that leverage will result in a minor gain if you have used your lifetime exemption and a lower return if you have not used your lifetime exemption.

The best leveraging scenario

A more positive use of leverage is when you expect to earn a significantly above-average return over a short time period. Assume that your favourite fund manager has suddenly reduced the cash portion of his portfolio from, say, 40 percent to 10 percent. That tells you that he expects a jump in the market. As a result you go out and borrow $100,000 to buy units of his fund, matching the $100,000 worth you already own. Your intention is to hold for one year. Table IX shows what happens if the fund appreciates by 30 percent over that one-year period. If you haven't used your lifetime exemption your net worth with leverage would increase by $55,320, about 48 percent more than the $37,320 you would show without leverage. If you had used your lifetime exemption your increase in net worth with leverage would be $42,450, about 49 percent more than the $28,545 without leverage.

Borrowing against your home

Many Canadians are house-rich but cash-poor. They have a substantial net worth, but it's tied up in a single asset.

Some mutual fund salespeople see this as an opportunity, both for the homeowner and for themselves. They might recommend that a homeowner borrow thousands of dollars using the home as collateral to invest in funds. A withdrawal plan would be used to finance the interest costs.

This type of program can be profitable, but what happens if interest rates skyrocket and the stock market plunges? This happened in 1981 when the prime lending rate reached a record 22.75 percent and the stock market fell by 43 percent over about eighteen months. The hapless homeowner would find his equity dissipating if he has to sell his mutual fund investment after the market has dropped in order to pay the higher interest charges.

Unless you can handle the interest payments out of your personal income, not the cash flow from the mutual fund, you shouldn't be in a leverage program that uses your home as security. The risks are simply too great.

Alternatively, you could borrow $100,000 and finance the interest out of cash flow as shown in Table X. Here's how you would fare over five years, if we assume a 15 percent rate of return.

At the end of five years your gain would be $101,136. The taxable capital gain would be 75 percent of this, or $75,852. Your lifetime capital gains exemption is $100,000, or $75,000 of taxable capital gains. But from that $75,000 you must subtract your accumulated investment loss, which in this case is five years of interest at $12,000 a year, or $60,000. So only $15,000 of your taxable capital gain is exempt from tax in the year you take your profit. You can claim the rest in subsequent years. In other words, you'll be paying tax on $60,852 of your gain, which will cost you $26,471. Therefore, your after-tax profit after five years is $74,665.

Your alternative to borrowing to invest is investing the cash that would otherwise have been used to service your debt. Annual cash flow of $7,320 invested at the end of each year and earning a rate of 15 percent annually would be worth $49,354 at the end of five years. Borrowing to invest gives you the higher return. But not before you've exposed yourself to much greater risk.

Leverage is sometimes used by investors to reduce taxes because the interest expense is deductible. However, the gains from a leverage strategy should be compared with the gains from just investing the cash that would have been available for investment. It could work to your benefit if you have some interest-paying investments such as guaranteed investment certificates or Canada Savings Bonds. You could borrow against these securities and use your loan to buy funds. Because your interest expense is offset by interest income, you will not have a cumulative net investment loss. Consequently, you will be able to use your lifetime exemption against your profits.

No "tax-free" withdrawals

A gimmick promoted by some fund salespeople – and one you should avoid – is the so-called "tax-free" withdrawal from RRSPs. It is a misnomer. Any money withdrawn from an RRSP is taxable.

What these salespeople really propose is a loan to purchase mutual funds. This loan is often secured by a mortgage although demand loans are also common with the interest payments financed by withdrawals from the client's RRSP. Because interest for investment purposes is deductible, the interest deduction offsets the increase in taxable income that stems from pulling money out of the RRSP. In the end, the client's tax bill remains the same – but the RRSP withdrawal is definitely taxable.

The idea behind the "tax-free" withdrawal, other than boosting sales commissions, is to convert a portfolio that will be fully taxed on withdrawal to one that will be taxed at capital gains rates or partially untaxed because of the capital gains exemption.

This strategy is far too risky for most people, especially those approaching retirement and whose major investment assets are their RRSPs. It converts a conservative investment program which is designed to finance retirement to one that leaves the investor exposed to unpredictable results if interest rates move higher.

When to use leverage

Leverage can be used successfully in some circumstances to meet specific objectives. For example, you might decide that you want to use part of your investment assets for speculation, perhaps 10 percent of the total. You could earmark these for specialty funds, such as gold funds, which you expect to do much better than broad-based funds in the short term. Alternatively, you might decide to borrow an amount equal to 10 percent of your investment assets and use the loan to buy a specialty fund in the hope of making a substantial gain of 50 percent or more within a year.

Just remember that the funds that are top performers in one period may turn out to be among the worst performers in a later period. As a result, be prepared to be nimble. And don't invest with borrowed funds for speculation unless you can afford to take a loss.

Also, don't second guess your fund manager. It makes little sense to borrow money to buy a fund that is heavily invested in cash because its manager believes the market is vulnerable. The time to use leverage is when your fund manager is bullish.

Trading mutual funds

You can make a lot of money by simply buying funds and holding them for a long time. A single investment of $10,000 earning 12 percent a year and held for thirty years would be worth almost $300,000. Investing $2,000 a year for thirty years at an average return of 12 percent would build to $540,000. In fact, most fund management companies recommend a buy-and-hold strategy.

Their argument is that the fund manager makes the decisions necessary to maximize gains and preserve capital, moving into those industry groups that offer the most potential at any given time and building cash when the market looks like it is going to move lower.

Some investors take a different tack. Rather than buying and holding, they trade funds. They try to buy in at the beginning of a trend and to sell at the top to lock in profits. People who invest this way are called market timers. They may trade their whole fund portfolio. Or they may trade only the specialty funds such as gold funds, energy funds or Japanese funds – groups that tend to have wide swings in rates of return over relatively short periods. The success of market timers depends on their own skills or those of their advisors. If you are going to trade funds, however, investigate trading costs before you start your program.

As a general rule, there is no charge to switch within a no-load group of funds. Among the groups selling load funds, the commission varies from group to group. The Guardian Group of funds does not charge for switching. The AGF Group has a maximum charge of 2 percent. Some other fund management companies state that the maximum commission applies when switching. However, most commissions are negotiable and most switching within groups can be done for commissions of 2 percent or less. Switching costs also vary among fund families with declining redemption fees. In some cases there is a service charge for switching. In others exchanges are not looked at as redemptions. It is all a matter of understanding the rules before you commit your funds.

If your fund portfolio includes funds of a number of management groups, your trading costs could be higher. Even so, you are unlikely to pay full commissions. Again, commissions are negotiable and you should be able to establish a rate with your dealer that reflects the volume of turnover in your portfolio.

A bit of advice: If you are going to trade funds, become familiar with the portfolios of the funds you plan to trade. You wouldn't want to cash in a specific fund because of worries about market direction, only to find out later that the manager had similar concerns and had moved to a heavy cash position to preserve capital. In the same vein, you wouldn't want to sell 20 percent of a Canadian equity fund to buy a gold fund, only to find out later that your manager had taken a 20 percent position in gold stocks. You can get the portfolio information from the latest fund quarterlies or your fund sales representative.

Diversification

Diversification is a very important investment concept. By diver-
sifying your investments, you spread your risk. If one investment
goes sour, it is more than offset by the other investments you hold.
Mutual funds are diversified portfolios – a mutual fund that invests
in stocks would generally have a minimum of twenty different
stocks.

Even so, you may want to diversify your fund holdings because
you're concerned about tying your fortunes to a single manager, one
market or one class of assets.

You can diversify a portfolio of mutual funds in two ways. The
first is by asset mix, using different types of funds such as Canadian
equity, American equity, fixed income and global investments. The
second is by using two or more funds of the same type but different
investment strategies – if one manager does poorly the others will
carry the day.

Diversification by asset mix is fairly common and makes sense.
Many people will hold a Canadian equity fund and a fixed income
fund in their RRSP and hold a global fund and an American fund
outside their RRSP. The actual mix depends largely on their age, the
capital available and how much exposure they want in a given class
of assets or a specific market.

Diversification within a specific type of fund also makes sense.
However, many investors who diversify within a specific type of
fund fail to meet their objective. They or their advisors neglect to
look at the portfolios or the managers of the funds they buy. Consequently, they end up with two or more funds with similar portfolios
and management styles. An extreme irony would be purchasing two
Canadian equity funds offered by competing fund organizations but
which, in fact, have the same fund manager.

CHAPTER 10

Fees, Loads and Commissions

IT'S IMPORTANT TO DEVELOP an understanding of all the fees and costs connected with mutual fund investment. First, they vary widely. Second, they can have a significant impact on the rate of return earned.

Fees and charges can be broken down into two broad categories: sales commissions and administrative and management fees. In some cases they overlap so that part of the administrative fee is, in reality, on-going compensation to a salesperson for either selling you a fund or for giving you continuing service. At the same time, virtually all major fund groups withhold a portion of the commission paid when you purchase a fund. This is used to finance incentive programs and advertising. But whether costs are included as sales commissions or administrative fees, they affect your net returns from holding mutual funds.

Sales fees have become more complex in recent years. In addition to the traditional no-load funds, which don't charge any commission, and the front-end load funds, which can be bought only on payment of an acquisition fee, there are funds that have flat redemption fees, funds that have declining sales charges and funds that have ongoing sales charges. Some funds even combine two types of sales fees so you'll pay a fee when you buy and when you redeem. A number of groups, such as the Dynamic Group, give you the option of buying either with an acquisition fee or a declining deferred redemption fee. A few funds have registration fees or administration fees. For example, London Life Canadian Equity Fund has a quarterly administration fee ranging from $10 to $15 quarterly.

Rates of return published in the *Financial Times of Canada* and similar tables do not take sales fees into consideration but do account for all administrative and management fees charged to the fund. If the published rate of return for a fund is 15 percent and its management fee is 2 percent, the fund actually returned 17 percent. The return that investors realize is 15 percent.

Management fees range from about 0.75 percent to more than 3 percent, depending on the fund. They include the fees paid to the portfolio manager and they may also include the expenses of operating the fund. In some cases they reflect compensation paid to the salesperson. Funds must disclose all compensation and incentive arrangements in their prospectuses, a requirement introduced by the Ontario Securities Commission in 1987. Over the past decade many mutual fund companies have offered various types of incentives to boost sales, a practice that is common in many industries. These incentives have ranged from giving salespeople small appliances for opening new accounts to providing fur coats for volume sales and offering travel points or all-expenses-paid educational conferences on luxury ocean liners or in exotic foreign resorts. The sales conference contests were the big draw and indeed, most companies which sell funds through stockbrokers and through mutual fund dealers found themselves offering sales conference contests if only to remain competitive with the leaders in the incentive field.

These contests have been widely covered in the business press. Concern that they create serious conflicts of interest or give the appearance of conflicts prompted regulators to consider prohibiting such conferences. As a result, regulators appear to be heading in the direction of not allowing any incentives other than the fees or commissions disclosed in a fund prospectus. Regulators, however, allow fund companies to sponsor bona fide sales conferences or educational seminars held in Canada and to pay food, lodging and transportation expenses of those persons attending.

No-load funds

Some funds do not carry any up-front sales fee or back-end redemption fee. Funds offered or sponsored by banks and trust companies generally, but not always, fall into this category. A few fund management companies offer these no-load funds through investment dealers as well as directly to investors. The fund companies compensate the dealer by paying them reciprocal commissions, orders to buy or sell stock for the fund.

Alternatively, a fund company may compensate a seller of its no-load fund by paying part of the management fee for as long as the client holds the fund. This payment, which ranges from 0.25 percent to 0.5 percent of the value of the client's holding, is called a "trailer." Many, if not most, load funds also pay trailers.

Rear-end load funds

During late 1989 and early 1990 many fund companies modified their commission schedules and dealer compensation programs. Competition from banks and trust companies which do not charge acquisition fees forced many fund companies to introduce declining deferred redemption fees as an option for purchasers. With these, you don't pay a commission when you buy into a mutual fund; all

Typical Back-End Charges

INDUSTRIAL HORIZON FUND

Year of Redemption	Charge
During first year	4.5%
During second year	4.0%
During third year	3.5%
During fourth year	3.0%
During fifth year	2.5%
During sixth year	2.0%
During seventh year	1.5%
During eighth year	1.0%
During ninth year	0.5%
After that	nil

TABLE XI

your money is invested for you. But, even though you don't pay an acquisition fee, the fund company pays your broker a commission of about 4 percent. You will have to pay a redemption charge only if you redeem within a specific period. The fee is highest in the first year and tapers down to zero, usually within six years. The fee differs between fund groups but usually ranges from about 5 per cent if you redeem within one year of purchase down to 1 percent if you redeem in the fifth year. If you redeem after the sixth year, you won't have to pay any redemption fee. These fees vary widely and are not negotiable. The redemption fee on Maritime Life Growth Fund, for instance, is 10 percent on first-year redemptions and declines by 1 percent a year until it reaches zero after the tenth year.

The largest declining back-end load fund is Industrial Horizon Fund, which was launched during the 1987 RRSP season and which had $1.5 billion in assets at the end of June 1991. Table XI shows its redemption charges.

Some brokers and dealers were initially reluctant to introduce their clients to funds with deferred declining sales charges because they were used to charging up to 9 percent. This reluctance has disappeared for the most part because of competitive pressures from banks and trust companies and their no-load funds.

Different fund groups have different bells and whistles. For instance, in some cases the redemption fee applies to the value of units at the time the investment was made, rather than the market value at the time of the redemption. Dividends reinvested may be exempt from the redemption fee and shares purchased with reinvested dividends are considered the first shares redeemed. You may also get exchange privileges within a fund group without triggering redemption fees. Also you may get the privilege of redeeming up to say, 10 percent of your holdings a year without triggering a redemption fee. This is an important privilege for someone who has an automatic withdrawal plan or who holds fund units inside a registered retirement income fund.

Load funds

No-load funds are a minority in Canada, but their numbers are growing as more banks and trust companies jump into the fund business. As well, declining deferred redemption fee sales have become increasingly important to funds which are sold by brokers and dealers. Still, a substantial portion of fund business written each year is in load funds – funds that pay a commission to the dealer or broker who places the order.

The most common form of load funds is the front-end load fund, which requires payment of a commission of up to a maximum 9 percent. Virtually all front-end load funds have tapered commission schedules, with the commission charged declining according to the size of the purchase.

There is no standard commission schedule and each mutual fund company can taper its commission rates in a different way. There can even be differences between the funds managed by one company. Typically, a fund would charge a maximum commission of 9 percent on purchases of up to $24,999 and 7 percent on purchases of $25,000 to $50,000; 5 percent on purchases from $50,000 to $100,000; 3 percent on $100,000 to $250,000; 2 percent on $250,000 to $500,000 and 1 percent on anything greater. Several preferred dividend funds have maximum commission rates of 5 percent. Some dealers will add up the purchases made within a year for commission-calculating purposes to give clients the commission rate that would be paid if all the purchases had been made at once. Mutual Diversico Ltd. calculates sales charges on lifetime purchases of all funds in the Mutual group of funds.

Negotiating commissions

Commissions charged on front-end load funds are generally negotiable. The phrase in the prospectus is "maximum sales charge" or "not to exceed." This phraseology allows a salesperson to discount commission to reflect a client's purchase of several funds so that the commission charged would be the same as if the client put all of his or her money in one fund. As well, it creates a competitive environment in which some brokers and salespeople are more willing to cut commissions

Typical Equity Fund Commission Schedule

DYNAMIC EQUITY FUNDS

Amount Paid	Maximum sales charge
Up to $14,999	9%
$15,000 to $24,999	8%
$25,000 to $49,999	7%
$50,000 to $99,999	5%
$100,000 to $249,999	4%
$250,000 to $499,999	3%
$500,000 to $999,999	2%
$1 million and over	1%

TABLE XII

than others. They might, for instance, accept a 3 percent commission on a $5,000 order rather than the maximum 9 percent. Of course, a broker who accepts 3 percent on a small order is unlikely to provide any service other than filling the forms and accepting your cheque.

Discount stockbrokers will generally place an order for half the maximum commission noted in a fund prospectus. But most dealers will cut commissions drastically if they aren't expected to provide any advice or service. As a group, stockbrokers are more likely to cut commissions than independent fund salespeople. But there are no hard and fast rules. Many salespeople won't cut commissions under any circumstances other than to reflect the total dollar value of a client's purchases spread among two or more funds. These salespeople usually provide detailed financial planning and feel they are compensated for their efforts only if they charge full commissions.

Fixed commissions

All major mutual fund groups allow commissions to be discounted. Templeton Growth Fund changed in 1988: it had required a fixed rate as a carryover from the days when the fund's prospectus was filed both in Canada and the United States. U.S. securities regulations prohibit discounting of fund commissions. Funds sold through insurance companies often have fixed commission rates. So do funds which have "captive" sales forces that sell only a specific family of funds. Rates do change from time to time. For example, Investors Group, which is the largest fund company, recently revised its commission structure to makes its funds more competitive.

Not all the commission paid when you buy a fund with a front-end load finds its way into the hands of the person who sold you the fund. Most major fund management companies that distribute through independent fund sales organizations and investment dealers have what is called a "hold-back." A hold-back is part of the sales commission that is retained by the fund management company to finance promotional activities. These include advertising campaigns jointly sponsored by a fund company and a broker, and, until recently, educational seminars held in exotic locations for salespeople who sell a specific amount of a fund. Some funds use holdbacks to pay bonuses to brokers whose sales exceed specific targets.

The hold-back varies among fund groups. In some cases it will be a flat percentage amount, such as one percentage point, so that if a salesperson sells a fund with a 9 percent commission, 8 per cent is returned to the broker and 1 percent is held back for promotion. If a salesperson sells a fund with a 4 percent commission, 3 per cent is returned to the broker and 1 percent is held back. In other cases, the hold-back is a constant fraction of the commission charged, perhaps 10 percent, so that the smaller the commission, the smaller the hold-back. Not surprisingly, salespeople are likely to be less generous about discounting a fund that has a flat percentage of the amount you invest as its hold-back.

Redemption fees

A handful of funds charge a flat fee when you redeem units. It can be a small amount, as is the case with Associate Investors Ltd., which charges a 1 percent redemption fee. Most funds can charge a redemption fee of up to 2 percent if an investor who paid less than 2 percent commission then redeems within a short time, usually within one year of purchase. In some cases management has the option of waiving this fee. This is often done as a good-will measure and depends on the circumstances.

Paying at both ends

A few fund groups such as the Viking Group of Funds charge a commission both when you buy and when you sell. Viking Group of Funds has a 3.5 per cent commission on purchases of all Viking Funds up to $25,000, and a redemption fee using the same scale. The total sales and redemption fee cannot exceed 9 percent of the amount invested.

Many fund groups apply a charge if you want to transfer your money to another fund within the group. Others allow transfers free of charge. While the fee can be as much as full commission rates, many groups charge a 2 percent fee for a transfer.

Management expense ratio

All fees, other than direct sales fees and specific fees such as RRSP trustee fees, are almost always reflected in the management expense ratio. This ratio, expressed as a percentage in prospectuses, includes the management fee and the expenses paid by the fund. Some funds pay all expenses out of the management fee. Others charge the expenses directly to the fund. However, the management expense ratio is all-inclusive and allows comparisons among funds.

Some fees, such as management fees, are charged directly to the client rather than to the fund by at least one fund. However, its published rates of return are net of fees. Consequently, investors can make valid comparisons. Management expense ratios vary widely. For some equity funds they are as low as 0.75 percent; others exceed 3 percent. Most range from 1.5 percent to 2.75 percent. Indeed, management expense ratios have been rising in recent years. Management expense ratios for income funds are marginally lower. Many fund groups have raised their management fees in recent years to reflect rising costs, including sales costs such as trailer fees (see next section). Consequently, management expense ratios have been rising for some but not all funds. While management expense ratios are reflected in fund rates of return, it is important for investors to make any necessary adjustments to historical rates of return to keep them in perspective. Funds disclose their latest five years' management expense ratios in their annual reports.

The management expense ratio is important because it is often the only part of a performance number that is predictable. For instance, few investors are going to worry about whether a management expense ratio is 1.5 percent or 2.5 percent if a fund's long-term rate of return is 15 percent or 16 percent. But in years when the markets are lacklustre or show negative returns, a one percentage point difference in management expense ratio becomes significant.

Trailer fees

Another shift in the mutual fund industry is toward trailer fees. Trailer fees are paid by management on an ongoing basis to the selling broker to encourage the broker to continue to service the client and to discourage switching. Trailer fees are usually one-quarter of the management fee.

If you've purchased your mutual fund units from one dealer and later switch your account to another firm, your trailer will move to the new firm provided your account shows you are dealing with the second firm. Therefore, a fund salesperson may insist you have all your dealings under one roof.

If you have purchased funds and aren't happy with the advice you've been getting, find a salesperson with whom you feel comfortable. Even if you don't purchase additional funds, the salesperson may be happy to give you advice provided the funds in question pay a trailer and he or she becomes involved with your account.

Trailers are a point of contention in the industry. Some want them banned entirely as a hidden charge, while others argue they are a payment made by the fund company, not the client, to encourage ongoing service. Provincial securities commissions are likely to require the fund industry to provide more detailed disclosure about trailers and the investors' rights, if any, to direct them.

Additional fees

Depending on the funds you hold, you may face additional charges. A few funds have nominal charges for pre-authorized purchases or cheques issued on redemption. Trustee fees for RRSPs are an additional charge for virtually all funds and are charged against your account or billed separately. The point is, fees vary widely, so you should know what they are before you commit to buy.

Load versus no-load

Every fee you pay will affect your final return. Table XIII compares the growth of an investment of $10,000 over thirty years in three

Comparing Load and No-Load Funds

Yr.	Front-End Load	Back-End Load	No Load	Yr.	Front-End Load	Back-End Load	No Load
1	$ 9,500	$ 9,550	$10,000	16	$ 49,948	$ 50,498	$ 58,518
2	10,612	10,694	11,250	17	55,792	56,255	65,833
3	11,853	11,976	12,656	18	62,320	62,668	74,062
4	13,240	13,410	14,238	19	69,611	69,812	83,319
5	14,789	15,016	16,018	20	77,756	77,771	93,734
6	16,519	16,813	18,020	21	86,853	86,637	105,451
7	18,452	18,826	20,273	22	97,015	96,513	118,632
8	20,611	21,078	22,807	23	108,366	107,516	133,461
9	23,022	23,600	25,658	24	121,045	119,773	150,144
10	25,716	26,422	28,865	25	135,207	133,427	168,912
11	28,725	29,434	32,473	26	151,026	148,638	190,026
12	32,085	32,790	36,532	27	168,697	165,582	213,779
13	35,839	36,528	41,099	28	188,434	184,459	240,502
14	40,033	40,692	46,236	29	210,481	205,487	270,564
15	44,717	45,331	52,016	30	235,107	228,912	304,385

TABLE XIII

funds which have different types of sales charges. Each fund earns the same rate of return of 14 percent before sales charges and management fees. The figures show what investors would receive if they redeemed at the beginning of any year.

The first fund is a front-end load fund with a management expense ratio of 2.3 percent, so its compound rate of return is 11.7 percent. The management expense ratio is the average for Canadian equity funds sold with front-end loads. We will assume the investor paid a 5 percent front-end load.

The second fund has a deferred declining sales charge of 4.5 percent in the first year decreasing by 0.5 percent each year to zero in the ninth year. This fund has a management expense ratio of 2.6 percent (an actual average), so its compound rate of return to the investor is 11.4 percent.

The third fund is a no-load fund with a management expense ratio of 1.5 percent, so its compound rate of return is 12.5 per cent.

The table suggests that, all other things being equal, investors who expect to hold a fund for a long time and are choosing between a front-end load fund and a deferred declining-sales-charge fund with a higher management fee are better off paying the front-end load. Of course, if the fund company gives you a choice of front-end or rear-end load on the same fund and you are a long term investor you are better off with the declining-sales-charge option.

If the choice is between a front-end load fund and a no-load fund, the decision depends on the difference in management fees. A no-load fund has the advantage for at least twenty-five years, even if its management expense ratio is one-quarter point higher.

Your best buy is a no-load fund with a low management fee, ignoring the value of service and advice you receive when buying a load fund. Very few funds meet this description. Two that do are MD Growth Investments Ltd. and CMA Investment Fund. However, they are available only to members of the Canadian Medical Association.

Investors shouldn't shop on the basis of price alone. The decision to purchase a fund should be based on the securities in which the fund invests and the expertise of the manager. Arguments can be made for allowing costs to determine the choice of fund, but many people who haven't the time to continuously follow their investments are probably better off getting professional advice – and paying for it.

CHAPTER 11

How to Pick a Fund

INDIVIDUAL INVESTORS AND fund advisors spend hours agonizing over performance figures, attending information meetings and reading annual and quarterly reports and prospectuses searching for something that will help them pick one fund over another.

Unfortunately, there is no way you can know for certain that any one fund will outperform another. The best you can do is choose funds whose investment policies are compatible with your own and which have performed well over time, particularly in the same type of market conditions you currently face (or whose current managers have demonstrated acceptable performance under similar market conditions).

The first thing you have to do is determine what type of fund meets your objectives. If you want long-term capital growth tied to the Canadian economy, look at Canadian equity funds. If you want stable growth based on income within your RRSP, look at bond funds, mortgage funds or both.

Examine past performance

Most funds are sold on their past performance. But past performance is not a perfect indicator of future performance. It may be a fair indication of how a specific manager performed under certain market conditions but it is not a guarantee.

A performance figure is a fund's rate of return or average rate of return over a specific period of time. If you look at several ending dates you'll likely find different funds among the top performers. You should also realize that many funds have grown from a few million dollars to hundreds of millions, a growth that could impact on both investment strategy and performance. The management styles and stock market trading responsible for superior perfor-

Equity Funds — RRSP-Eligible

Southam variability ranking	Max. sales fee %	Codes	Total assets $ mil.	% fgn	Divi-dend $	Net asset value $	Mutual Fund	1 mo.	3 mo.	1 yr.	3 yr.	5 yr.	10 yr.
N/A		R	171	6		3.79	20/20 Cdn Asset Allocation	0.3	3.6	15.8			
N/A		R	23			12.30	20/20 Cdn Growth Fund	-2.1	0.0	13.8			
N/A		R	19	3		11.11	20/20 RSP Growth Fund	-2.5	-0.2	11.5			
17 2.07			97	7		13.52	20/20 Sunset Fund	0.4	4.0	17.4	9.7	8.2	
16 2.03		NLP	8		0.044	5.63	ABC Fully Managed Fund	-0.4	-2.5	17.3	13.7		
N/A		NLP	2			5.71	ABC Fundamental Value Fund	-1.6	-5.1	25.8			
61 4.19	9.00		316			8.32	AGF Canadian Equity Fund	-3.8	-3.4	5.6	-0.6	0.6	10.0
98 5.68	9.00		32	2		7.57	AGF Cdn Resources Fund	-3.6	-4.0	-15.4	1.1	4.4	0.3
29 2.50	9.00		16	13		8.31	AGF Convertible Income Fund	0.1	1.7	13.0	2.7		
92 5.21	9.00		83			9.93	AGF Growth Equity Fund	-3.0	-0.6	11.0	2.6	0.9	6.9
97 5.57	9.00		9	14		11.52	AIC Advantage Fund	-3.4	-1.7	31.7	6.0	4.2	
N/A		R	6			4.81	Admax Canadian Performance	-2.2	-1.2	3.7			
34 2.80	8.00		12			13.37	All-Canadian Compound Fund	-0.5	-2.8	-0.3	3.3	4.0	9.0
34 2.81	8.00		13			9.43	All-Canadian Dividend Fund	-0.5	-2.8	-0.4	3.3	4.0	8.6
89 5.02		NL	!	2		4.62	Allied Canadian Fund	-1.9	-3.8	13.8	4.9	-0.6	
N/A			82	2		9.74	AltaFund	-1.9	-0.3				
49 3.76		NL	31	2		10.26	Altamira Balanced Fund	0.2	1.7	1.8	2.1	0.9	
53 3.98		NLP	7	5	0.030	8.98	Altamira Capital Growth Fund	-2.1	0.8	7.7	8.4	6.3	9.8
44 3.37		NLP	82	5		17.70	Altamira Equity Fund	-1.0	2.2	14.0	22.7		
12 1.96		NLP	31	6	0.100	5.82	Altamira Growth & Income Fund	0.9	5.5	14.9	11.3	10.5	
N/A			4			5.60	Altamira Resource	-2.3	1.1	7.9			
70 4.43		NL	10	7		8.45	Altamira Special Growth Fund	-1.6	0.8	18.0	12.1	5.3	
52 3.92		R	2			9.34	BPI Cdn Equity Fund	-3.1	-2.9	5.3	1.6		
36 2.91		R	17	4		10.67	BPI One Decision Fund	0.0	4.0	15.8	7.0	5.3	
16 2.02			5	8	0.079	6.51	Barrtor Canadian Fund	0.6	3.9	16.8	9.8	7.6	
35 2.84			5	12		12.14	Batirente-Section Action	-2.8	-1.9	7.6	1.2		
7 1.68			14	3		13.67	Batirente-Section Diversifiee	1.8	5.0	17.4	8.8		
75 4.62		NL	2	16		16.01	Bissett Canadian Equity	-2.1	-0.3	14.9	7.3	6.3	
61 4.18	9.00		64	14		14.23	Bolton Tremblay Cda Cum Fund	-1.9	-0.6	10.9	3.6	3.3	7.6
20 2.16	9.00		4	8	0.100	4.72	Bolton Tremblay Cdn Balanced	0.4	2.8	14.3	7.1		
44 3.36	9.00		4			4.78	Bolton Tremblay Discovery	-2.0	-1.2	17.9	2.6		
* 56 4.01			5	14		6.76	Bolton Tremblay Optimal Cdn	0.0	-1.2	10.4	4.5	3.9	
99 5.96	9.00		17			10.82	Bolton Tremblay Planned Res	-3.3	-4.3	-0.3	5.7	3.5	5.2
6 1.64	9.00	P	1	6		9.95	Bullock Balanced Fund	-0.3	2.4	13.7	5.1		
80 4.75	9.00		6	9		2.27	Bullock Growth Fund	-1.3	-0.3	17.0	3.6	2.4	4.4
19 2.16		X	10			33.26	CDA RSP Balanced Fund	0.2	3.1	15.6	9.4	8.4	11.5
60 4.16		X	36	10		17.04	CDA RSP Common Stock Fund	-1.8	0.8	13.1	7.4	7.9	13.2
10 1.88		NL	75	6	0.108	10.82	CIBC Bal Income & Growth Fund	0.0	3.0	14.9	9.1		
N/A		NL	36		0.041	9.74	CIBC Canadian Equity Fund	-3.6	-5.2	2.1			
22 2.21			19	4		23.07	Caisse de Sec du Spectacle	0.7	4.2	18.1	9.1	7.3	11.7
N/A		R	5	13		5.48	Caldwell Securities Associate	-0.3	3.8				

TABLE XIV

mance when a fund was small may not work as well in a larger fund.

Southam Business Communications Inc. prepares a monthly survey of investment funds published by the *Financial Times of Canada* and other papers. The survey includes six performance figures for each fund. Three are short-term returns covering the change in value of a fund, including dividends reinvested, for one-month, three-month and one-year periods. The other figures are average annual compound rates of return for three years, five years and ten years. These show the average annual return of the fund each year, assuming all income is reinvested. Average annual compound rates of return are a more accurate method of measuring performance than simply taking the average annual performance of the fund. *The Financial Post* and *The Globe and Mail Report On Business* also publish monthly performance tables.

Southam publishes two other products widely used by mutual fund professionals and, to a lesser extent, by individual investors. One is the Mutual Fund Sourcedisk and the other is the Mutual Fund Sourcebook.

The Mutual Fund Sourcedisk, which can be used on an IBM PC or compatible computer, is a computer disk of mutual fund data that is updated monthly. It provides the performance information included in the *Financial Times'* monthly survey, plus additional historical performance information. It allows investors to rank funds globally or within fund types using a broad range of criteria. You could, for example, rank Canadian equity funds with assets equal to or greater than $25 million. The Sourcedisk can also provide information on individual funds and average data on any group of funds.

The Mutual Fund Sourcebook includes performance information as well as details covering such matters as commission rates, trustee fees, the names of the fund managers and the addresses of the management companies.

Best Financial Network Inc. provides an on-line service of mutual fund performance tables to people who sell mutual funds as well as tables covering guaranteed investment rates and insurance and annuity premiums.

Most people who work in the fund business emphasize the longer-term rates of return, arguing that most investors buy funds as long-term investments. They feel that many investors are misled by short-term performance. However, short-term performance is also important because it can act as an indicator of a change in a manager's investment strategy. For instance, if a top-performing fund started to lag behind its competition in a rising market, it might indicate that the manager is building cash in anticipation of a market correction. If your fund starts to fall behind other performers, you might want to investigate. It could mean a change in investment strategy or it could signal something more serious, such as a change in fund manager.

It makes sense to look at performance over various periods of time if you're holding for long-term growth. If a fund has good long- and short-term performance but poor medium-term performance, don't reject it outright. Try to determine why performance fluctuated. It's possible the manager called the market wrong for a relatively short period but then corrected the error. Even though the error in strategy was corrected, it will be reflected in the performance figures for several years.

When judging the performance of specialty funds, particularly volatile ones such as golds and Japanese funds, short-term performance figures are probably more important than long-term figures. You are more likely to buy specialty funds for a relatively short-term hold. And, your decision will probably be based on how such a fund has performed recently rather than over ten, five or even three years.

If you're considering a relatively new fund, you only have short-term performance to examine. Just remember that there is little correlation between short-term and long-term performance. If you buy a fund on the basis of short-term performance, don't be surprised if its long-term performance fails to meet your expectations.

In fact, some investors buy funds that have good long-term performance but which have lagged the pack recently. Their view is that every dog has its day.

If you ask your broker, fund dealer or a fund company for information about how well a fund has performed relative to competing funds, you'll probably get a copy of a performance table from the *Financial Times* or a printout from the Sourcedisk.

It's not that the fund companies and people who sell funds don't want to give you more but because provincial securities regulatory authorities severely restrict the information fund companies and salespeople can provide investors. The restrictions are included in National Policy 39, Section 16 which governs mutual fund advertising and applies in all provinces.

At the time of writing regulators were reviewing these restrictions. Fund companies are also severely restricted in television and radio advertising by another set of regulations.

Besides performance you should also consider volatility, particularly when considering funds whose objective is growth or a combination of growth and income. The *Financial Times'* monthly survey of investment funds ranks funds by volatility, or the stability of monthly rates of return. The survey uses two measures. One is a percentage figure, the second is a statistical measure called standard deviation. Standard deviation is the relative volatility of monthly rates of return. The lower the figure, the less volatile the monthly rate of return. A money market fund would have a very low standard deviation, a gold fund would have a very high one.

The percentage figure ranks funds by volatility within fund groups. Within Canadian growth and income funds one would expect balanced funds to have a low percentage figure while gold funds and energy funds to have high percentage figures. Most funds fall in the middle range, between 15 percent and 85 per cent. If you are trying to decide between two funds as long-term investments and they have similar performance histories, the fund with the lower volatility would be your choice.

On the other hand, if you're looking for a short-term trading position, you might want the fund that has shown the largest swings in performance as measured by the volatility rating. Funds which tended to have large swings in the past will likely be the funds that have large swings in the future. If you're nimble you can buy low and sell high.

Look at the fund's attributes

Another way to choose a fund is by examining the fund's attributes – specific characteristics such as its yield, cash component, size of companies in its portfolio – and choosing one whose attributes match your views on market. For example, if you believe interest rates will decline sharply you would look for a bond fund whose average maturity is ten years or greater rather than a fund which is primarily invested in treasury bills and bonds which mature within five years.

Investors who expect a period of economic expansion would choose funds which are growth oriented rather than invested in mature companies. Conversely, investors who expect a recession would invest in funds which have defensive characteristics, such as a high component of cash and high-yielding stocks.

Portfolio Analytics Limited of Toronto has looked at this issue closely, arriving at the conclusion that differences in fund performance result primarily from the allocation of assets and, within asset types, management style or strategy. It has also concluded that future performance will be affected more by a fund's current attributes than its past performance. By analysing the holdings within fund portfolios Portfolio Analytics determines the attributes of different funds, information which investors can then use in making their decisions.

Investors who want a diversified portfolio of funds would look at fund attributes so they can choose funds which complement, rather than duplicate, each other. For example, they might pick a fund invested in companies with small capitalization as a balance against a fund invested in mature, large-cap companies.

Who is the manager?

You and your fund advisor should also look at who is managing the fund and consider his or her experience. This information is available from most fund management companies. Indeed, many fund salespeople place more emphasis on the manager than on the fund's recent performance record. After all, it doesn't make sense to buy a fund on the basis of its ten-year performance if the person who was responsible for that performance has left for another job. Similarly, it doesn't make sense to reject a fund with poor performance if a new manager with a superior track record has just been put in charge.

Besides looking at the manager, look at the management organization. Is there adequate back-up if the manager takes a vacation or quits? What type of analytical support is behind the manager? There is nothing wrong with investing in a fund whose manager has limited back-up. Just be prepared to be nimble if the manager leaves.

When should I switch?

No manager is infallible. From time to time a manager may make a bad decision that has an impact on performance. A manager may build cash prematurely in a rising market and consequently underperform the competition. Or, he or she may not sell soon enough and tumble with the general market.

Don't make a decision to sell on the basis of short-term performance. You should, however, determine whether the manager has corrected any misjudgments and is back on track. It can be difficult to know whether the manager has, in fact, made an error. Some managers habitually "sell too soon," only to outperform their competition in the subsequent market downturn. Three to five years is probably the minimum period over which to judge a fund manager.

What you can expect

Pick up the financial pages of any newspaper and you'll likely see ads for mutual funds. Generally, the results they display are impressive. In 1989 when long-term rates were high, many showed ten-year average annual compound rates of return of 16 percent, 18 per cent, even 22 percent. Some ads for newer funds emphasize short-term performance that may be significantly higher. During the summer of 1990 few funds were advertising long-term rates because they were much lower.

There aren't any guarantees that future results will be similar to past performance. However, historically, people who have invested for long-term growth using equity funds have done better than people who invested in guaranteed investments. Moreover, people who have invested in equity funds have outpaced inflation.

Over the ten years ended June 30, 1987, the average annual compound rate of return for Canadian equity funds was 17.2 percent, while the average return for bond and mortgage funds was 11.1 per cent. In comparison, an investment in Government of Canada treasury bills would have given an average return of 11 per cent. Using the ten years to June 30, 1988, which includes the October 1987 crash, the average return for Canadian equity funds was 14.5 percent, still substantially above a T-bill return of 11.1 percent. For the ten years ended June 30, 1989, the average return for Canadian equity funds was 12.6 percent; for the ten years ended June 30, 1990, that return was only 9.5 percent. However, the starting point of that period, July 1980, was near a market cycle peak. The stock market declined 39.2 percent in the twelve months ended June 30, 1982. Even without a crystal ball it is likely that in one year when investors look at the ten-year rate for the period ended June 30, 1992, that rate will be higher than the June 1990 ten-year rate and the June 1991 ten-year rate of 8.5 percent.

No one can predict the rates of return that funds will achieve in the future. But given the structure of the economy, it seems safe to say that people who buy equities for the long term will continue to do better than people who take less risk and buy fixed-income investments.

Legal registration of funds

Open-end funds are either mutual fund corporations, mutual fund trusts or insurance company variable life policies. Their common element is an underlying portfolio of securities or investments, which determines the share or unit value of the fund.

It doesn't really matter to most investors which of the three they own. But there are some subtle differences, particularly with insurance company variable life policies, that can have a bearing on making investment decisions.

For tax purposes, mutual fund trusts must "flow through" to investors all Canadian dividends, interest and capital gains. It would also flow foreign income through to investors but it would generally charge expenses against foreign income and interest income to reduce the potential tax liability of unitholders.

Mutual fund corporations also flow through Canadian dividends and capital gains. However, they are not allowed to flow through interest and foreign income. Rather, it is taxable in the fund's hands. But mutual fund corporations generally charge expenses against interest income and foreign income, effectively cutting their tax liability.

There are some circumstances in which a mutual fund corporation's Canadian income can become taxable in the fund's hands rather than flow through to shareholders. If 25 percent or more of the shares of a mutual fund corporation were held by one shareholder – an unlikely event – its income would be taxable. Similarly, if 25 percent or more of its income was interest income, it would be taxable in the corporation's hands. This can happen if a fund manager, anticipating a declining stock market, decides to hold a major portion of the portfolio in treasury bills and other short-term investments.

Having income taxed in the fund's hands is a disadvantage for RRSP holders, who would pay no tax if the income were flowed through. Even so, on a per-unit basis this is of little consequence, especially when weighed against the alternative of not preserving capital in a falling market.

Mutual fund corporations must hold annual meetings but trusts do not. This is not a significant difference since both mutual fund corporations and trusts must issue detailed annual and semi-annual financial statements to investors. Most of them issue quarterly reports as well. Trusts generally don't issue certificates, although many will on request. This is of little importance to most people. In fact, certificates can be a bother, particularly if you have distributions automatically reinvested to buy additional units in a fund. After a few years you could end up with a stack of certificates. Alternatively, you would be constantly having your certificates replaced to reflect your increased holdings.

In some circumstances having certificates can be helpful. If you borrow money from a bank using your fund holdings as security, the bank may want the certificate as security for the loan. However, the certificate isn't really necessary. You can assign the units as collateral so that the bank's name would appear on the fund's list of unitholders. Virtually all fund management companies have procedures covering this and can explain them to bank or trust company managers, if necessary.

All in all, it makes little difference whether you hold units in a mutual fund corporation or mutual fund trust. However, overtures – unsuccessful to date – have been made to Ottawa by the funds industry to allow mutual fund corporations to flow through dividends, interest and realized capital gains to shareholders in the same manner as mutual fund trusts.

Creditor-proof funds

Insurance company segregated funds are effectively insurance policies on which the value varies with the underlying assets. On the death of the investor or at maturity, the holder of the policy or his or her estate receives either the market value of the policy or 75 percent of the value of contributions, whichever is greater. Moreover, as an insurance policy, the investment can be made creditor-proof under certain circumstances by designating a beneficiary within the immediate family. (A recent ruling in a Saskatchewan court has led analysts to question whether insurance policy investments are in fact creditor-proof.) Also, these policies give holders the option of rolling the funds into an annuity at guaranteed rates, although these rates are generally quite low.

For tax purposes, dividends, interest and capital gains received by insurance company segregated funds are flowed through to investors. But an important caveat for people who invest with borrowed money is that interest on money borrowed to buy a segregated fund may not be deductible from income for tax purposes.

All funds have similar mechanisms to protect investors. The fund portfolio is the property of the investors, not the fund management company, and the securities are held by a custodian, generally a bank or trust company. The portfolio is not part of the assets of the fund management company and cannot be used by the manager to support its business. If the fund management company goes bankrupt, the investors in the funds are protected.

Avoiding commissions

Should you buy a no-load fund and avoid commissions? The answer depends on your own personal situation. In some cases the answer is "absolutely." In other cases it's a definite "no." In many cases it's a "maybe." It all depends on your objectives, how much work you do on your own and whether you need professional advice. Moreover, with the choice of funds available with deferred declining sales charges or redemption fees, the question is becoming academic in many cases, especially when management fees are comparable.

Some no-load fund groups have employees who can provide advice. But the majority of fund specialists sell load funds or funds with redemption fees and are paid commissions. If you decide to use a broker or fund specialist, make sure the person you pick has the expertise and can provide a level of service that justifies the commission you pay.

As far as performance is concerned, no-loads, as a group, are just as good as load funds. Both groups include funds that are excellent performers as well as funds that are poor performers. In fact, some investment managers manage both types of funds, but the funds are marketed through different fund-management distribution companies.

If you are a sophisticated, experienced investor who knows what you want, then by all means buy no-load funds and save yourself the commission. Even if you aren't an investment wizard but have a good idea which funds suit your objectives – perhaps you want a bond fund for your RRSP or a mortgage fund for income – then check out the no-loads offered by the banks and trust companies with which you deal.

The vast majority of no-loads are offered by banks and trust companies. However, a handful of investment counsellors such as Sceptre Investment Counsel Ltd. offer no-loads directly to the public. As well, several organizations such as the Canadian Medical Association and Ontario Teachers' Group offer families of funds to their members.

If you buy a fund from a bank or trust company the quality of advice you'll get, if any, depends on the expertise of the individual who comes to the counter. This can be a hit-or-miss situation, depending on the experience and education of the institution's employee.

Securities regulators have taken steps to improve the proficiency of bank and trust company funds salespeople. As well as the IFIC mutual fund course and the Canadian Securities Institute course, regulatory authorities accept for registration requirements courses offered by the Institute of Canadian Bankers and Trust Companies Institute.

The onus is on you to determine whether the person advising you has sufficient training and experience. It is generally a good idea to ask for the manager. And don't be too shy to ask what training he or she has. Just remember that if you use no-load funds you've assumed the responsibility of monitoring performance and making changes to your fund portfolio when necessary. You've also assumed the task of making sure the portfolio of funds you've chosen meets your needs and objectives.

CHAPTER 12

How to Pick an Advisor

THE MAJORITY OF FUND owners in Canada buy funds through an intermediary. It can be an investment dealer or stockbroker, a mutual fund specialist, a trust company employee, or an insurance agent selling insurance company segregated funds or mutual funds.

Some intermediaries will sell funds offered by several fund management companies; others will sell only a single group of funds. Firms that advertise themselves as independent dealers, such as Regal Capital Planners Ltd., offer funds from many of the major fund management companies. In contrast, sales representatives employed by Investors Group, or its subsidiary Investors Syndicate Ltd., will offer only the Investors funds. Similarly, many insurance agents will sell only the specific family of funds that is affiliated with their insurance company. Stockbrokers will generally offer funds from the major fund management companies. In addition, some will offer funds affiliated with their firms. It's expected that brokerage houses owned by banks may soon be distributing bank-managed mutual funds along with other funds.

Should you use an advisor who offers a single family of funds or someone who offers many? All advisors will, or should, offer you the best they have. The question is whether a sales representative handling a single family of funds has the best. While many fund companies have top performers, none has a monopoly on top performance in all types of funds – RRSP equity, RRSP bond, foreign equity, specialty funds and so on. An independent salesperson who handles many funds has access to a wider range than a captive representative who has only a single family to offer. Further, many of the top-performing funds are available only through independent salespeople. But as the ranking table indicates, some of the funds sold only through captive sales forces have done quite well, as have some of the no-load funds.

Of course, there is nothing stopping you from dealing with more than one sales organization and indeed many people do have several dealers.

Much depends on the individual sales representative and whether he or she can tailor a fund portfolio to suit your needs. The key point is that if you are going to need advice and guidance, the salesperson you choose must be an expert. A mutual fund specialist, whether employed by an investment dealer, independent fund sales organization, insurance agency or part of a captive sales force should have a detailed understanding of how to use funds to meet clients' objectives. He or she should monitor fund performance closely and be in touch with fund management companies to be aware of any changes in strategy or investment personnel that may have an impact on client returns.

While there is a tendency among many fund salespeople not to second-guess portfolio managers, some salespeople demand detailed explanations of current investment policy. This helps them determine whether specific funds continue to meet the criteria on which they base their recommendations. Take the time to choose your fund advisor carefully and with thought. Making the wrong choice can be financially and emotionally expensive.

Licensing requirements

Sales of mutual funds are regulated by provincial securities commissions. Firms selling mutual funds must meet certain capital requirements and their officers and managers must demonstrate specific levels of expertise. Individuals selling mutual funds must also meet certain standards.

To receive registration to sell mutual funds, individuals must complete an investment course. Salespeople who are employed by investment dealers must have completed the Canadian Securities Course. This course covers the investment spectrum but includes a section on mutual funds. It also meets the requirement for licensing of people employed by mutual fund dealers. The Canadian Investment Funds Course is designed specifically for people seeking registration to sell mutual funds and as additional education for people who are registered to sell securities. During 1988 the banking and trust company associations decided to develop their own educational programs which would meet licensing requirements for their employees. Until recently, bank and trust company employees marketing funds were considered exempt from registration. However, the recent trend is to eliminate exemptions and require all people involved in selling securities to the public to meet minimum training levels.

The Canadian Investment Funds Course is sponsored by the education division of the Investment Funds Institute of Canada. IFIC is the umbrella organization of the fund industry and is recognized as such by provincial securities commissions. The educational standards of the industry are constantly being upgraded. However, the quality of people giving advice on mutual funds varies widely, just as in any other profession. It's up to you to determine whether a specific fund salesperson meets your needs.

If you do most of your own work and know specifically which funds you want, almost any dealer can handle your order at a discounted commission. If you only want your purchase order executed and nothing else, expect to pay between one-third and one-half of the maximum commission in the fund prospectus for the amount of money you're investing. If you buy funds with a declining deferred redemption fee you will not get a break on the redemption fee whether you buy from a full service or discount broker.

If you want full service, including detailed advice and monitoring of your holdings, and you are buying funds sold only with an acquisition fee expect to pay higher commissions – up to, but not necessarily, the full rates. Full service should include an analysis of your investment objectives and needs along with recommendations on the funds that meet your requirements. Many sales representatives will confine their analysis to your investment needs; others will extend their analysis to every aspect of your finances including your life insurance needs, tax returns, pension plans and personal balance sheet.

You should determine in advance what type of ongoing service you can expect from a fund salesperson. Is his or her analysis of funds limited to reviewing rates of return? Or does the analysis include reviews of portfolio managers' investment strategies and comparisons with other funds? Many fund salespeople do this on their own, while others depend on specialists within their firms to do this work. It is essential that your advisor have access to this type of information on a continuous basis in order to advise you when conditions have changed. Your advisor should be able to give you

detailed explanations behind all purchase recommendations, especially those that involve switching funds. He or she should also provide you with periodic statements of your holdings and their
performance, generally monthly or quarterly, depending on how active you are in the market.

The use of personal computers has allowed many fund
salespeople to develop their own report packages. These often include monthly statements showing how your funds have performed. Other reports include such items as projected returns using
recent performance figures along with account histories and performance summaries of each fund held plus a detailed portfolio summary and performance comparison of clients' holdings.

Not every investor wants detailed reports. What it really comes
down to is making sure that you are comfortable with the salesperson you choose. Do his or her recommendations fit your investment
objectives? Do they take into consideration your other investment
holdings? Have the risks been explained in detail? Will your situation be monitored constantly and, if so, how? Will you get service
even if you don't make any subsequent purchases? Does your advisor have substantial investment or business experience? Unfortunately, many fund salespeople may not fully appreciate the risks
involved in the strategies they recommend.

Financial planning

Many people selling funds call themselves financial planners. However, financial planning is unregulated. Anyone can call himself or
herself a financial planner, whether or not they know anything
about financial planning or produce a financial plan for their
clients.

The fund industry is trying to set some standards. The Canadian
Institute of Financial Planning, which is affiliated with IFIC, has
developed a program of six correspondence courses covering areas
relevant to financial planning. Successful completion of the course
leads to the designation of chartered financial planner.

A voluntary association of personal financial planners, the
Canadian Association of Financial Planners, has been formed as an
industry group and has also set standards for membership. And
provincial securities commissions have been considering registering
financial planners as a separate category. Should the commissions
proceed – and there is a wide range of opinion in the fund industry

about whether they should – they will likely require that people who call themselves financial planners show their expertise either through completing specific courses or by demonstrating relevant experience.

CHAPTER 13

Inside the Prospectus

WHILE VIRTUALLY EVERY fund uses glossy sales material to promote itself, the offer to sell fund shares or units is made only through the fund's prospectus. This is a legal document that discloses all pertinent information about the fund.

When you first inquire about a fund you may be given the prospectus or, more likely, the condensed prospectus summary statement. No-load funds routinely send out prospectuses in response to requests for information. But many load funds do not because their salespeople prefer to stick with the more easily understood brochures.

When you actually get down to buying a fund, the seller is required by law to provide a prospectus, the latest annual financial statements and subsequent quarterly statements, if any. Generally, these will be mailed to you along with the slip confirming your purchase order.

Most people don't bother to read prospectuses and financial statements and, frankly, most people are not any worse off since they can get enough information from sales material or their salesperson. Nevertheless, you might take the time to at least skim through the prospectus.

Each fund actually files two prospectuses, the second being a shorter form or summary statement of the first. This summary prospectus includes the main points of the full prospectus in plain language. Real estate funds are the exception. They file only the full prospectus.

The shorter version was introduced in response to requests from the fund industry in the belief that a condensed version would not only save the funds money on postal and printing costs but would also more likely be read by investors.

If you request a prospectus or agree to invest in a fund, you'll almost certainly receive the shorter version. Even if you don't want to read it thoroughly, leaf through the first couple of pages of the section that summarizes the document.

There are a number of areas you can look at quickly. Make sure the fund's investment policies and objectives are compatible with yours. It's also important that you understand the sales charges, if any, and whether they are negotiable. You should also be aware of ongoing management fees. Every fund has management fees that, with the rare exception, are charged to the fund and not to individual investors. Management fees cover the cost of portfolio management and the other expenses of running a fund. Since they can vary widely and have a significant impact on the rate of return you receive, you should look at the explanation of how these fees are calculated and paid.

Some funds absorb all expenses, such as legal and audit fees, as part of their management fees. Others charge certain expenses directly to the fund. If you want to compare directly expenses of different funds, check the management expense ratio. This takes into account all fees charged to the fund, excluding brokerage commissions, and allows for direct comparisons among funds.

The summary prospectus begins by telling you that it is only an outline of the information you should have before making a decision to buy and that additional information is available in the prospectus or annual information form, which you can get by writing to the issuer.

The summary prospectus also explains your statutory rights. Generally speaking, you can back out of an agreement to buy mutual fund shares or units within two days after receipt of the simplified prospectus or within forty-eight hours of receiving the confirmation of the purchase of such securities. Very few people use this right of rescission. But if you read the prospectus and you find that the fund's investment objectives aren't compatible with yours or that the fund is undesirable for any other reason, you have the right to withdraw from your agreement to purchase.

You have other rights, too. Some provinces provide for cancelling the purchase and allow for damages if the prospectus includes misrepresentations. There are time limits, however, on exercising these rights.

The next item in a prospectus is the name and address of the fund and information on its incorporation. This is followed by a brief summary of the fund's investment policies.

The summary statement may include a section outlining risks. This isn't included in all short-form prospectuses. Rather, it is required only if a fund is speculative or has significant risk factors. The value of all funds, except money market funds, will fluctuate with changes in the value of their underlying securities. This is disclosed in all summary prospectuses. However, not every fund calls this a risk factor.

Following the summary statement is a description of the shares or units, which provides information on dividend rights, voting rights and the like.

Other important items include how the manager calculates the price at which sales are offered and redeemed, how the shares will be distributed, as well as information on minimum purchases and sales charges, management fees, dividend records, the tax consequences of sales, rules governing dividends and redemptions. Every prospectus will provide the name and address of the auditor.

Since the rules on exactly where all this information must appear aren't rigid, some of this information may be found in the annual report, rather than the summary statement.

CHAPTER 14

The Largest Funds

TO MAKE THE TASK OF choosing a fund easier, we have included listings of 100 of the largest funds offered in Canada within five categories – fifty Canadian equity funds, ten balanced funds, fifteen U.S. equity funds, fifteen bond and mortgage funds and ten international funds. This is not to say you should restrict your search to these 100 funds. But the list is representative of the more than 600 currently offered in Canada.

Before you begin comparing funds, go through the following steps every investor needs to take before deciding on a particular investment:

1. Get your financial house in order. Make sure your insurance needs are taken care of, your will is up to date, personal debts are paid off and your affairs are structured so you don't pay any more taxes than necessary. Eliminating personal debts is the best high-return, no-risk investment you can make. Also, make sure you understand how different types of investment income are taxed so you can set up your mutual fund investment program in a way that will keep taxes to a minimum.

2. Next, list your specific investment objectives, such as saving for retirement, saving for your children's education or maximizing current income. With this in mind, choose the fund type or types that are most suitable for your goals. Remember, the shorter the saving time frame, the more conservative you should be. Conversely, if you can invest for the long term, it's to your advantage to take some risk.

3. Then, decide on the strategies that can help you meet your objectives. These might include opening an RRSP to use tax-assisted dollars to save for retirement; beginning an accumulation or dollar-averaging plan; opening a withdrawal plan; or even borrowing money from the bank to invest. Of course, if you do borrow, don't

overlook the risks should the market plummet. Also, consider the potential impact of tax reform on your expected returns.

4. At this point, decide whether to make all your own decisions about investment funds or whether to seek an advisor. If you decide to use an advisor, make sure he or she is a specialist. Any broker or mutual fund salesperson can execute orders. Pick an experienced specialist who stays on top of developments in the fund industry and understands your objectives.

5. Finally, understand all the costs associated with your investment and the criteria used to choose a specific fund. Costs vary widely and can have a significant impact on rates of return. The time to investigate is before you buy, not after years of holding a fund. Two other things: make sure that a fund's objective is compatible with your personal objectives and don't forget to compare a fund's performance with other funds that have similar objectives.

How the listings work

The funds are listed alphabetically within the five groups and ranked by assets which the funds managed on June 30, 1991.

Each list includes much of the information you need to decide whether a fund meets your needs:

- The name and address so you can contact the fund to obtain its prospectus and annual and latest quarterly reports.
- The date the fund was established so you'll know how long it has been in operation.
- The provinces in which the fund is available.
- Whether the fund can be registered as an RRSP.
- The maximum sales charge, if any.
- The maximum redemption charge, if any.
- The management expense ratio. This is the ratio of management and other administrative fees charged to the fund as a percentage of a fund's total assets, as reported in its latest annual report or prospectus.
- The total returns for each twelve-month period ended June 30, going back as far as fourteen years. These periods include some of the strongest markets as well as some weak ones. This enables you to determine and compare how funds have performed in bull and bear markets.

	Rank 10	31
Canadian Equity	AGF Canadian Equity Fund Limited AGF Management Ltd. 31st Floor, T-D Bank Tower Toronto, Ont. M5K 1E9 (416) 367-1900 1-800-387-1780 Fax: (416) 865-4197	AGF Growth Equity Fund Limited AGF Management Ltd. 31st Floor, T-D Bank Tower Toronto, Ont. M5K 1E9 (416) 367-1900 1-800-387-1780 Fax: (416) 865-4197
Fund Established	June 12, 1963	October 22, 1964
Where Sold	Everywhere in Canada	Everywhere in Canada
Maximum Sales Charge	9%	9%
Maximum Redemption Fee	4.5%	4.5%
Management Expense Ratio	2.65%	2.69%
RRSP Eligible	Yes	Yes
Net Assets($ million)	292.9	89.2
Total Return		
1990	-1.2	2.4
1989	-9.1	-4.1
1988	9.2	4.4
1987	-7.0	-17.0
1986	12.0	20.3
1985	27.2	33.2
1984	35.5	21.5
1983	2.6	-7.6
1982	80.4	90.9
1981	-31.5	-49.8
1980	31.8	27.4
1979	21.7	53.8
1978	40.9	61.2
1977	28.6	42.6

Rank	40	38
Canadian Equity	**Altamira Equity Fund** Altamira Investment Services Inc. 250 Bloor St. E., Suite 301 Toronto, Ont. M4W 1E6 (416) 925-1623 1-800-263-2824 Fax: (416) 925-5352	**Bolton Tremblay Canada Cumulative Fund** Bolton Tremblay Funds Inc. 70 University Ave., Suite 1050 Toronto, Ont. M5J 2M4 (416) 595-5200 Fax: (416) 595-5382
Fund Established	.... September 30, 1987	.... April 21, 1972
Where Sold	.. Everywhere in Canada	.. Everywhere in Canada
Maximum Sales Charge	.... No Load	.... 9%
Maximum Redemption Fee	.... N/A	.... N/A
Management Expense Ratio	.... 2.5%	.... 2.70%
RRSP Eligible	.... Yes	.... Yes
Net Assets($ million)	.... 64.8	.... 66.5
Total Return		
1990	.... 13.7	.... -0.9
1989	.... 18.0	.... -4.6
1988	.... 32.7	.... 16.0
1987		.... -7.7
1986		.... 10.7
1985		.... 19.4
1984		.... 11.7
1983		.... -2.0
1982		.... 80.0
1981		.... -32.4
1980		.... 33.7
1979		.... 22.8
1978		.... 28.4
1977		.... 22.6

16	11	39
Canada Life Canadian Equity S-9	**Canada Trust RSP-Equity**	**Canadian Investment Fund, Ltd.**
Canada Life Assurance Co.	Canada Trust Co.	
330 University Ave.	Fund Administration Ser-	Calvin Bullock Ltd.
Toronto, Ont. M5G 1R8	vices	630 Rene Levesque Blvd.
(416) 597-1456	320 Bay St.	W., Ste. 2690
Fax: (416) 597-3892	Toronto, Ont. M5H 2P6	Montreal, Que. H3B 1X1
	(416) 361-8191	(514) 866-5421
	Fax: (416) 361-8106	1-800-363-0260
		Fax: (514) 866-4659
.... August, 1969	.... October 31, 1957	..... November 16, 1932
.. Everywhere in Canada	.. Everywhere in Canada	.. Everywhere in Canada
.... 1%	.... N/A	.... 9%
.... 2.5%	.... N/A	.... N/A
.... 2%	................0.99%	.................2.0%
.................Yes	...................Yes	.................Yes
...................194.1	...................289.0	....................66.4
.... 0.7	.... 3.4	................-1.4
................-5.2	................-0.1	.... 0.4
.... 16.5	.... 11.2	.... 15.4
.... 1.7	................-9.8	................-7.8
.... 14.0	.... 16.8	.... 11.1
.... 23.0	.... 18.4	.... 15.1
.... 31.1	.... 27.3	.... 27.3
................-1.0	................-8.1	................-5.1
.... 64.3	.... 70.2	.... 66.4
................-26.8	................-31.7	................-22.7
.... 19.4	.... 22.9	.... 14.7
.... 25.9	.... 25.1	.... 13.8
.... 36.2	.... 44.5	.... 30.7
.... 12.4	.... 12.1	.... 11.9

Rank	48	32
Canadian Equity	**Cdn Anaes Mutual Accumulating Fund** Canadian Anaesthetists' Mutual Accumulating Fund Ltd. 94 Cumberland St., Suite 503 Toronto, Ont. M5R 1A3 (416) 923-1449 Fax: (416) 920-7843	**Crown Life Pensions Equity** Crown Life 120 Bloor St. E. Toronto, Ont. M4W 1B8 (416) 928-4500 Fax: (416) 928-7631
Fund Established	.... September 13, 1957	1965
Where Sold	.. Everywhere in Canada except P.E.I.	.. Everywhere in Canada
Maximum Sales Charge	..............No Load	..............No Load
Maximum Redemption Fee	.... N/A	.... N/A
Management Expense Ratio	.... 0.93%	.... 0.70%
RRSP Eligible	..................Yes	..................Yes
Net Assets($ million)	...................57.3	...................84.1
Total Return		
1990	.... 1.7	.... 3.8
1989	.... 0.6	.... 1.6
1988	.... 11.9	.... 15.5
1987	.... -3.7	.... -3.6
1986	.... 20.4	.... 18.2
1985	.... 21.7	.... 26.9
1984	.... 27.2	.... 36.0
1983	.... -2.6	.... -12.1
1982	.... 59.5	.... 53.6
1981	.... -25.3	.... -28.1
1980	.... 30.4	.... 12.3
1979	.... 30.8	.... 13.3
1978	.... 54.4	.... 39.7
1977	.... 17.7	.... 10.8

23	17	50
Dynamic Fund of Canada Ltd	**Empire Equity Growth Fund #1**	**Empire Group Equity Growth Fund #6**
Dynamic Fund Management Ltd.	Empire Life Insurance Co.	Empire Life Insurance Co.
6 Adelaide St. E., 9th Floor	243-259 King St. E.	243-259 King St. E.
Toronto, Ont. M5C 1H6	Kingston, Ont. K7L 3A8	Kingston, Ont. K7L 3A8
(416) 363-5621	(613) 548-1881	(613) 548-1881
1-800-268-8186	Fax: (613) 541-3050	Fax: (613) 541-3050
Fax: (416) 363-5850		
...................1957	........December, 1964	..........October 1970
.. Everywhere in Canada	.. Everywhere in Canada	.. Everywhere in Canada
...................9%	...................9%	..............No Load
...............4.5%	.................N/A	.................N/A
...................2%	................1.44%	.................N/A
...................Yes	...................Yes	...................Yes
...................158.5	...................185.0	...................46.7
...............2.4	...............3.0	...............9.8
...............1.2	...............-1.8	...............-2.8
...............12.5	...............14.6	...............13.0
...............-1.9	...............3.5	...............-3.2
...............25.3	...............16.9	...............12.1
...............15.2	...............23.5	
...............23.0	...............31.9	
...............-6.5	...............-9.4	
...............65.2	...............85.9	
...............-31.1	...............-26.0	
...............23.7	...............37.3	
...............26.8	...............22.6	
...............45.2	...............33.6	
...............31.7	...............25.9	

Rank	45	29
Canadian Equity	**Ethical Growth Fund** VanCity Investment Services Ltd. 515 West 10th Ave. Vancouver, B.C. V5Z 4A8 (604) 877-7613 Fax:(604) 877-7639	**Fidelity Capital Builder Fund** Fidelity Investments Canada Ltd. 100 Simcoe St., Suite 300 Toronto, Ont. M5H 3G2 (416) 971-6170 1-800-263-4077 Fax: (416) 971-7678
Fund Established	. . . . .Feb. 3, 1986	. . . . . . .February 1, 1988
Where Sold	. . Everywhere in Canada except Quebec	. . Everywhere in Canada
Maximum Sales Charge	. . . . .5%	. . . . .4%
Maximum Redemption Fee	. . . . N/A	. . . . 4.5%
Management Expense Ratio	. . . . .2%	. . . . 2.5%
RRSP Eligible	. . . . .Yes	. . . . .Yes
Net Assets($ million)	. . . . .59.9	. . . . .99.5
Total Return		
1990	. . . . 7.3	. . . . 13.9
1989	. . . . 4.0	. . . . 1.3
1988	. . . . 16.0	. . . . 14.3
1987	. . . . 13.9	. . . .
1986	. . . . 9.1	. . . .
1985	. . . .	. . . .
1984	. . . .	. . . .
1983	. . . .	. . . .
1982	. . . .	. . . .
1981	. . . .	. . . .
1980	. . . .	. . . .
1979	. . . .	. . . .
1978	. . . .	. . . .
1977	. . . .	. . . .

26	30	15
FuturLink Canadian Growth Fund	**Global Strategy Canadian Fund**	**Great-West Life Equity Index Investment**
Central Guaranty Trust Co. Funds Services	Global Strategy Financial Inc.	Great-West Life Assurance Co.
The Atrium on Bay, Tower C	2 Bloor St. W., Suite 3400	100 Osborne St. N.
20 Dundas St. W.	Toronto, Ont. M4W 3E2	Winnipeg, Man. R3C 3A5
Box 95, Suite 933	(416) 927-9344	(204) 946-1190
Toronto, Ont. M5G 2C2	1-800-387-1229	Fax: (204) 946-8622
(416) 345-5911	Fax: (416) 927-9168	
Fax: (416) 345-5906		

. . . . . .September 1, 1987	. . . . . . .December, 1987	. . . . . . February 28, 1983
. . Everywhere in Canada	. . Everywhere in Canada	. . Everywhere in Canada
. . . . .No Load	. . . . N/A	. . . . No Load
. . . . N/A	. . . . .4.5%	. . . . N/A
. . . . 2.33%	. . . . .3.21%	. . . . .1.8%
. . . . .Yes	. . . . Yes	. . . . Yes
. . . . .125.2	. . . . .93.1	. . . . .200.5
. . . . 1.8	. . . . 4.2	. . . . 0.0
. . . .-1.0	. . . .-0.2	. . . .-3.9
. . . . 15.2	. . . . 13.0	. . . . 11.2
		. . . .-6.8
		. . . . 22.5
		. . . . 14.0
		. . . .-18.4
		. . . . 40.5

	Rank	25	33
Canadian Equity		Great-West Life Equity Investment Great-West Life Assurance Co. 100 Osborne St. N. Winnipeg, Man. R3C 3A5 (204) 946-1190 Fax: (204) 946-8622	Imperial Growth Canadian Equity Fund Imperial Life Assurance Co. 95 St. Clair Ave. W. Toronto, Ont. M4V 1N7 (416) 926-2668 Fax: (416) 923-1599
Fund Established		January 31, 1987	1969
Where Sold		Everywhere in Canada	Everywhere in Canada
Maximum Sales Charge		No Load	5%
Maximum Redemption Fee		N/A	N/A
Management Expense Ratio		2.04%	1.5%
RRSP Eligible		Yes	Yes-RRSP
Net Assets($ million)		126.7	81.5
Total Return			
1990		3.7	3.0
1989		1.8	-5.9
1988		9.9	27.4
1987		-12.5	17.3
1986			31.3
1985			23.1
1984			28.9
1983			-5.0
1982			71.3
1981			-27.4
1980			17.0
1979			27.5
1978			44.4
1977			8.3

19	42	27
Industrial Dividend Fund	**Industrial Equity Fund**	**Industrial Future Fund**
Mackenzie Financial Corp.	Mackenzie Financial Corp.	Mackenzie Financial Corp.
150 Bloor St. W., 4th Floor	150 Bloor St. W., 4th Floor	150 Bloor St. W., 4th Floor
Toronto, Ont. M5S 3B5	Toronto, Ont. M5S 3B5	Toronto, Ont. M5S 3B5
(416) 922-5322	(416) 922-5322	(416) 922-5322
Fax: (416) 922-0399	Fax: (416) 922-0399	Fax: (416) 922-0399

..........March, 1950	..........January, 1969	..... December 23, 1987
.. Everywhere in Canada	.. Everywhere in Canada	.. Everywhere in Canada
.... 9%	.... 9%	.... 5%
.... N/A	.... N/A	.... N/A
.... 2.41%	.... 2.53%	.... 2.49%
.... Yes	.... Yes	.... Yes
...................177.1	...................63.8	...................113.4
...................-8.7	...................-12.5	...................-0.9
...................-5.8	...................-13.0	...................-2.6
.... 2.7	...................-2.9	.... 11.0
.... 6.1	...................-0.5	....
.... 27.4	.... 31.4	....
.... 16.5	.... 18.1	....
.... 33.2	.... 16.8	....
.... 6.5	.... 0.3	....
.... 69.7	.... 88.1	....
...................-21.4	...................-25.4	....
.... 16.8	.... 10.5	....
...................-1.3	.... 20.2	....
.... 40.8	.... 27.1	....
.... 16.7	.... 35.0	....

Rank	2	1
Canadian Equity	**Industrial Growth Fund** Mackenzie Financial Corp. 150 Bloor St. W., 4th Floor Toronto, Ont. M5S 3B5 (416) 922-5322 Fax: (416) 922-0399	**Industrial Horizon Fund** Mackenzie Financial Corp. 150 Bloor St. W., 4th Floor Toronto, Ont. M5S 3B5 (416) 922-5322 Fax: (416) 922-0399
Fund Established	October, 1967	January 28, 1987
Where Sold	Everywhere in Canada	Everywhere in Canada
Maximum Sales Charge	9%	No Load
Maximum Redemption Fee	N/A	4.5%
Management Expense Ratio	2.36%	2.40%
RRSP Eligible	Yes	Yes
Net Assets($ million)	1339.1	1511.0
Total Return		
1990	-1.5	0.4
1989	-2.5	-1.7
1988	8.4	10.1
1987	4.5	15.2
1986	27.7	
1985	16.4	
1984	27.1	
1983	2.8	
1982	77.7	
1981	-17.1	
1980	8.6	
1979	24.9	
1978	28.1	
1977	25.1	

34	9	35
Industrial Pension Fund Mackenzie Financial Corp. 150 Bloor St. W., 4th Floor Toronto, Ont. M5S 3B5 (416) 922-5322 Fax: (416) 922-0399	**Investors Canadian Equity Fund** Investors Group One Canada Centre 447 Portage Ave. Winnipeg, Man. R3C 3B6 (204) 943-0361 Fax: (204) 943-0021	**Investors Group Trust Pooled Equity** Investors Group One Canada Centre 447 Portage Ave. Winnipeg, Man. R3C 3B6 (204) 956-8240 Fax: (204) 943-2698
.... February, 1971	.... September, 1983	.... September, 1958
.. Everywhere in Canada	.. Everywhere in Canada	.. Everywhere in Canada
.... 9%	.... 5%	..................3.5%
.... N/A	.... 1%	.... N/A
.... 2.49%	.... N/A	..................0.04%
.... Yes	.... Yes	.... Yes
.... 73.3	....................326.3	....................69.4
.... -9.8	.... 6.6	.... 4.3
.... -7.9	.... 2.1	....................-1.1
.... 3.5	.... 9.1	.... 12.2
.... 4.3	....................-6.9	....................-3.0
.... 23.4	.... 10.1	.... 15.7
.... 20.8	.... 27.9	.... 15.4
.... 30.6	.... 25.5	.... 27.0
.... 0.6		....................-4.8
.... 84.0		.... 64.9
....................-21.2		....................-27.0
.... 11.6		.... 16.4
....................-2.4		.... 26.7
.... 37.4		.... 43.8
.... 21.0		.... 9.5

Rank	6	4
Canadian Equity	**Investors North American Growth Fund**	**Investors Retirement Mutual Fund**
	Investors Group	Investors Group
	One Canada Centre	One Canada Centre
	447 Portage Ave.	447 Portage Ave.
	Winnipeg, Man. R3C 3B6	Winnipeg, Man. R3C 3B6
	(204) 943-0361	(204) 943-0361
	Fax: (204) 943-0021	Fax: (204) 943-0021
Fund Established	.... September 10, 1957	...... November, 1971
Where Sold	.. Everywhere in Canada	.. Everywhere in Canada
Maximum Sales Charge	.... 5%	.... 5%
Maximum Redemption Fee	.... 1%	.... 1%
Management Expense Ratio	.... 1.33%	.... N/A
RRSP Eligible	.... No	.... Yes
Net Assets($ million)	.... 523.7	.... 970.9
Total Return		
1990	.... 7.3	.... 1.9
1989	.... 7.9	.... -2.7
1988	.... 21.8	.... 12.7
1987	.... -9.8	.... 4.6
1986	.... 18.8	.... 20.4
1985	.... 25.5	.... 13.6
1984	.... 28.5	.... 26.7
1983	.... -7.4	.... -3.9
1982	.... 69.2	.... 58.3
1981	.... -23.7	.... -27.0
1980	.... 15.7	.... 15.8
1979	.... 28.5	.... 27.9
1978	.... 38.9	.... 42.7
1977	.... 5.2	.... 8.2

46	21	3
Investors Summa Fund Ltd. Investors Group One Canada Centre 447 Portage Ave. Winnipeg, Man. R3C 3B6 (204) 943-0361 Fax: (204) 943-0021	**London Life Canadian Equity Fund** London Life Insurance Co. 255 Dufferin Ave. London, Ont. N6A 4K1 (519) 432-5281 Fax: (519) 432-9035	**MD Equity Fund** MD Management Limited 1867 Alta Vista Drive Ottawa, Ont. K1G 3Y6 (613) 731-4552 1-800-267-4022 Fax: (613) 526-1352
October, 1986	1961	March 1, 1966
Everywhere in Canada	Everywhere in Canada	Everywhere in Canada
5%	5%	No Load
1%	N/A	N/A
1.46%	1.5%	1%
Yes	Yes	Yes
59.8	170.5	1071.0
1.9	1.1	0.9
-3.3	-8.1	0.1
12.5	15.0	10.6
-3.1	-0.3	6.1
	21.0	20.5
	19.0	20.5
	28.7	33.9
	-3.8	2.3
	65.3	62.0
	-21.3	-12.1
	15.7	12.1
	26.4	17.8
	44.0	30.3
	14.1	10.4

Rank	**47**	**13**
Canadian Equity	**Mackenzie Equity Fund**	**Manulife 1 Equity Fund**
	Mackenzie Financial Corp.	Manulife Financial
	150 Bloor St. W., 4th Floor	500 King St. N.
	Toronto, Ont. M5S 3B5	Waterloo, Ont. N2J 4C6
	(416) 922-5322	(519) 747-7000
	Fax: (416) 922-0399	Fax: (519) 747-9835
Fund Established	. . . . May, 1973	1963
Where Sold	. . Everywhere in Canada	. . Everywhere in Canada
Maximum Sales Charge	. . . . .9%	. . . . 4.0%
Maximum Redemption Fee	. . . . N/A	. . . . N/A
Management Expense Ratio	. . . . .2%	. . . . 1.59%
RRSP Eligible	. . . . .Yes	. . . . .Yes
Net Assets($ million)	. . . . .57.3	. . . . .228.4
Total Return		
1990	. . . . -8.6	. . . . 3.7
1989	. . . . -7.1	. . . . -1.9
1988	. . . . 6.5	. . . . 10.5
1987	. . . . 4.8	. . . . -6.1
1986	. . . . 20.8	. . . . 20.3
1985	. . . . 23.1	. . . . 9.8
1984	. . . . 29.6	. . . . 22.5
1983	. . . . 3.0	. . . . -7.3
1982	. . . . 67.9	. . . . 63.4
1981	. . . . -26.8	. . . . -19.1
1980	. . . . 25.7	. . . . 17.1
1979	. . . . 25.1	. . . .
1978	. . . . 44.6	. . . .
1977	. . . . 14.5	. . . .

14	**22**	**43**
Manulife 2 Equity Fund Manulife Financial 500 King St. N. Waterloo, Ont. N2J 4C6 (519) 747-7000 Fax: (519) 747-9835	**Maritime Life Growth Fund** Maritime Life Assurance Co. 2701 Dutch Village Road Halifax, N.S. B3J 2X5 (902) 453-4300 Fax: (902) 453-7041	**Montreal Trust RRSP/RRIF:** **Equity** Montreal Trust Co. Place Montreal Trust 1800 McGill College Ave. Montreal, Que. H3A 3K9 (514) 982-7000 Fax: (514) 982-7069
. 1963	. . . . .April, 1968	. . . . .February, 1958
. .Everywhere in Canada	. . Everywhere in Canada	. . Everywhere in Canada
. . . . .No Load	. . . . .No Load	. . . . N\L
. . . . 3.5%	. . . . N/A	. . . . N/A
. . . . 1.59%	. . . . .1.5%	. . . . .1.78%
. . . . .Yes	. . . . Yes	. . . . .Yes
. . . . .228.4	. . . . .166.2	. . . . .63.1
. . . . 2.9	. . . .-1.0	. . . . 4.4
. . . .-2.7	. . . .-4.0	. . . .-2.0
. . . . 9.7	. . . . 13.5	. . . . 11.7
. . . .-6.8	. . . .-11.1	. . . .-6.1
. . . . 19.4	. . . . 15.2	. . . . 20.9
. . . . 9.0	. . . . 24.7	. . . . 17.7
. . . . 21.6	. . . . 34.8	. . . . 25.0
. . . .-8.0	. . . .-2.8	. . . .-9.7
. . . . 62.3	. . . . 73.2	. . . . 69.3
. . . .-19.7	. . . .-30.9	. . . .-29.5
. . . . 16.2	. . . . 15.1	. . . . 17.2
. . . .	. . . . 24.7	. . . . 24.8
. . . .	. . . . 40.1	. . . . 40.5
. . . .	. . . . 17.0	. . . . 11.7

Rank	37	28
Canadian Equity	**Mutual Equifund** Mutual Investco Inc. 227 King St. S. Waterloo, Ont. N2J 4C5 (519) 888-2472 Fax: (519) 888-2990	**National Trust Equity Fund** National Trust National Trust Tower One Financial Place 1 Adelaide St. E. Toronto, Ont. M5C 2W8 (416) 361-5553 Fax: (416) 361-5563
Fund Established	. . . . January 2, 1985	. . . . .Dec. 23, 1957
Where Sold	. . Everywhere in Canada	. . Everywhere in Canada except New Brunswick, Nfld and P.E.I.
Maximum Sales Charge	. . . . 6%	. . . . .No Load
Maximum Redemption Fee	. . . . N/A	. . . . N/A
Management Expense Ratio	. . . . 1.54%	. . . . 1.3%
RRSP Eligible	. . . . .Yes	. . . . .Yes
Net Assets($ million)	. . . . 68.4	. . . . 105.8
Total Return		
1990	. . . . -1.9	. . . . 6.7
1989	. . . . -8.3	. . . . 0.8
1988	. . . . 20.4	. . . . 10.9
1987	. . . . -6.2	. . . . -9.7
1986	. . . . 7.9	. . . . 14.6
1985	. . . . 26.7	. . . . 24.9
1984	. . . .	. . . . 31.0
1983	. . . .	. . . . -5.9
1982	. . . .	. . . . 50.9
1981	. . . .	. . . . -20.5
1980	. . . .	. . . . 19.9
1979	. . . .	. . . . 25.3
1978	. . . .	. . . . 40.7
1977	. . . .	. . . . 10.0

36	49	44
PH&N Pooled Pension Trust	**Phillips, Hager & North**	**Prudential Growth Fund**
Phillips, Hager & North	**Canadian Fund**	**Canada Ltd.**
Ltd.	Phillips, Hager & North	Prudential Family of
1700-1055 West Hastings	Ltd.	Funds
St.	1700-1055 West Hastings	200 Consilium Place
Vancouver, B.C. V6E 2H3	St.	Scarborough, Ont. M1H
(604) 684-4361	Vancouver, B.C. V6E 2H3	3E6
1-800-661-6141	(604) 684-4361	(416) 296-0777
Fax: (604) 684-5120	1-800-661-6141	Fax: (416) 296-3186
	Fax: (604) 684-5120	

. . . . 1966	. . . . June 1, 1971	. . . . July 29, 1970
. . Everywhere in Canada (Not to the general public)	. . Everywhere in Canada	. . Everywhere in Canada
. . . . N/A	. . . . No Load	. . . . .8.5%
. . . . N/A	. . . . N/A	. . . . N/A
. . . . 0.5%	. . . . .1.18%	. . . . .1.48%
. . . . Yes	. . . . Yes	. . . . Yes
. . . . .68.9	. . . . .56.2	. . . . .61.3
. . . . 1.9	. . . . 1.3	. . . .-1.0
. . . . 3.6	. . . . 4.1	. . . .-4.0
. . . . 14.9	. . . . 18.2	. . . . 12.1
. . . .-4.7	. . . .-2.9	. . . .-15.6
. . . . 18.7	. . . . 16.1	. . . . 27.9
. . . . 23.8	. . . . 29.7	. . . . 23.7
. . . . 28.6	. . . . 28.1	. . . . 27.9
. . . .-3.5	. . . .-5.5	. . . .-5.8
. . . . 85.8	. . . . 88.7	. . . . 74.7
. . . .-34.6	. . . .-40.9	. . . .-35.5
. . . . 19.7	. . . . 36.5	. . . . 14.8
. . . . 24.3	. . . . 25.4	. . . . 24.3
. . . . 27.9	. . . . 33.0	. . . . 44.5
. . . . 14.3	. . . . 32.0	. . . . 13.1

Rank	5	12
Canadian Equity	**RoyFund Equity Ltd.** Royal Bank of Canada 4th Floor, North Tower Royal Bank Plaza Toronto, Ont. M5J 2J2 (416) 974-0616 Fax: (416) 974-4076	**Royal Trust Canadian Stock Fund** Royal Trust Co. Suite 3900, Royal Trust Tower Toronto-Dominion Centre Toronto, Ont. M5W 1P9
Fund Established	. . . . April, 1967	. . . . July 29, 1966
Where Sold	. . Everywhere in Canada	. . Everywhere in Canada
Maximum Sales Charge	. . . . No Load	. . . . No Load
Maximum Redemption Fee	. . . . N/A	. . . . N/A
Management Expense Ratio	. . . . 1.88%	. . . . 1.416%
RRSP Eligible	. . . . Yes	. . . . Yes
Net Assets($ million)	. . . . 678.7	. . . . 251.1

Total Return		
1990	. . . . -6.3	. . . . 2.6
1989	. . . . 0.1	. . . . -4.3
1988	. . . . 10.2	. . . . 15.1
1987	. . . . -8.3	. . . . -5.7
1986	. . . . 12.1	. . . . 17.8
1985	. . . . 34.9	. . . . 11.3
1984	. . . . 35.2	. . . . 24.6
1983	. . . . -0.9	. . . . -8.6
1982	. . . . 82.1	. . . . 79.0
1981	. . . . -40.7	. . . . -34.1
1980	. . . . 24.4	. . . . 14.6
1979	. . . . 37.6	. . . . 28.8
1978	. . . . 48.1	. . . . 43.3
1977	. . . . 15.5	. . . . 11.0

41	7	8
Talvest Growth Fund Inc.	**Trimark Canadian Fund**	**Trimark Select Canada Fund**
Talvest Fund Management	Trimark Investment	Trimark Investment
1800 Place du Canada	Management Inc.	Management Inc.
Montreal, Que. H3B 2N2	Suite 5200, P.O. Box 205	Suite 5200, P.O. Box 205
(514) 875-9090	Scotia Plaza	Scotia Plaza
1-800-465-1657	Toronto, Ont. M5H 3Z3	Toronto, Ont. M5H 3Z3
Fax: (514) 875-9304	(416) 362-7181	(416) 362-7181
	1-800-387-9823	1-800-387-9823
	Fax: (416) 362-8515	Fax: (416) 362-8515

July 3, 1947	July 10, 1981	August 9, 1988.
	First offered Sept., 1981	First offered Sept.,1988
Everywhere in Canada	Everywhere in Canada	Everywhere in Canada
5%	9%	No Load
4.5%	N/A	4.5%
2.40%	1.72%	2.14%
Yes	Yes	Yes
64.2	489.2	402.8
10.6	5.1	7.9
-1.3	3.1	2.4
8.8	16.9	
-0.6	1.6	
25.7	19.6	
15.4	18.1	
27.5	31.5	
-2.8	-0.9	
52.8	85.1	
-29.8		
40.6		
5.7		
37.3		
12.1		

Rank	24	20
Canadian Equity	**United Accumulative Retirement Fund** United Financial Management Ltd. 200 King St. W., Suite 1202 Toronto, Ont. M5H 3W8 (416) 598-7777 1-800-263-1867 Fax: (416) 598-7821	**Universal Canadian Equity Fund Limited** Universal Group 401 Bay St., 12th Floor Toronto, Ont. M5H 2Y4 (416) 364-1145 1-800-268-9374 Fax: (416) 364-2969
Fund Established	. . . . .November 30, 1978	. . . . April, 1965
Where Sold	. . Everywhere in Canada	. . Everywhere in Canada
Maximum Sales Charge	. . . . .9%	. . . . .9%
Maximum Redemption Fee	. . . . 5.0%	. . . . 5.5%
Management Expense Ratio	. . . . 1.88%	. . . . 2.60%
RRSP Eligible	. . . . .Yes	. . . . .Yes
Net Assets($ million)	. . . . .146.0	. . . . .172.5
Total Return		
1990	. . . . 9.5	. . . . -6.5
1989	. . . . -4.3	. . . . -7.0
1988	. . . . 16.0	. . . . 7.6
1987	. . . . -2.2	. . . . 11.0
1986	. . . . 4.8	. . . . 17.1
1985	. . . . 22.3	. . . . 24.3
1984	. . . . 42.9	. . . . 31.1
1983	. . . . 2.4	. . . . 1.3
1982	. . . . 54.4	. . . . 54.4
1981	. . . . -29.0	. . . . -13.4
1980	. . . . 28.0	. . . . 12.2
1979	. . . . 28.1	. . . . 17.4
1978	. . . . 69.4	. . . . 43.0
1977	. . . . 9.8	. . . . 27.5

18

Viking Canadian Fund Ltd.
Laurentian Funds Manage-
ment Inc.
310 Front St. W.
Toronto, Ont. M5V 3B8
(416) 343-5222
Fax: (416) 343-5214

. . . . September, 1971

. . Everywhere in Canada
except the Yukon,
Northwest
. . . . 3.5%

. . . . 3.5%

. . . . 2.20%

. . . . Yes

. . . . 177.6

. . . . 1.6
. . . . -11.2
. . . . 16.9
. . . . -2.6
. . . . 11.1
. . . . 20.6
. . . . 25.9
. . . . -2.4
. . . . 66.8
. . . . -29.8
. . . . 19.2
. . . . 26.6
. . . . 42.4
. . . . 11.0

Rank	11	6
U. S. Equity	**20/20 U.S. Growth Fund** 20/20 Group Financial Inc. 2010 Winston Park Drive, Suite 500 Oakville, Ont. L6H 5R7 (416) 829-2020 1-800-268-8690 Fax: (416) 829-3863	**AGF American Growth Fund Limited** AGF Management Ltd. 31st Floor, T-D Bank Tower Toronto, Ont. M5K 1E9 (416) 367-1900 1-800-387-1780 Fax: (416) 865-4197
Fund Established	. . . . June 30, 1989	. . . . April 18, 1957
Where Sold	. . Everywhere in Canada	. . Everywhere in Canada
Maximum Sales Charge	. . . . 9%	. . . . 9%
Maximum Redemption Fee	. . . . 6%	. . . . 4.5%
Management Expense Ratio	. . . . N/A	. . . . 2.43%
RRSP Eligible	. . . . No	. . . . No
Net Assets($ million)	. . . . 46.6	. . . . 82.2
Total Return		
1990	. . . . 5.1	. . . . -2.6
1989	. . . . 10.8	. . . . 5.0
1988		. . . . 21.2
1987		. . . . -15.0
1986		. . . . 8.4
1985		. . . . 27.0
1984		. . . . 33.3
1983		. . . . -6.0
1982		. . . . 62.9
1981		. . . . -5.3
1980		. . . . 43.2
1979		. . . . 27.9
1978		. . . . 17.6
1977		. . . . 8.6

4	7	13
AGF Special Fund Limited	**Bullock American Fund**	**Canada Life U.S. and Intl.**
AGF Management Ltd.	Calvin Bullock Ltd.	**Equity S-34**
31st Floor, T-D Bank	630 Rene Levesque Blvd.	Canada Life Assurance Co.
Tower	W., Ste. 2690	330 University Ave.
Toronto, Ont. M5K 1E9	Montreal, Que. H3B 1X1	Toronto, Ont. M5G 1R8
(416) 367-1900	(514) 866-5421	(416) 597-1456
1-800-387-1780	1-800-363-0260	Fax: (416) 597-3892
Fax: (416) 865-4197	Fax: (514) 866-4659	

. . . . .September 19, 1968	. . . . .September 14, 1977	. . . . April 1, 1984
. . Everywhere in Canada	. . Everywhere in Canada	. . Everywhere in Canada
. . . . 9%	. . . . 9%	. . . . 1%
. . . . 4.5%	. . . . N/A	. . . . .2.5%
. . . . 2.55%	. . . . .2.0%	. . . . 2%
. . . . No	. . . . No	. . . . .No
. . . . .133.7	. . . . 72.2	. . . . .33.8
. . . . 4.7	. . . . 22.4	. . . . 3.0
. . . . 8.2	. . . . 32.1	. . . . 13.3
. . . . 15.3	. . . . 15.8	. . . . 17.1
. . . .-8.2	. . . .-20.7	. . . .-7.4
. . . . 10.5	. . . . 21.2	. . . . 13.3
. . . . 31.2	. . . . 56.0	. . . . 31.7
. . . . 23.4	. . . . 16.8	. . . . 27.8
. . . .-10.3	. . . .-16.2	. . . .
. . . . 96.1	. . . . 62.6	. . . .
. . . .-12.6	. . . .-16.0	. . . .
. . . . 47.5	. . . . 46.4	. . . .
. . . . 33.2	. . . . 17.9	. . . .
. . . . 30.7	. . . .-0.9	. . . .
. . . . 35.8	. . . .	. . . .

	Rank 9	12
U. S. Equity	Dynamic American Fund Dynamic Fund Management Ltd. 6 Adelaide St. E., 9th Floor Toronto, Ont. M5C 1H6 (416) 363-5621 1-800-268-8186 Fax: (416) 363-5850	Green Line U.S. Index Fund Toronto Dominion Securities Inc. Investment Management Group T-D Bank Twr, 20th Floor Toronto-Dominion Centre P.O. Box 100 Toronto, Ont. M5K 1A2 (416) 982-6432 1-800-268-8166
Fund Established	August 31, 1979	July 11, 1986
Where Sold	Everywhere in Canada	Everywhere in Canada
Maximum Sales Charge	9%	No Load
Maximum Redemption Fee	4.5%	N/A
Management Expense Ratio	2%	1.17%
RRSP Eligible	No	No
Net Assets($ million)	48.3	37.2
Total Return		
1990	-4.0	5.4
1989	7.5	14.0
1988	16.4	17.8
1987	-8.1	-7.8
1986	22.7	
1985	22.3	
1984	31.1	
1983	2.9	
1982	58.5	
1981	-11.1	
1980	39.7	
1979		
1978		
1977		

1	2	14
Industrial American Fund	**Investors U.S. Growth Fund Ltd.**	**Landmark American Fund**
Mackenzie Financial Corp.	Investors Group	Bolton Tremblay Funds Inc.
150 Bloor St. W., 4th Floor	One Canada Centre	70 University Ave., Suite 1050
Toronto, Ont. M5S 3B5	447 Portage Ave.	Toronto, Ont. M5J 2M4
(416) 922-5322	Winnipeg, Man. R3C 3B6	(416) 595-5200
Fax: (416) 922-0399	(204) 943-0361	Fax: (416) 595-5382
	Fax: (204) 943-0021	
July 1975	November, 1961	June 1989
Everywhere in Canada	Everywhere in Canada	Everywhere in Canada
No Load	5%	No Load
4.5%	1%	4.5%
2.26%	1.35%	N/A
No	No	No
272.7	255.4	31.2
-1.1	8.0	7.4
7.7	7.7	7.0
8.3	15.8	
-6.3	-14.4	
18.4	18.5	
26.3	25.3	
29.9	27.2	
-1.3	-12.2	
55.9	66.5	
-5.1	-14.8	
38.9	23.7	
14.8	25.2	
23.3	12.2	
17.8	11.6	

	Rank 15	3
U. S. Equity	London Life U.S. Equity Fund London Life Insurance Co. 255 Dufferin Ave. London, Ont. N6A 4K1 (519) 432-5281 Fax: (519) 432-9035	PH&N U.S. Pooled Pension Fund Phillips, Hager & North Ltd. 1700-1055 West Hastings St. Vancouver, B.C. V6E 2H3 (604) 684-4361 1-800-661-6141 Fax: (604) 684-5120
Fund Established	.... January, 1988	1980
Where Sold	.. Everywhere in Canada	.. Everywhere in Canada (Not to the general public)
Maximum Sales Charge	..................5%	.... N/A
Maximum Redemption Fee	.... N/A	.... N/A
Management Expense Ratio	.... N/A	.... 0.5%
RRSP Eligible	.... No	................Yes
Net Assets($ million)	...................27.4	...................237.4
Total Return		
1990	.... -2.9	.... 10.5
1989	.... -7.4	.... 19.4
1988	.... 18.6	.... 13.8
1987		.... -8.8
1986		.... 8.7
1985		.... 28.7
1984		.... 33.4
1983		.... -8.4
1982		.... 82.0
1981		.... -3.6
1980		
1979		
1978		
1977		

5	8	10
Phillips, Hager & North U.S. Fund	**Royal Trust American Stock Fund**	**Universal American Fund**
Phillips, Hager & North Ltd.	Royal Trust Co.	Universal Group
1700-1055 West Hastings St.	Suite 3900, Royal Trust Tower	401 Bay St., 12th Floor
Vancouver, B.C. V6E 2H3	Toronto-Dominion Centre	Toronto, Ont. M5H 2Y4
(604) 684-4361	Toronto, Ont. M5W 1P9	(416) 364-1145
1-800-661-6141		1-800-268-9374
Fax: (604) 684-5120		Fax: (416) 364-2969

......September 1, 1964	.... July 29, 1966	.... November 1978
.. Everywhere in Canada	.. Everywhere in Canada	.. Everywhere in Canada
.... No Load	.... No Load	.... 9%
.... N/A	.... N/A	.................5.5%
.... 1.18%	...............1.476%	................2.61%
.... No	.... No	.................No
...................87.8	...................59.1	...................46.7
.... 9.7	.... 1.8	.... 0.0
.... 17.6	.... 18.2	.... 9.4
.... 13.1	.... 16.1	.... 8.8
.................-10.6	.................-15.6	.................-5.8
.... 8.1	.... 16.8	.... 18.9
.... 28.8	.... 31.8	.... 26.8
.... 32.4	.... 21.9	.... 27.6
.................-15.8	.................-11.9	.... 2.5
.... 86.2	.... 45.4	.... 37.4
.................-4.2	.................-5.6	.... 4.2
.... 38.8	.... 22.9	.... 61.5
.... 14.8	.... 11.1	.................-3.5
.... 16.3	.... 15.5	....
.... 26.4	.... 6.8	....

Rank	9	4
International Equity	Bolton Tremblay International Fund Bolton Tremblay Funds Inc. 70 University Ave., Suite 1050 Toronto, Ont. M5J 2M4 (416) 595-5200 Fax: (416) 595-5382	Cundill Value Fund Ltd. Peter Cundill & Associates Ltd. 1200 Sun Life Plaza 1100 Melville St. Vancouver, B.C. V6E 4A6 (604) 685-4231 1-800-663-0156 Fax: (604) 689-9532
Fund Established	March 14, 1961	January 16, 1967
Where Sold	Everywhere in Canada	Everywhere in Canada
Maximum Sales Charge	9%	8.75%
Maximum Redemption Fee	N/A	N/A
Management Expense Ratio	2.54%	2.0%
RRSP Eligible	No	No
Net Assets($ million)	176.6	358.4
Total Return		
1990	-5.5	-5.8
1989	13.0	1.7
1988	11.2	10.4
1987	-15.2	10.4
1986	19.5	16.5
1985	41.1	22.4
1984	25.4	13.5
1983	1.1	5.5
1982	67.6	67.2
1981	-9.2	-0.3
1980	45.5	40.0
1979	12.9	6.6
1978	17.2	43.2
1977	12.5	42.1

10	5	7
Industrial Global Fund	**Investors Global Fund Ltd.**	**Investors Japanese Growth**
Mackenzie Financial Corp.	Investors Group	**Fund Ltd.**
150 Bloor St. W., 4th Floor	One Canada Centre	Investors Group
Toronto, Ont. M5S 3B5	447 Portage Ave.	One Canada Centre
(416) 922-5322	Winnipeg, Man. R3C 3B6	447 Portage Ave.
Fax: (416) 922-0399	(204) 943-0361	Winnipeg, Man. R3C 3B6
	Fax: (204) 943-0021	(204) 943-0361
		Fax: (204) 943-0021

. . . . .September 1985	. . . . June, 1986	. . . . March 1971
. . Everywhere in Canada	. . Everywhere in Canada	. . Everywhere in Canada
. . . . .No Load	. . . . 5%	. . . . 5%
. . . . 4.5%	. . . . 1%	. . . . 1%
. . . . 2.54%	. . . . N/A	. . . . .1.32%
. . . . No	. . . . No	. . . . .No
. . . . .154.0	. . . . .280.1	. . . . .226.5
. . . .-14.1	. . . .-6.4	. . . .-9.5
. . . . 8.6	. . . . 20.5	. . . .-1.7
. . . . 2.8	. . . . 3.2	. . . .-2.6
. . . .-1.4	. . . .-14.9	. . . . 4.5
. . . . 32.1		. . . . 31.8
		. . . . 87.9
		. . . . 7.2
		. . . . 14.4
		. . . . 34.3
		. . . .-15.7
		. . . . 66.0
		. . . . 1.1
		. . . .-4.8
		. . . . 38.6

Rank	2	1
International Equity	**MD Growth Investments Limited**	**Templeton Growth Fund Ltd.**
	MD Management Limited 1867 Alta Vista Drive Ottawa, Ont. K1G 3Y6 (613) 731-4552 1-800-267-4022 Fax: (613) 526-1352	Templeton Management Ltd. 4 King St. W. P.O. Box 4070, Station A Toronto, Ont. M5W 1M3 (416) 364-4672 Ontario: 1-800-387-0814 National: 1-800-387-0830 Fax: (416) 364-1163
Fund Established	. . . . .July 18, 1969	. . . . . September 1, 1954
Where Sold	. . Everywhere in Canada	. . Everywhere in Canada
Maximum Sales Charge	. . . . .No Load	. . . . 8.5%
Maximum Redemption Fee	. . . . N/A	. . . . N/A
Management Expense Ratio	. . . . .1%	. . . . 0.89%
RRSP Eligible	. . . . No	. . . . No
Net Assets($ million)	. . . . .785.8	. . . . .1005.6
Total Return		
1990	. . . . -9.5	. . . . -4.0
1989	. . . . 10.1	. . . . 11.0
1988	. . . . 8.7	. . . . 15.4
1987	. . . . -5.2	. . . . -10.4
1986	. . . . 25.8	. . . . 19.3
1985	. . . . 36.9	. . . . 31.8
1984	. . . . 37.2	. . . . 28.1
1983	. . . . 0.7	. . . . 6.7
1982	. . . . 74.3	. . . . 56.2
1981	. . . . -16.9	. . . . -14.1
1980	. . . . 42.9	. . . . 28.3
1979	. . . . 16.2	. . . . 17.0
1978	. . . . 33.6	. . . . 24.4
1977	. . . . 34.8	. . . . 33.5

3	8	6
Trimark Fund	**Trimark Select Growth Fund**	**United Accumulative Fund Ltd.**
Trimark Investment Management Inc.	Trimark Investment Management Inc.	United Financial Management Ltd.
Suite 5200, P.O. Box 205	Suite 5200, P.O. Box 205	200 King St. W., Suite 1202
Scotia Plaza	Scotia Plaza	Toronto, Ont. M5H 3W8
Toronto, Ont. M5H 3Z3	Toronto, Ont. M5H 3Z3	(416) 598-7777
(416) 362-7181	(416) 362-7181	1-800-263-1867
1-800-387-9823	1-800-387-9823	Fax: (416) 598-7821
Fax: (416) 362-8515	Fax: (416) 362-8515	

..........July 10, 1981 First offered Sept., 1981	......February 15, 1989	..........May 27, 1957
.. Everywhere in Canada	.. Everywhere in Canada	.. Everywhere in Canada
................9%	..............No Load	................9%
................N/A	................4.5%	................5.0%
..............1.69%	..............2.66%	..............1.88%
................No	................No	................No
................606.4	................203.4	................243.5
................0.7	................0.0	................8.4
................8.6	................11.4	................3.4
................14.9		................25.7
................-0.5		................-14.9
................17.5		................11.7
................31.2		................34.3
................26.5		................32.7
................-1.6		................10.6
................82.8		................39.8
		................-17.9
		................30.5
		................27.9
		................46.8
		................2.8

Rank	6	8
Balanced	**Canada Life Managed Fund S-35** Canada Life Assurance Co. 330 University Ave. Toronto, Ont. M5G 1R8 (416) 597-1456 Fax: (416) 597-3892	**Industrial Income Fund** Mackenzie Financial Corp. 150 Bloor St. W., 4th Floor Toronto, Ont. M5S 3B5 (416) 922-5322 Fax: (416) 922-0399
Fund Established	. . . . .April 1, 1984	. . . . July, 1974
Where Sold	. . Everywhere in Canada	. . Everywhere in Canada
Maximum Sales Charge	. . . . .1%	. . . . .9%
Maximum Redemption Fee	. . . . 2.5%	. . . . N/A
Management Expense Ratio	. . . . .2%	. . . . 1.84%
RRSP Eligible	. . . . .Yes	. . . . .Yes
Net Assets($ million)	. . . . .310.6	. . . . .234.3
Total Return		
1990	. . . . 6.1	. . . . 8.8
1989	. . . . -0.7	. . . . -1.4
1988	. . . . 13.0	. . . . 12.6
1987	. . . . 3.5	. . . . 13.2
1986	. . . . 11.4	. . . . 12.3
1985	. . . . 20.0	. . . . 18.6
1984	. . . . 27.4	. . . . 38.0
1983	. . . .	. . . . -0.5
1982	. . . .	. . . . 39.0
1981	. . . .	. . . . 5.9
1980	. . . .	. . . . -7.0
1979	. . . .	. . . . -5.0
1978	. . . .	. . . . 7.3
1977	. . . .	. . . . 8.5

10	1	5
Investors Growth Portfolio Fund	**Investors Income Plus Portfolio Fund**	**Investors Income Portfolio Fund**
Investors Group	Investors Group	Investors Group
One Canada Centre	One Canada Centre	One Canada Centre
447 Portage Ave.	447 Portage Ave.	447 Portage Ave.
Winnipeg, Man. R3C 3B6	Winnipeg, Man. R3C 3B6	Winnipeg, Man. R3C 3B6
(204) 943-0361	(204) 943-0361	(204) 943-0361
Fax: (204) 943-0021	Fax: (204) 943-0021	Fax: (204) 943-0021

.... August 15, 1989	.... August 15, 1989	.... August 15, 1989
.. Everywhere in Canada	.. Everywhere in Canada	.. Everywhere in Canada
.... 5.0%	.... 5.0%	.... No Load
.... 1%	.... 1%	.................3.0%
.... N/A	.... N/A	.... N/A
.... No	.... Yes	.... Yes
..................141.7	..................432.9	..................315.4
.................-1.2	.... 10.9	.... 14.2
.... 7.1	.... 3.5	.... 4.5

Rank	4	7
Balanced	Investors Mutual of Canada Ltd. Investors Group One Canada Centre 447 Portage Ave. Winnipeg, Man. R3C 3B6 (204) 943-0361 Fax: (204) 943-0021	Investors Retirement Plus Portfolio Fund Investors Group One Canada Centre 447 Portage Ave. Winnipeg, Man. R3C 3B6 (204) 943-0361 Fax: (204) 943-0021
Fund Established	. . . . October, 1948	. . . . August 15, 1989
Where Sold	. . Everywhere in Canada	. . Everywhere in Canada
Maximum Sales Charge	. . . . 5%	. . . . 5.0%
Maximum Redemption Fee	. . . . 1%	. . . . 1%
Management Expense Ratio	. . . . 1.3%	. . . . N/A
RRSP Eligible	. . . . No	. . . . Yes
Net Assets($ million)	. . . . 320.8	. . . . 263.3
Total Return		
1990	. . . . 8.1	. . . . 6.7
1989	. . . . -0.7	. . . . 3.4
1988	. . . . 11.6	. . . .
1987	. . . . -1.9	. . . .
1986	. . . . 18.4	. . . .
1985	. . . . 12.7	. . . .
1984	. . . . 21.6	. . . .
1983	. . . . -5.9	. . . .
1982	. . . . 68.6	. . . .
1981	. . . . -19.7	. . . .
1980	. . . . 12.3	. . . .
1979	. . . . 21.7	. . . .
1978	. . . . 29.7	. . . .
1977	. . . . 7.4	. . . .

3	2	9
Manulife 1 Diversified Fund	**Manulife 2 Diversified Fund**	**Viking Commonwealth**
Manulife Financial	Manulife Financial	**Fund Ltd.**
500 King St. N.	500 King St. N.	Laurentian Funds Manage-
Waterloo, Ont. N2J 4C6	Waterloo, Ont. N2J 4C6	ment Inc.
(519) 747-7000	(519) 747-7000	310 Front St. W.
Fax: (519) 747-9835	Fax: (519) 747-9835	Toronto, Ont. M5V 3B8
		(416) 343-5222
		Fax: (416) 343-5214

. . . . 1970	 1970	. . . . April, 1932
. . Everywhere in Canada	. . Everywhere in Canada	. . Everywhere in Canada except the Yukon, Northwest
. . . . 4%	. . . . N/A	. . . . 3.5%
. . . . N/A	. . . . 3.5%	. . . . 3.5%
. . . . 1.48%	. . . . 1.48%	. . . . 2.23%
. . . . Yes	. . . . Yes	. . . . No
. . . . 379.5	. . . . 379.5	. . . . 176.0
. . . . 6.4	. . . . 5.6	. . . . -1.7
. . . . 0.5	. . . . -0.3	. . . . 6.5
. . . . 10.7	. . . . 9.9	. . . . 14.4
. . . . -1.2	. . . . -2.0	. . . . -3.4
. . . . 18.3	. . . . 17.5	. . . . 21.2
. . . . 13.1	. . . . 12.3	. . . . 30.4
. . . . 21.6	. . . . 20.7	. . . . 24.3
. . . . -2.9	. . . . -3.6	. . . . 0.7
. . . . 46.5	. . . . 45.5	. . . . 55.0
. . . . -3.2	. . . . -3.9	. . . . -7.7
. . . . 9.4	. . . . 8.6	. . . . 30.9
. . . .	. . . .	. . . . 4.7
. . . .	. . . .	. . . . 14.5
. . . .	. . . .	. . . . 11.8

Rank	6	12
Bond, Mortgage and Bond Mortgage	AGF Canadian Bond Fund AGF Management Ltd. 31st Floor, T-D Bank Tower Toronto, Ont. M5K 1E9 (416) 367-1900 1-800-387-1780 Fax: (416) 865-4197	CIBC Mortgage Investment Fund CIBC Securities Inc. Toronto Mutual Funds Centre P.O. Box 51 Commerce Court Postal Station Toronto, Ont. M5L 1A2 1-800-465-Fund Fax: (416) 362-1967
Fund Established	. . . . August 15, 1962	. . . . . . December 6, 1974
Where Sold	. . Everywhere in Canada	. . Everywhere in Canada
Maximum Sales Charge	. . . . 9%	. . . . No Load
Maximum Redemption Fee	. . . . 4.5%	. . . . N/A
Management Expense Ratio	. . . . 1%	. . . . 1.25%
RRSP Eligible	. . . . Yes	. . . . Yes
Net Assets($ million)	. . . . 475.5	. . . . 213.0
Total Return		
1990	. . . . 10.0	. . . . 17.1
1989	. . . . 1.4	. . . . 7.2
1988	. . . . 12.2	. . . . 9.4
1987	. . . . 7.5	. . . . 7.5
1986	. . . . 5.8	. . . . 8.8
1985	. . . . 20.4	. . . . 10.3
1984	. . . . 31.6	. . . . 15.3
1983	. . . . 3.5	. . . . , . 8.6
1982	. . . . 31.2	. . . . 21.6
1981	. . . . 18.4	. . . . 15.4
1980	. . . . -3.8	. . . . 3.8
1979	. . . . 3.1	. . . . 8.2
1978	. . . . 7.2	. . . .
1977	. . . . 8.0	. . . .

5	10	9
First Canadian Mortgage Fund	**Great-West Life Bond Investment**	**Great-West Life Mortgage Investment**
Bank of Montreal Investment Management Ltd.	Great-West Life Assurance Co.	Great-West Life Assurance Co.
First Bank Tower	100 Osborne St. N.	100 Osborne St. N.
1 First Canadian Place	Winnipeg, Man. R3C 3A5	Winnipeg, Man. R3C 3A5
Toronto, Ont. M5X 1A1	(204) 946-1190	(204) 946-1190
(416) 867-5793	Fax: (204) 946-8622	Fax: (204) 946-8622
Fax: (416) 867-7305		
. . . . 1974	. . . . April 30, 1976	. . . . July 1, 1966
. . Everywhere in Canada	. . Everywhere in Canada	. . Everywhere in Canada except Ontario
. . . . No Load	. . . . No Load	. . . . No Load
. . . . N/A	. . . . N/A	. . . . N/A
. . . . 1.10%	. . . . .2.04%	. . . . .2.04%
. . . . .Yes	. . . . .Yes	. . . . .Yes
. . . . .658.7	. . . . .292.7	. . . . .310.6
. . . . 19.2	. . . . 13.3	. . . . 13.3
. . . . 7.8	. . . . 0.0	. . . . 3.5
. . . . 9.0	. . . . 10.6	. . . . 10.8
. . . . 9.2	. . . . 7.4	. . . . 7.8
. . . . 9.2	. . . . 5.9	. . . . 6.7
. . . . 11.5	. . . . 14.7	. . . . 12.5
. . . . 18.4	. . . . 26.0	. . . . 18.8
. . . . 8.5	. . . . 1.9	. . . . 5.3
. . . . 21.4	. . . . 29.0	. . . . 24.9
. . . . 18.4	. . . . 10.1	. . . . 15.7
. . . . 3.3	. . . .-6.1	. . . . -3.2
. . . . 9.0	. . . . 2.4	. . . . 4.4
. . . . 8.2	. . . .	. . . .
. . . . 9.2	. . . .	. . . .

Rank	4	2
Bond, Mortgage and Bond Mortgage	Industrial Bond Fund Mackenzie Financial Corp. 150 Bloor St. W., 4th Floor. Toronto, Ont. M5S 3B5 (416) 922-5322 Fax: (416) 922-0399	Investors Bond Fund Investors Group One Canada Centre 447 Portage Ave. Winnipeg, Man. R3C 3B6 (204) 943-0361 Fax: (204) 943-0021
Fund Established	. . . . January 12, 1989	. . . . April, 1979
Where Sold	. . Everywhere in Canada	. . Everywhere in Canada
Maximum Sales Charge	. . . . No Load	. . . . No Load
Maximum Redemption Fee	. . . . 3.5%	. . . . 1%
Management Expense Ratio	. . . . 1.98%	. . . . 1.37%
RRSP Eligible	. . . . Yes	. . . . Yes
Net Assets($ million)	. . . . 946.3	. . . . 1103.5
Total Return		
1990	. . . . 12.6	. . . . 13.3
1989	. . . . 1.2	. . . . 3.3
1988	. . . .	. . . . 11.5
1987	. . . .	. . . . 7.4
1986	. . . .	. . . . 6.4
1985	. . . .	. . . . 16.3
1984	. . . .	. . . . 28.5
1983	. . . .	. . . . 0.0
1982	. . . .	. . . . 28.3
1981	. . . .	. . . . 13.7
1980	. . . .	. . . . -7.7
1979	. . . .	. . . . -1.1
1978	. . . .	. . . .
1977	. . . .	. . . .

1	15	13
Investors Mortgage Fund Investors Group One Canada Centre 447 Portage Ave. Winnipeg, Man. R3C 3B6 (204) 943-0361 Fax: (204) 943-0021	**Investors Pooled Mortgage Fund** Investors Group One Canada Centre 447 Portage Ave. Winnipeg, Man. R3C 3B6 (204) 956-8240 Fax: (204) 943-2698	**London Life Bond Fund** London Life Insurance Co. 255 Dufferin Ave. London, Ont. N6A 4K1 (519) 432-5281 Fax: (519) 432-9035
August, 1973	September, 1958	1961
Everywhere in Canada	Everywhere in Canada	Everywhere in Canada
No Load	3.5%	5%
3%	N/A	N/A
1.35%	0.26 of 1%	1.5%
Yes	Yes	Yes
1612.6	169.5	195.8
15.7	16.8	5.2
7.1	8.7	3.2
9.0	9.9	13.2
8.8	9.5	5.3
8.4	9.3	4.2
11.4	12.4	21.2
18.5	20.4	41.3
7.0	7.1	2.0
23.8	27.4	31.6
16.7	15.1	13.5
3.7	0.7	-1.9
7.6	5.4	3.8
7.4	7.7	7.3
9.6	9.4	7.6

Rank	8	14
Bond, Mortgage and Bond Mortgage	Mackenzie Income Fund Mackenzie Financial Corp. 150 Bloor St. W., 4th Floor Toronto, Ont. M5S 3B5 (416) 922-5322 Fax:(416) 922-0399	Phillips, Hager & North Bond Fund Phillips, Hager & North Ltd. 1700-1055 West Hastings St. Vancouver, B.C. V6E 2H3 (604) 684-4361 1-800-661-6141 Fax: (604) 684-5120
Fund Established	.... December, 1974	...... December 4, 1970
Where Sold	.. Everywhere in Canada	.. Everywhere in Canada
Maximum Sales Charge	.... 9%	.... No Load
Maximum Redemption Fee	.... N/A	.... N/A
Management Expense Ratio	.... 1.85%	.... 0.68%
RRSP Eligible	.... Yes	.... Yes
Net Assets($ million)	.... 323.6	.... 176.5
Total Return		
1990	.... 9.6	.... 14.2
1989	.... -0.9	.... 3.2
1988	.... 12.9	.... 13.2
1987	.... 13.0	.... 9.5
1986	.... 12.5	.... 9.4
1985	.... 17.6	.... 18.6
1984	.... 30.3	.... 34.0
1983	.... 4.3	.... -3.2
1982	.... 27.6	.... 44.8
1981	.... 14.2	.... 9.0
1980	.... 0.9	.... -8.9
1979	.... 8.0	.... 0.3
1978	.... 8.0	.... 8.4
1977	.... 8.0	.... 6.8

11	7	3
RoyFund Bond Fund	**Royal Trust Bond Fund**	**Royal Trust Mortgage Fund**
Royal Bank of Canada	Royal Trust Co.	Royal Trust Co.
4th Floor, North Tower	Suite 3900, Royal Trust	Suite 3900, Royal Trust
Royal Bank Plaza	Tower	Tower
Toronto, Ont. M5J 2J2	Toronto-Dominion Centre	Toronto-Dominion Centre
(416) 974-0616	Toronto, Ont. M5W 1P9	Toronto, Ont. M5W 1P9
Fax: (416) 974-4076		

................1973	.........July 29, 1966	.......October 1, 1968
.. Everywhere in Canada	.. Everywhere in Canada	.. Everywhere in Canada
..............No Load	..............No Load	..............No Load
.... N/A	.... N/A	.... N/A
.... 1.42%	...............1.105%	...............1.391%
.................Yes	.................Yes	.................Yes
.................223.2	.................409.1	.................949.4
.... 13.4	.... 13.6	.... 15.7
.... 3.0	.... 1.9	.... 8.6
.... 9.4	.... 11.0	.... 8.5
.... 7.8	.... 7.3	.... 9.2
.... 6.8	.... 6.2	.... 8.7
.... 15.7	.... 16.5	.... 11.3
.... 23.9	.... 30.0	.... 16.8
.... 1.0	.... 1.3	.... 8.6
.... 23.4	.... 35.5	.... 20.8
.... 8.6	.... 11.7	.... 18.7
.... 0.9	.................-2.1	.... 5.2
.... 13.3	.... 1.3	.... 7.9
.... 6.5	.... 7.3	.... 8.3
.... 8.0	.... 7.8	.... 9.3

CHAPTER 15

The Best Performers

Best One Year Performers

1	ABC Fundamental Value	27.1
2	Bullock American	22.4
3	Pursuit American	21.9
4	First Canadian Mortgage	19.2
5	ABC Fully-Managed	17.7
6	CIBC Mortgage	17.1
7	Investors Pooled Mortgage	16.8
8	Crown Life Pensions Mort	16.5
9	London Life Mortgage	16.4
10	Allied Canadian	16.3
11	Margin of Safety Fund	16.3
12	United Security Fixed Income	16.3
13	Green Line Mortgage	16.2
14	Sceptre Bond	16.1
15	Trust Pret & Revenu H	15.9
16	Investors Mortgage	15.7
17	Royal Trust Mortgage	15.7
18	Empire Fixed Income #4	15.6
19	Fd des Prof du Que-Bond	15.5
20	Canada Trust RSP-Mortgage	15.4
21	Investors Trust Bond	15.3
22	GBC Canadian Growth	15.2
23	McLean Budden Amer Growth	15.2
24	Trust General Mortgage	15.2
25	Standard Life Bond 2000	15.1

One-year figures show percentage rate of return, including dividends and capital gains distributions, for year to June 30, 1991.

26	FuturLink Mortgage	15.0
27	Altamira Income	14.9
28	Fds Desjardins Hypotheq	14.8
29	United Mortgage	14.7
30	Bolton Tremblay Bond & Mort	14.6
31	Montreal Trust RRSP Mortgage	14.6
32	AIC Advantage	14.5
33	Confed Mortgage	14.5
34	Montreal Trust Mortgage	14.5
35	Bissett Fiduciary	14.4
36	McLean Budden Fixed Inc	14.4
37	Altamira Special Growth	14.3
38	Central Guaranty Trust Mort	14.2
39	Investors Income Portfolio	14.2
40	Manulife 1 Bond	14.2
41	PH&N Bond	14.2
42	CDA RSP Bond & Mortgage	14.1
43	Fonds SNF Obligations	14.1
44	Empire Bond #2	14.0
45	Fd des Prof du Que-Bal	14.0
46	GBC Canadian Bond Fund	14.0
47	Strata Income	14.0
48	Fds Desjardins Obligat	13.9
49	Fidelity Capital Builder	13.9
50	Canada Trust Income Invest	13.8
51	Endurance Government Bond	13.8

Best Three Year Performers

1	Bullock American	23.3
2	Altamira Equity	21.2
3	Barrtor American Fund	17.9
4	ABC Fully-Managed	14.9
5	Everest International	14.6
6	NW Equity	14.5
7	PH&N U.S. Pooled Pension	14.5
8	Vintage Fund	13.6
9	PH&N U.S.	13.5
10	Pursuit American	13.4
11	Investors Special	13.1
12	Green Line U.S. Index	12.3
13	Investors N.A. Growth	12.1
14	United Accumulative	12.1
15	Everest Money Market	12.0
16	United Canadian Money Market	12.0
17	Elliott & Page Money	11.9
18	First Canadian Mortgage	11.9
19	Guardian Short Term Money	11.9
20	Investors Pooled Mortgage	11.8
21	Royal Trust American Stock	11.8
22	Counsel Real Estate	11.7
23	Green Line Cdn Money Market	11.7
24	Talvest Money	11.7
25	Industrial Cash Management	11.6
26	PH&N Money Market	11.6
27	Spectrum Savings	11.6
28	CDA RSP Money Market	11.5
29	Green Line Mortgage	11.5
30	Bolton Tremblay Money	11.4
31	Capstone Cash Management	11.4
32	Templeton Treasury Bill	11.4
33	Waltaine Instant $$	11.4
34	AGF Money Market	11.3
35	Altamira Income	11.3
36	Prudential Money Market	11.3

Three-year, five-year and ten-year rates are average annual compound rates of return, including dividends and capital gains, for year to June 30, 1991.

37	Spectrum Cash Reserve	11.3
38	Trimark Interest	11.3
39	United American	11.3
40	Crown Life Pen Short	11.2
41	Manulife 1 Short Term	11.2
42	Montreal Trust Money Market	11.2
43	O.I.Q. Fonds d'Monetaire	11.2
44	RoyFund Money Market	11.2
45	Sceptre Money Market	11.2
46	Viking Money Market	11.2
47	CIBC Mortgage	11.1
48	Finsco Cdn Money Market	11.1
49	Montreal Trust RRSP Money Market	11.1
50	Canada Life US & International Equity S-34	11.0
51	Canada Trust RSP-Mortgage	11.0
52	Confed Mortgage	11.0

Best Five-Year Performers

1	Imperial Growth Equity	13.7
2	Counsel Real Estate	12.7
3	Bullock American	12.5
4	MD Realty A	11.1
5	First Canadian Mortgage	10.8
6	Investors Pooled Mortgage	10.8
7	MD Realty B	10.8
8	Elliott & Page Money	10.6
9	Green Line Mortgage	10.5
10	Vintage Fund	10.5
11	Altamira Income	10.4
12	Guardian Short Term Money	10.4
13	Altamira Growth & Income	10.2
14	Bolton Tremblay Money	10.2
15	Trust Pret & Revenu H	10.2
16	Canada Trust RSP-Mortgage	10.1
17	Crown Life Pen Short	10.1
18	Fds Desjardins Hypotheq	10.1
19	First City RealFund	10.1
20	Industrial Cash Management	10.1
21	London Life Mortgage	10.1
22	Royal Trust Mortgage	10.1
23	Viking Money Market	10.1
24	AGF Money Market	10.0
25	CDA RSP Money Market	10.0
26	Confed Mortgage	10.0
27	Crown Life Pensions Mort	10.0
28	Ethical Growth	10.0
29	F.M.O.Q. Fd de Placements	10.0
30	O.I.Q. Fonds d'Monetaire	10.0
31	St-Laurent Fonds D'Epargne	10.0
32	CIBC Mortgage	9.9
33	Finsco Cdn Money Market	9.9
34	PH&N Bond	9.9
35	Allied Income	9.8
36	Investors Mortgage	9.8

Three-year, five-year and ten-year rates are average annual compound rates of return, including dividends and capital gains, for year to June 30, 1991.

37	Investors Trust Bond	9.8
38	Manulife 1 Short Term	9.8
39	Montreal Trust Mortgage	9.8
40	Investors Money Market	9.7
41	Dynamic Money Market	9.6
42	Guardian Balanced	9.6
43	Trust General Mortgage	9.6
44	Great-West Life Money Market	9.5
45	Montreal Trust RRSP Mortgage	9.5
46	Royal Trust Energy	9.5
47	Talvest Money	9.5
48	Allied Money	9.4
49	Cambridge Growth	9.4
50	CDA RSP Bond & Mortgage	9.4
51	MD Money Fund	9.4

Best Ten-Year Performers

1	PH&N U.S. Pooled Pension	15.2
2	London Life Mortgage	14.6
3	PH&N Bond	14.5
4	Crown Life Pensions Mort	14.4
5	Universal Canadian Bond	14.3
6	Bullock American	14.1
7	Talvest Bond	14.1
8	Industrial Income	13.9
9	O.I.Q. Fonds d'Obligations	13.9
10	Investors Trust Bond	13.8
11	AGF Canadian Bond Fund	13.7
12	Mackenzie Income & Mortgage	13.7
13	PH&N U.S.	13.7
14	AGF Japan	13.6
15	Cambridge Growth	13.5
16	Imperial Growth Equity	13.5
17	Investors Pooled Mortgage	13.5
18	MD Growth Investments	13.5
19	London Life Bond	13.4
20	CDA RSP Bond & Mortgage	13.2
21	Trust General Bond	13.2
22	Viking Income	13.2
23	First Canadian Mortgage	13.1
24	Manulife 1 Bond	13.0
25	Montreal Trust RRSP Income	13.0
26	Royal Trust Bond	13.0
27	Trust General Mortgage	13.0
28	Dynamic Income	12.9
29	F.M.O.Q. Omnibus	12.9
30	MD Equity Fund	12.9
31	National Trust Income	12.9
32	Altamira Income	12.8
33	Cundill Value	12.8
34	Fds Desjardins Hypotheq	12.8
35	AGF Special	12.7
36	Cambridge Balanced	12.7

Three-year, five-year and ten-year rates are average annual compound rates of return, including dividends and capital gains, for year to June 30, 1991.

37	Templeton Growth	12.7
38	Bolton Tremblay Intl	12.6
39	Canada Life Fixed Inc S-19 & Mortgage	12.6
40	Canada Trust RSP-Income	12.6
41	Confed Mortgage	12.6
42	Fds Desjardins Obligat	12.6
43	Montreal Trust Income	12.6
44	Prudential Income & Mortgage	12.6
45	Royal Trust Mortgage	12.6
46	Trust Pret & Revenu H	12.6
47	Viking Commonwealth	12.6
48	Green Line Mortgage	12.5
49	Investors Bond	12.5
50	Investors Mortgage	12.5

CHAPTER 16

Directory of Fund Management Companies

AIC Limited
86 Queen St. N.
Kitchener, Ont. N2H 2H5
(519) 578-6760
Fax: (519) 570-0767

AIC Advantage
AIC Value

Admax International Investments Ltd.
200 King St. W., 8th Floor
Toronto, Ont. M5H 3W3
(416) 586-6265
Fax: (416) 586-6789

Admax American Performance
Admax Canadian Performance

AGF Management Ltd.
P.O. Box 50, T-D Centre
Toronto, Ont. M5K 1E9
(416) 367-1900
1-800-387-1780
Fax: (416) 865-4197

AGF American Growth
AGF Canadian Bond
AGF Canadian Equity
AGF Canadian Resource
AGF Convertible Income
AGF Global Government Bond
AGF Growth Equity
AGF High Income
AGF Japan
AGF Money Market
AGF Option Equity
AGF Special
Corporate Investors Ltd
Corporate Investors Stock

Allied Capital Management Inc.

6 Adelaide St. E.,
9th Floor,
Toronto, Ont. M5C 1H6
(416) 363-5621
1-800-268-8186
Fax: (416) 363-5850

Allied Canadian
Allied Dividend
Allied Income
Allied International
Allied Money

Altamira Investment Services Inc.

250 Bloor St. E., Suite 301
Toronto, Ont. M4W 1E6
(416) 925-1623
1-800-263-2824
Fax: (416) 925-5352

Altamira Balanced
Altamira Canadian Bond
Altamira Canadian Equity
Altamira Capital Growth
Altamira Diversified
Altamira Growth & Income
Altamira Resource
Altamira Special Growth
Gyro Bond
Gyro Equity

Associate Investors Ltd.

8 King St. E., Suite 2001
Toronto, Ont. M5C 1B6
(416) 864-1120
Fax: (416) 864-1491

Associate Investors

Bank of Montreal Investment Management Ltd.

First Bank Tower
1 First Canadian Place
Toronto, Ont. M5X 1A1
(416) 867-5793
Fax: (416) 867-7305

First Canadian Balanced
First Canadian Bond
First Canadian Equity Index
First Canadian Money Market
First Canadian Mortgage

Bissett & Associates Investment Management Ltd.

750, 205 5th Ave. S.W.
Calgary, Alta. T2P 2V7
(403) 266-4664
Fax: (403) 237-2334

Bissett Balanced
Bissett Canadian
Bissett Fiduciary
Bissett Special

Bolton Tremblay Funds Inc.
70 University Ave., Suite 1050
Toronto, Ont. M5J 2M4
(416) 595-5200
Fax: (416) 595-5382

Bolton Tremblay Bond & Mortgage
Bolton Tremblay Canada Cumulative
Bolton Tremblay Canadian Balanced
Bolton Tremblay Discovery
Bolton Tremblay Income
Bolton Tremblay International
Bolton Tremblay Money Market
Bolton Tremblay Optimal Canadian
Bolton Tremblay Planned Resources
Bolton Tremblay Taurus
Landmark American
Landmark Bond & Mortgage
Landmark Canadian
Landmark International
Landmark Short Term Interest

BPI Capital Management Corp.
141 Adelaide St. W., Suite 1009
Toronto, Ont. M5H 3L5
(416) 861-9811
1-800-263-2427
Fax: (416) 861-9415

BPI Canadian Bond
BPI Canadian Equity
BPI Emerging Growth
BPI Europe & Far East
BPI Global Equity
BPI Global Income
BPI High Yield
BPI Money Market
BPI One Decision
BPI Option Equity

Burns Fry Ltd.
P.O. Box 150
1 First Canadian Place
Toronto, Ont. M5X 1H3
(416) 365-4000
Fax: (416) 365-4707

Burns Fry Bond
Burns Fry Canadian
Burns Fry Fund

Calvin Bullock Ltd.
630 Rene Levesque Blvd. W.
Suite 2690
Montreal, Que. H3B 1X1
(514) 866-5421
1-800-363-0260
Fax: (514) 866-4659

Bullock American
Bullock Balanced
Bullock Bond
Bullock Dividend
Bullock Growth
Bullock Money Market
Canadian Investment Fund

Canada Life Assurance Co.
330 University Ave.
Toronto, Ont. M5G 1R8
(416) 597-1456
Fax: (416) 597-3892

Canada Life Balanced Equity Income E-2
Canada Life Canadian Equity S-9
Canada Life Fixed Income S-19
Canada Life Managed S-35
Canada Life Money Market S-29
Canada Life U.S. & Intl Equity S-34

Canada Trust Co.
Fund Administration Services
320 Bay St.
Toronto, Ont. M5H 2P6
(416) 361-8191
Fax: (416) 361-8106

Canada Trust Income Investment
Canada Trust Investment-Equity
Canada Trust Investment-Income
Canada Trust RSP-Equity
Canada Trust RSP-Income
Canada Trust RSP-Mortgage

Canadian Anaestheists' Mutual
Accumulating Fund Ltd.
Suite 503, 94 Cumberland St.
Toronto, Ont. M5R 1A3
(416) 923-1449
Canadian Anaestheists' Mutual
Accumulating

CDSPI
2 Lansing Sq., Suite 600
Willowdale, Ont. M2J 4Z3
(416) 497-7117
Fax: (416) 497-9257

CDA RSP Balanced
CDA RSP Bond & Mortgage
CDA RSP Common Stock
CDA RSP Money Market

Central Asset Management
1 First Canadian Place
Suite 2500
Toronto, Ont. M5X 1G4
(416) 345-4600
Fax: (416) 345-4579

Central Guaranty Property
FuturLink Canadian Growth
FuturLink Government Bond
FuturLink Income
FuturLink Select
FuturLink Money Market
FuturLink Mortgage
Guaranty Trust Balanced Income & Growth
Guaranty Trust Investors Equity
Guaranty Trust Investors Income
Guaranty Trust Mortgage

The Central Group
P.O. Box 7320
Ancaster, Ont. L9G 3N6
(416) 648-2025
Fax: (416) 648-5422

All-Canadian Compound
All-Canadian Dividend
All-Canadian Income
Natural Resources Growth
Univest Growth

Century DJ Fund
4 King St. W., Suite 301
Toronto, Ont. M5H 1B6
(416) 860-0495
Fax: (416) 363-1954

Century DJ

Chou & Associates Management Inc.
70 Dragoon Crescent
Scarborough, Ont. M1V 1N4
(416) 299-6749

Chou Associates
Chou RRSP

Church Street Financial Corp.
26 Wellington St. E., Suite 900
Toronto, Ont. M5E 1S2
(416) 865-1985
Fax: (416) 865-9241

Church Street Balanced
Church Street Equity
Church Street Income
Church Street Money Market

CIBC Securities Inc.
Toronto Mutual Fund Centre
P.O. Box 51
Commerce Court Postal Station
Toronto, Ont. M5L 1A2
(416) 980-Fund
1-800-465-Fund
Fax: (416) 362-1967

CIBC Balanced Income & Growth
CIBC Canadian Equity
CIBC Fixed Income
CIBC Global Equity
CIBC Money Market
CIBC Mortgage

The Citadel Assurance
1075 Bay St.
Toronto, Ont. M5S 2W5
(416) 928-8500
Fax: (416) 928-1553

Citadel Premier

Confed Funds
321 Bloor St. E.
Toronto, Ont. M4W 1H1
(416) 323-8999
1-800-263-2820
Fax: (416) 323-4100

Confed Growth
Confed Mortgage

Counsel Trust Co.
36 Toronto St., Suite 300
Toronto, Ont. M5C 2C5
(416) 365-0094
Fax: (416) 365-1634

Counsel Trust Real Estate Fund

Crown Life
120 Bloor St. E.
Toronto, Ont. M4W 1B8
(416) 928-4500
Fax: (416) 928-7631

Crown Life Commitment
Crown Life Pension Balanced
Crown Life Pension Bond
Crown Life Pension Equity
Crown Life Pension Foreign Equity
Crown Life Pension Mortgage
Crown Life Pension Short Term

C.S.A. Management Ltd.
P.O. Box 68, IBM Tower
Toronto-Dominion Centre
Toronto, Ont. M5K 1E7
(416) 865-0326
Fax: (416) 865-9636

Goldfund
Goldtrust

CT Investment Counsel Inc.
110 Yonge St., Suite 800
Toronto, Ont. M5C 1T4
(416) 869-6391
1-800-268-8777
Fax: (416) 869-5903

Everest Balanced
Everest Bond
Everest Growth
Everest International
Everest Short Term Asset
Everest Special Equity

Dean Witter Reynolds (Canada) Inc.
Scotia Plaza, Suite 3300
40 King St. W.
Toronto, Ont. M5H 1B5
(416) 369-8900
1-800-387-1840
Fax: (416) 369-8778

Dean Witter American High Yield
Dean Witter American Liquid Asset

Dynamic Funds Management Ltd.
6 Adelaide St. E., 9th Floor
Toronto, Ont. M5C 1H6
(416) 363-5621
1-800-268-8186
Fax: (416) 363-5850

Dynamic American
Dynamic Dividend
Dynamic Fund of Canada
Dynamic Global Bond
Dynamic Global
Dynamic Income
Dynamic Managed Portfolio
Dynamic Money Market
Dynamic Partners
Dynamic Precious Metals
Europe 1992

Elliot & Page Ltd.
120 Adelaide St. W., Suite 1120
Toronto, Ont. M5H 1V1
(416) 365-8300
Fax: (416) 365-2156

Elliot & Page Balanced
Elliot & Page Bond
Elliot & Page Equity
Elliot & Page Money

Empire Life Insurance Co.
243-259 King St. E.
Kingston, Ont. K7L 3A8
(613) 548-1881
Fax: (613) 541-3050

Empire Balanced #8
Empire Bond #2
Empire Equity Growth #1
Empire Equity Growth #3
Empire Equity Growth #5
Empire Fixed Income #4
Empire Group Equity Growth #6
Empire International #9
Empire Money Market #7

Environmental Investment Funds
225 Brunswick Ave.
Toronto, Ont. M5S 2M6
(416) 978-4397
Fax: (416) 978-3824

EIF Canadian
EIF International

Extro Funds Management Inc.
149 Union St. E.
Waterloo, Ont. N2J 1C4
(519) 579-4040
Fax: (519) 579-4212

Extro International

Fidelity Investments Canada Ltd.
100 Simcoe St., Suite 300
Toronto, Ont. M5H 3G2
(416) 971-6170
1-800-263-4077
Fax: (416) 971-7678

Fidelity Capital Balanced
Fidelity Capital Builder
Fidelity Capital Conservation
Fidelity International Portfolio

Fiducie Desjardins
1 Complexe Desjardins
P.O. Box 34
Montreal, Que. H5B 1E4
(514) 286-5883
Fax: (514) 849-3228

Caisse de Section du Spectacle
Fonds Desjardins Action
Fonds Desjardins Equilibre
Fonds Desjardins Hypotheqeues
Fonds Desjardins Internationale
Fonds Desjardins Marche Monetaire
Fonds Desjardins Obligations
Ordre Ingenieurs Marche Monetaire
Ordre Ingenieurs Actions
Ordre Ingenieurs Equilibre
Ordre Ingenieurs Obligations

Finsco Services Ltd.
110 Yonge St., Suite 500
Toronto, Ont. M5C 1T4
(416) 368-3863
Fax: (416) 368-6011

Finsco Bond
Finsco Canadian Money Market
Finsco Canadian T-Bill
Finsco U.S. Dollar Money Market
Jarislowsky Finsco American Equity
Jarislowsky Finsco Balanced
Jarislowsky Finsco Canadian Equity

First City Trust Co.
777 Hornby St.
Vancouver, B.C. V6C 1S4
(604) 685-2489
Fax: (604) 661-4892

First City Growth
First City Income
First City RealFund
First City Government Money

F.M.O.Q.
1440 St. Catherine W.
Suite 1100
Montreal, Que. H5B 1E4
(514) 286-5883
Fax: (514) 849-3328

F.M.O.Q. Fonds de Placements
F.M.O.Q. Monetaire
F.M.O.Q. Omnibus

Fonds des Professionnels du Quebec
2 Complexe Desjardins, Suite 3000
P.O. Box 216, Sucursal Desjardins
Montreal, Que. H5B 1G8
(514) 843-3536
1-800-363-6713
Fax: (514) 843-3536

Fund des Professionales du Quebec-Balanced
Fund des Professionales du Quebec-Bond
Fund des Professionales du Quebec-Equity
Fund des Professionales du Quebec-Money Mkt

Global Strategy Financial Inc.
2 Bloor St. W., Suite 3400
Toronto, Ont. M4W 1A1
(416) 927-9344
1-800-387-1229
Fax: (416) 927-9168

Global Strategy Americas
Global Strategy Canadian
Global Strategy Corporation
Global Strategy Europe
Global Strategy Far East
Global Strategy Fund
Global Strategy Intl Real Estate
Global Strategy T-Bill Savings
Global Strategy U.S. Money
Global Strategy World Bond
Global Strategy World Money

Gordon-Daly Grenadier Securities
224 Richmond St. W.
Toronto, Ont. M5V 1V6
(416) 593-0144
Fax: (416) 593-4922

Canadian Natural Resources

Great-West Life Assurance Co.
100 Osborne St. N.
Winnipeg, Man. R3C 3A5
(204) 946-1190
Fax: (204) 946-8622

Great-West Life Bond
Great-West Life Diversified RS
Great-West Life Equity Index
Great-West Life Equity
Great-West Life Equity/Bond
Great-West Life Money Market
Great-West Life Mortgage
Great-West Life Real Estate

Guardian Group of Funds
110 Yonge St., 18th Floor
Toronto, Ont. M5C 1T4
(416) 947-4099
1-800-668-7327
Fax: (416) 947-0601

Canada Income Plus 1987
Guardian American Equity
Guardian Balanced
Guardian Canadian Equity
Guardian Enterprise
Guardian Global Equity
Guardian International Income
Guardian North American
Guardian Pacific Rim
Guardian Preferred Dividend
Guardian Short Term Money
Guardian Strategic Income
Guardian U.S. Money Market
Guardian Vantage Balanced
Guardian Vantage Bond
Guardian Vantage Equity
Guardian Vantage International
Guardian Vantage U.S. Equity

Guardian Timing Services
130 Bloor St. W.
11th Floor
Toronto, Ont. M5S 1N5
(416) 924-1522
Fax: (416) 924-0878

Canadian Protected
Protected American

Guardian Trust Co.
555 Rene Levesque Blvd. W.,
3rd Floor
Montreal, Que. H2Z 1B1
(514) 842-7161
Fax: (514) 393-1085

Cooperants Group American Equity
Cooperants Group Balanced
Cooperants Group Canadian Equity
Cooperants Group Income
Cooperants Group Real Estate

Hodgson Roberton Laing Ltd.
390 Bay St., Suite 1608
Toronto, Ont. M5H 2Y2
(416) 368-1428
1-800-268-9622
Fax: (416) 869-1653

Waltaine Balanced
Waltaine Dividend Growth
Waltaine Income
Waltaine Instant $$

Hong Kong Bank of Canada
130 Adelaide St. W.
Toronto, Ont. M5H 3R2
(416) 868-8398
Fax: (416) 361-6011

Lloyds Bank Balanced
Lloyds Bank Equity Index
Lloyds Bank Money Market

Hughes, King & Co. Ltd.
Suite 401
One University Ave.
Toronto, Ont. M5J 2P1
(416) 863-0687
Fax: (416) 863-0841

Capstone Investment Trust

I.A. Michael Investment Counsel Ltd.
10 King St. E., Suite 1010
Toronto, Ont. M5C 1C3
(416) 365-9696
Fax: (416) 367-8059

ABC Fully-Managed
ABC Fundamental Value

Imperial Life Assurance Co.
95 St. Clair Ave. W.
Toronto, Ont. M4V 1N7
(416) 926-2668
Fax: (416) 923-1599

Imperial Growth Canadian Equity
Imperial Growth Diversified
Imperial Growth Money Market
Imperial Growth North American Equity

Interga Balanced Fund
55 University Ave.
Suite 1100, P.O. Box 42
Toronto, Ont. M5J 2H7
(416) 367-0404
Fax: (416) 367-0351

Interga Balanced

InvesNAT Group
600 La Gauchetiere W.
6th Floor
Montreal, Que. H3B 4L2
(514) 394-8858
Fax: (514) 394-8229

InvesNAT Balanced
InvesNAT Equity
InvesNAT Income

Investors Group
One Canada Centre
447 Portage Ave.
Winnipeg, Man. R3C 3B6
(204) 943-0361
Fax: (204) 943-0021

Investors Bond
Investors Canadian Equity
Investors Dividend
Investors Global
Investors Growth
Investors Growth Plus Portfolio
Investors Growth Portfolio
Investors Income Plus Portfolio
Investors Income Portfolio
Investors Japanese Growth
Investors Money Market
Investors Mortgage
Investors Mutual of Canada
Investors Pooled Equity
Investors Pooled Mortgage
Investors Real Property
Investors Retire Growth Portfolio
Investors Retire Plus Portfolio
Investors Retirement Mutual
Investors Special
Investors Summa
Investors Trust Bond
Investors U.S. Growth

Ivory & Sime Pembroke Inc.
55 University Ave., Suite 616
P.O. Box 19
Toronto, Ont. M5J 2H7
(416) 366-2550
1-800-668-7383
Fax: (416) 366-6833

GBC Bond
GBC Canada
GBC Money Market
GBC North American

John D. Hillery Investment Counsel Inc.
4000 Weston Road
Weston, Ont. M9L 2W8
(416) 743-1400
Fax: (416) 746-1311

Margin of Safety
Margin of Safety Canadian

Jones Heward Investment Management
770 Sherbrooke St. W., Suite 1700
Montreal, Que. H3A 1G1
(514) 286-5462
Fax: (514) 286-7226

Jones Heward American
Jones Heward Fund

Keltic Investment Trust
1690 Hollis St.
Halifax, N.S. B3J 3M3
(902) 429-9911
Fax: (902) 423-5316

Keltic Investment Trust

Laurentian Funds Management Inc.
310 Front St. W.
Toronto, Ont. M5V 3B8
(416) 343-5222
Fax: (416) 343-5214

Endurance Canadian Balanced
Endurance Canadian Equity
Endurance Global Equity
Endurance Government Bond
Viking Canadian
Viking Commonwealth
Viking Dividend
Viking Growth
Viking Income
Viking International
Viking Money Market

London Life Insurance Co.
255 Dufferin Ave.
London, Ont. N6A 4K1
(519) 432-5281
Fax: (519) 432-9035

London Life Bond
London Life Canadian Equity
London Life Diversified
London Life Money Market
London Life Mortgage
London Life U.S. Equity

Mackenzie Financial Corp.
150 Bloor St. W., 4th Floor
Toronto, Ont. M5S 3B5
(416) 922-5322
Fax: (416) 922-0399

Industrial American
Industrial Bond
Industrial Cash Management
Industrial Dividend
Industrial Equity
Industrial Future
Industrial Global
Industrial Growth
Industrial Horizon
Industrial Income
Industrial Pension
Mackenzie Equity
Mackenzie Mortgage & Income
Mackenzie Sentinel American Equity
Mackenzie Sentinel Canada Bond
Mackenzie Sentinel Canada Equity
Mackenzie Sentinel Canada Money Market

Manulife Financial
500 King St. N.
Waterloo, Ont. N2J 4C6
(519) 747-7000
Fax: (519) 747-9835

Manulife Bond
Manulife Capital Gains Growth
Manulife Diversified
Manulife Equity
Manulife Short Term Securities

Maritime Life Assurance Co.
2701 Dutch Village Road
Halifax, N.S. B3J 2X5
(902) 453-4300
Fax: (902) 453-7041

Maritime Life Balanced
Maritime Life Growth

Marlborough Fund Ltd.
250 Consumers Road
Suite 200
Willowdale, Ont. M2J 4V6
(416) 494-3039
Fax: (416) 497-0678

Marlborough Fund

McLean Budden Ltd.
390 Bay St., Suite 1000
Toronto, Ont. M5H 2Y2
(416) 862-9800
Fax: (416) 862-0167

McLean Budden American Growth
McLean Budden American Value
McLean Budden Balanced
McLean Budden Balanced Growth
McLean Budden Equity Growth
McLean Budden Fixed Income
McLean Budden Money Market

MD Management Ltd.
1867 Alta Vista Drive
Ottawa, Ont. K1G 3Y6
(613) 731-4552
1-800-267-4022
Fax: (613) 526-1352

CMA Investment
CMA Short Term Deposit
MD Bond
MD Growth Investments
Perpetual Growth
Perpetual Growth II

MD Management Ltd.
2283 St. Laurent Blvd.
Suite 200
Ottawa, Ont. K1G 5A2
(613) 526-3691
Fax: (613) 526-2609

MD Realty Fund A
MD Realty Fund B

**Merritt Easton Rae
Management Ltd.**
1703-1166 Alberni St.
Vancouver, B.C. V6E 3Z3
(604) 688-9531
M.E.R. Equity

Metfin Real Estate Growth Fund
Suite 200, 360 Bay St.
Toronto, Ont. M5H 2V6
(416) 363-7507
Fax: (416) 869-0249

Metfin Real Estate Growth

MetLife Funds
99 Bank St.
Ottawa, Ont. K1P 5A3
(613) 560-7978
Fax: (613) 560-6985

MetLife MVP Balanced
MetLife MVP Bond
MetLife MVP Equity

Metropolitan Canadian Mutual Funds Ltd.
2700 Metropolitan Place
10303 Jasper Ave.
Edmonton, Alta. T5J 3N6
(403) 421-2020
Fax: (403) 421-2022

Metropolitan Bond
Metropolitan Canadian
Metropolitan Collective
Metropolitan Growth
Metropolitan Protection
Metropolitan Speculators
Metropolitan Venture

M.K. Wong Management Ltd.
2520-1066 West Hastings St.
Vancouver, B.C. V6E 3X1
(604) 669-4555
Fax: (604) 669-2756

Lotus Fund

MOF Management Ltd.
P.O. Box 10379, Pacific Centre
2020-609 Granville St.
Vancouver, B.C. V7T 1G6
(604) 688-8151
Fax: (604) 687-6532

Multiple Opportunities
Special Opportunities

Montreal Trust Co.
Place Montreal Trust
1800 McGill College Ave.
Montreal, Que. H3A 3K9
(514) 982-7000
Fax: (514) 982-7069

Montreal Trust Balanced
Montreal Trust Dividend
Montreal Trust Equity
Montreal Trust Income
Montreal Trust International
Montreal Trust Money Market
Montreal Trust Mortgage
Montreal Trust Total Return
Montreal Trust RRSP/RRIF Balanced
Montreal Trust RRSP/RRIF Equity
Montreal Trust RRSP/RRIF Income
Montreal Trust RRSP/RRIF Money Market
Montreal Trust RRSP/RRIF Mortgage
Montreal Trust RRSP/RRIF Total Return

Mutual Life of Canada
227 King St. S.
Waterloo, Ont. N2J 4C5
(519) 888-2472
Fax: (519) 888-2990

Mutual Amerifund
Mutual Canadian Indexfund
Mutual Diversifund 25
Mutual Diversifund 40
Mutual Diversifund 55
Mutual Dividend
Mutual Equifund
Mutual Money Market

National Trust Co.
21 King St. E., 11th Floor
Toronto, Ont. M5C 1B3
(416) 361-5553
Fax: (416) 361-5563

National Trust Equity
National Trust Income
National Trust PRO

NN Financial
One Concorde Gate
Don Mills, Ont. M3C 3N6
(416) 391-2200
Fax: (416) 391-8431

NN Balanced
NN Bond
NN Canadian 35 Index
NN Canadian Growth
NN Global
Mony Gold Bullion

NW Fund Management Ltd
1040 West Georgia St., Suite 800
Vancouver, B.C. V6E 4H1
(604) 689-1211
Fax: (604) 682-2013

NW Canadian
NW Equity

Northern Funds Management Inc.
20 Toronto St., 9th Floor
Toronto, Ont. M5C 2T1
(416) 866-2950
Fax: (416) 866-2979

CGF Fund 4000
CGF International Growth
CGF Venture
MMF Dividend
MMF Growth
MMF Income
MMF Resource
MMF Worldwide
Northern Eagle
Northern Voyageur
Resource of Canada

Noram Capital Management Inc.
390 Bay St., Suite 1400
Toronto, Ont. M5H 2Y2
(416) 364-2642
Fax: (416) 364-1928

Noram Canadian Convertible
Securities
Noram Convertible Securities

Ontario Teachers' Group
60 Mobile Dr.
Toronto, Ont. M4A 2P3
(416) 751-8300
Fax: (416) 751-3394

OTG Aggressive Equity
OTG Balanced
OTG Diversified

Peter Cundill & Associates Ltd.
1200 Sun Life Plaza
1100 Melville St.
Vancouver, B.C. V6E 4A6
(604) 685-4231
1-800-663-015
Fax: (604) 689-9532

Cundill Security
Cundill Value

Phillips, Hager & North Ltd.
1700-1055 West Hastings St.
Vancouver, B.C. V6E 2H3
(604) 684-4361
1-800-661-6141
Fax: (604) 684-5120

PH&N Balanced
PH&N Bond
PH&N Canadian
PH&N Dividend Income
PH&N Money Market
PH&N Pooled Pension
PH&N RSP Equity
PH&N U.S.
PH&N U.S. Pooled Pension
Vintage Fund

Prudential Funds
200 Consilium Place
Scarbrough, Ont. M1H 3E6
(416) 296-0777
Fax: (416) 296-3186

Prudential Diversified
Prudential Dividend
Prudential Growth
Prudential Income
Prudential Money Market
Prudential Natural Resources
Prudential Precious Metals

Pursuit Financial Management Corp.
44 Victoria St., Suite 1715
Toronto, Ont. M5C 1Y2
(416) 947-9216
1-800-668-1314
Fax: (416) 947-1585

Pursuit American
Pursuit Canadian Equity
Pursuit Income
Pursuit Money Market

RBC Dominion Pemberton Securities Inc.
P.O. Box 11105, Royal Centre
1420-1055 West Georgia St.
Vancouver, B.C. V6E 3P3
(604) 665-0160
Fax: (604) 665-0180

Pacific Growth
Pacific Retirement Balanced
Pacific U.S. Growth

Royal Bank Investment Management Inc.
26th Floor, South Tower
Royal Bank Plaza
Toronto, Ont. M5J 2J5
(416) 974-0616
Fax: (416) 974-4076

RoyFund Balanced
RoyFund Bond
RoyFund Equity
RoyFund Money Market

Royal Trust Co.
Suite 3900, Royal Trust Tower
Toronto-Dominion Centre
Toronto, Ont. M5W 1P9
(416) 981-7000
Fax: (416) 981-6286

Royal Lepage Commercial Real Estate
Royal Trust Advantage Balanced
Royal Trust Advantage Growth
Royal Trust Advantage Income
Royal Trust American Stock
Royal Trust Bond
Royal Trust Canadian Money Market
Royal Trust Canadian Stock
Royal Trust Energy
Royal Trust Global Investment
Royal Trust Japanese Stock
Royal Trust Mortgage
Royal Trust Precious Metals
Royal Trust Preferred Blue Chip

RoyCom Advisor Ltd.
1959 Upper Water St.
Suite 1506
Halifax, N.S. B3J 3J5
(902) 421-1223
1-800-565-1979
Fax: (902) 420-0559

Roycom-Summit Realty
Roycom-summit TDF

Sagit Management Ltd.
Suite 900, 789 West Pender St.
Vancouver, B.C. V6C 1H2
(604) 685-3193
1-800-663-1003
Fax: (604) 681-7536

Cambridge American
Cambridge Balanced
Cambridge Diversified
Cambridge Growth
Cambridge Pacific
Cambridge Resource
Cambridge Special Equity
Trans-Canada Bond
Trans-Canada Equity
Trans-Canada Income
Trans-Canada Money Market

Saxon Funds
Suite 1904, P.O. Box 95
Cadillac Fairview Tower
20 Queen St. W.
Toronto, Ont. M5H 3R3
(416) 979-1818
Fax: (416) 979-7424

Saxon Balanced
Saxon Small Cap
Saxon Stock
Saxon World Growth

Sceptre Investment Counsel Ltd.
26 Wellington St. E., Suite 1200
Toronto, Ont. M5E 1W4
(416) 360-4826
Fax: (416) 367-8716

Sceptre Balanced
Sceptre Bond
Sceptre Equity
Sceptre International
Sceptre Money Market

Scotia Funds
1 Richmond St. W., Suite 200
Toronto, Ont. M5H 3W4
(416) 866-4574
Fax: (416) 866-2108

Scotia American Equity Growth
Scotia Canadian Balanced
Scotia Canadian Equity Growth
Scotia Defensive Income
Scotia Income
Scotia Stock & Bond

Sovereign Life Insurance Co.
Suncor Tower
500 Fourth Ave., S.W.
Calgary, Alta. T2P 2V6
(403) 298-5433
Fax: (403) 298-5576

Sovereign Capital Security Bond
Sovereign Growth Equity
Sovereign Revenue Growth
Sovereign Save & Prosper

Spectrum Mutual Funds
55 University Ave., Mezzanine
Toronto, Ont. M5J 2H7
(416) 360-2200
Fax: (416) 360-2180

Spectrum Canadian Equity
Spectrum Cash Reserve
Spectrum Diversified
Spectrum Dividend
Spectrum Government Bond
Spectrum Interest
Spectrum International Equity
Spectrum Savings

St-Laurent Financial Corp.
425 de Maisonneuve Blvd. W.
Suite 1740
Montreal, Que. H3A 3G5
(514) 288-9258
Fax: (514) 288-7692

St-Laurent Actions
St-Laurent Epargne
St-Laurent Obligations
St-Laurent Retraite

Strata Mutual Funds Ltd.
101 Frederick St.
P.O. Box 9032
Kitchener, Ont. N2G 4R8
(519) 888-5022
Fax: (519) 888-5925

Strata Growth
Strata Income
Strata Money Market
StrataFund 40
StrataFund 60

Standard Life Assurance Co.
1245 Sherbrooke St. W.
Montreal, Que. H3G 1G3
(514) 284-6711
Fax: (514) 499-4908

Balanced 2000
Bond 2000
Equity 2000

Talvest Fund Management
1900 Place du Canada
Montreal, Que. H3B 2N2
(514) 875-7040
Fax: (514) 875-9304

Talvest American
Talvest Bond
Talvest Diversified
Talvest Global Diversified
Talvest Growth
Talvest Income
Talvest Money

Templeton Management Ltd.
4 King St. W.
P.O. Box 4070, Station A
Toronto, Ont. M5W 1M3
(416) 364-4672
Fax: (416) 364-1163

Developing Growth Stock
Templeton Canadian
Templeton Global Income
Templeton Growth
Templeton Heritage Bond
Templeton Heritage
Templeton Heritage Retirement
Templeton Treasury Bill

Top Fifty Financial Group Ltd.
Suite 1650, 999 West Hastings
Vancouver, B.C. V6C 2W2
(604) 682-6446
Fax: (604) 662-8594

Top Fifty Equity
Top Fifty T-Bill/Bond

Toronto Dominion Securities Inc.

Investment Management Group
T-D Bank Tower, 9th Floor
Toronto-Dominion Centre
P.O. Box 100
Toronto, Ont. M5K 1A2
(416) 982-6432
1-800-268-8558
Fax: (416) 982-6625

Green Line Canadian Balanced
Green Line Canadian Bond
Green Line Canadian Equity
Green Line Canadian Index
Green Line Canadian Money Market
Green Line Canadian Mortgage
Green Line U.S. Index
Green Line U.S. Money Market

Total Return Fund Inc.

Place Air Canada
500 Bd Rene-Levesque W.,
Suite 1005
Montreal, Que. H2Z 1W7
(514) 398-0435
Fax: (514) 875-6779

Total Return Fund

Tradex Investment Fund Ltd.

77 Metcalfe St., Suite 701
Ottawa, Ont. K1P 5L6
(613) 233-3394

Tradex Investment
Tradex Security

Trimark Investment Management Inc.

Suite 5200, Scotia Plaza
P.O. Box 205
Toronto, Ont. M5H 3Z3
(416) 362-7181
1-800-387-9823
Fax: (416) 362-8515

Trimark Canadian
Trimark Fund
Trimark Income Growth
Trimark Interest
Trimark Select Balanced
Trimark Select Canada
Trimark Select Growth

Trust General Investment Funds

1100 University St.
Montreal, Que. H3B 2G7
(514) 871-7530
Fax: (514) 871-8525

Trust General Balanced
Trust General Bond
Trust General Canadian Equity
Trust General Growth
Trust General International
Trust General Money Market
Trust General Mortgage
Trust General U.S. Equity

Trust La Laurentienne du Canada
1981 McGill College Ave.
15th Floor
Montreal, Que. H3A 2Y2
(514) 284-7007
Fax: (514) 284-3210

Trust La Laurentienne Actions
Trust La Laurentienne Equilibre
Trust La Laurentienne Obligations

Trust Prêt et Revenu
850, place d'Youville
Quebec City, Que. G1K 7P3
(418) 692-1221
Fax: (418) 692-1675

Trust Pret Revenu Fonds H
Trust Pret Revenu American
Trust Pret Revenu Obligations
Trust Pret Revenu Retraite
Trust Pret Revenu Canadien

20/20 Group Financial Inc.
IBM Tower, Suite 2802
79 Wellington St.
Toronto, Ont. M5K 1H1
(416) 862-2020
1-800-268-8690
Fax: (416) 862-9981

20/20 American Tactical Asset
Allocation
20/20 Canadian Asset Allocation
20/20 Canadian Growth
20/20 Dividend
20/20 Income
20/20 Money Market
20/20 RSP Growth
20/20 Sunset
20/20 U.S. Growth
20/20 World
Sunrise Fund

United Financial Management Ltd.
200 King St. W.
Toronto, Ont. M5H 3W8
(416) 598-7777
1-800-263-1867
Fax: (416) 598-7821

United Accumulative
United Accumulative Retirement
United American
United Canadian Money Market
United Mortgage
United Portfolio of Funds
United Portfolio of RSP Funds
United Security Fixed Income
United U.S. Dollar Money Market
United Venture
United Venture Retirement

Universal Group
401 Bay St., 12th Floor
Toronto, Ont. M5H 2Y4
(416) 364-1145
1-800-268-9374
Fax: (416) 364-2969

Universal American
Universal Canadian Bond
Universal Canadian Equity
Universal Canadian Resource
Universal Global
Universal Pacific
Universal Sector American
Universal Sector Canadian
Universal Sector Currency
Universal Sector Global
Universal Sector Pacific
Universal Sector Resource

VanCity Investment Services Ltd.
515 West 10th Ave.
Vancouver, B.C. V5Z 4A8
(604) 877-7639
Fax: (604) 877-7639

Ethical Growth

The Growth of an Investment

This table shows:

1. How an investment of $100 a month (ignoring acquisition fees) would have grown if invested in a typical Canadian equity fund during the ten years ended June 30, 1991 and,

2. A withdrawal plan in which $100,000 (ignoring any acquisition or redemption fees) was invested at June 30, 1981 and $1,000 a month was withdrawn for the subsequent ten years.

Month	Return	Cumulative Contribution	Value of Plan	Cumulative Withdrawal	Value of Plan
1981-07	-3.1%	$100	$97	$1,000	$95,902
08	-3.6%	$200	$190	$2,000	$91,468
09	-9.2%	$300	$263	$3,000	$82,098
10	-1.5%	$400	$358	$4,000	$79,899
11	5.6%	$500	$483	$5,000	$83,338
12	0.8%	$600	$588	$6,000	$83,040
1982-01	-6.8%	$700	$642	$7,000	$76,412
02	-3.3%	$800	$717	$8,000	$72,896
03	-3.0%	$900	$793	$9,000	$69,716
04	-2.7%	$1,000	$868	$10,000	$66,806
05	-2.1%	$1,100	$948	$11,000	$64,395
06	-7.0%	$1,200	$974	$12,000	$58,878
07	3.5%	$1,300	$1,112	$13,000	$59,928
08	10.3%	$1,400	$1,336	$14,000	$65,089
09	0.3%	$1,500	$1,440	$15,000	$64,254
10	9.2%	$1,600	$1,682	$16,000	$69,174
11	2.6%	$1,700	$1,829	$17,000	$69,995
12	6.7%	$1,800	$2,058	$18,000	$73,682
1983-01	5.9%	$1,900	$2,285	$19,000	$77,013
02	3.4%	$2,000	$2,466	$20,000	$78,632
03	2.5%	$2,100	$2,630	$21,000	$79,585
04	6.0%	$2,200	$2,892	$22,000	$83,327
05	2.0%	$2,300	$3,053	$23,000	$84,027
06	-0.5%	$2,400	$3,138	$24,000	$82,620

Month	Return	Cumulative Contribution	Value of Plan	Cumulative Withdrawal	Value of Plan
07	1.9%	$2,500	$3,301	$25,000	$83,229
08	0.3%	$2,600	$3,411	$26,000	$82,477
09	1.0%	$2,700	$3,545	$27,000	$82,263
10	-3.7%	$2,800	$3,512	$28,000	$78,256
11	5.2%	$2,900	$3,799	$29,000	$81,326
12	0.4%	$3,000	$3,915	$30,000	$80,643
1984-01	-1.2%	$3,100	$3,967	$31,000	$78,683
02	-2.9%	$3,200	$3,949	$32,000	$75,405
03	-0.9%	$3,300	$4,014	$33,000	$73,750
04	-2.8%	$3,400	$4,000	$34,000	$70,717
05	-3.2%	$3,500	$3,968	$35,000	$67,438
06	-0.6%	$3,600	$4,044	$36,000	$66,034
07	-4.8%	$3,700	$3,944	$37,000	$61,850
08	9.0%	$3,800	$4,408	$38,000	$66,421
09	1.3%	$3,900	$4,567	$39,000	$66,279
10	-2.0%	$4,000	$4,571	$40,000	$63,927
11	0.3%	$4,100	$4,684	$41,000	$63,093
12	2.3%	$4,200	$4,892	$42,000	$63,518
1985-01	7.9%	$4,300	$5,387	$43,000	$67,550
02	-0.7%	$4,400	$5,447	$44,000	$66,062
03	-0.7%	$4,500	$5,507	$45,000	$64,582
04	2.5%	$4,600	$5,747	$46,000	$65,198
05	6.1%	$4,700	$6,203	$47,000	$68,159
06	0.7%	$4,800	$6,349	$48,000	$67,657
07	0.9%	$4,900	$6,510	$49,000	$67,298
08	1.5%	$5,000	$6,708	$50,000	$67,301
09	-4.7%	$5,100	$6,486	$51,000	$63,115
10	1.9%	$5,200	$6,714	$52,000	$63,341
11	6.9%	$5,300	$7,284	$53,000	$66,706
12	3.4%	$5,400	$7,635	$54,000	$67,976
1986-01	0.6%	$5,500	$7,780	$55,000	$67,369
02	-0.7%	$5,600	$7,823	$56,000	$65,889
03	6.1%	$5,700	$8,409	$57,000	$68,929
04	-0.6%	$5,800	$8,458	$58,000	$67,515
05	0.8%	$5,900	$8,629	$59,000	$67,076
06	-1.3%	$6,000	$8,612	$60,000	$65,172
07	-3.2%	$6,100	$8,434	$61,000	$62,095
08	4.5%	$6,200	$8,922	$62,000	$63,918
09	-0.2%	$6,300	$9,002	$63,000	$62,774
10	1.1%	$6,400	$9,197	$64,000	$62,434
11	1.5%	$6,500	$9,436	$65,000	$62,363
12	-1.2%	$6,600	$9,424	$66,000	$60,632

Month	Return	Cumulative Contribution	Value of Plan	Cumulative Withdrawal	Value of Plan
198701	7.0%	$6,700	$10,191	$67,000	$63,881
02	3.4%	$6,800	$10,641	$68,000	$65,049
03	6.8%	$6,900	$11,469	$69,000	$68,461
04	0.6%	$7,000	$11,640	$70,000	$67,882
05	1.0%	$7,100	$11,852	$71,000	$67,527
06	2.0%	$7,200	$12,193	$72,000	$67,890
07	4.9%	$7,300	$12,901	$73,000	$70,246
08	-0.3%	$7,400	$12,968	$74,000	$69,070
09	-2.1%	$7,500	$12,796	$75,000	$66,634
10	-15.4%	$7,600	$10,914	$76,000	$55,393
11	-0.4%	$7,700	$10,972	$77,000	$54,182
12	3.7%	$7,800	$11,486	$78,000	$55,207
1988-01	-1.3%	$7,900	$11,431	$79,000	$53,469
02	3.4%	$8,000	$11,922	$80,000	$54,281
03	3.6%	$8,100	$12,456	$81,000	$55,239
04	1.0%	$8,200	$12,685	$82,000	$54,807
05	-1.6%	$8,300	$12,585	$83,000	$52,949
06	4.1%	$8,400	$13,209	$84,000	$54,139
07	-1.1%	$8,500	$13,167	$85,000	$52,560
08	-1.7%	$8,600	$13,042	$86,000	$50,667
09	0.3%	$8,700	$13,183	$87,000	$49,826
10	3.1%	$8,800	$13,689	$88,000	$50,348
11	-3.1%	$8,900	$13,359	$89,000	$47,780
12	2.4%	$9,000	$13,786	$90,000	$47,941
1989-01	5.7%	$9,100	$14,681	$91,000	$49,685
02	-0.5%	$9,200	$14,703	$92,000	$48,424
03	-0.2%	$9,300	$14,781	$93,000	$47,350
04	1.7%	$9,400	$15,140	$94,000	$47,175
05	3.1%	$9,500	$15,705	$95,000	$47,614
06	2.5%	$9,600	$16,193	$96,000	$47,783
07	5.1%	$9,700	$17,131	$97,000	$49,241
08	0.9%	$9,800	$17,393	$98,000	$48,703
09	-0.9%	$9,900	$17,342	$99,000	$47,283
10	-0.4%	$10,000	$17,372	$100,000	$46,093
11	1.6%	$10,100	$17,754	$101,000	$45,836
12	0.5%	$10,200	$17,945	$102,000	$45,070
1990-01	-5.7%	$10,300	$17,011	$103,000	$41,489
02	1.0%	$10,400	$17,282	$104,000	$40,490
03	0.4%	$10,500	$17,444	$105,000	$40,048
04	-7.3%	$10,600	$16,257	$106,000	$36,111
05	7.4%	$10,700	$17,565	$107,000	$37,777
06	-0.6%	$10,800	$17,564	$108,000	$36,563

Month	Return	Cumulative Contribution	Value of Plan	Cumulative Withdrawal	Value of Plan
07	0.5%	$10,900	$17,753	$109,000	$35,745
08	-4.5%	$11,000	$17,055	$110,000	$33,148
09	-4.0%	$11,100	$16,467	$111,000	$30,819
10	-2.2%	$11,200	$16,208	$112,000	$29,152
11	2.5%	$11,300	$16,721	$113,000	$28,889
12	1.8%	$11,400	$17,131	$114,000	$28,422
91-01	0.8%	$11,500	$17,365	$115,000	$27,643
02	4.9%	$11,600	$18,315	$116,000	$27,988
03	2.1%	$11,700	$18,794	$117,000	$27,565
04	-0.6%	$11,800	$18,785	$118,000	$26,406
05	2.7%	$11,900	$19,392	$119,000	$26,115
06	-1.3%	$12,000	$19,244	$120,000	$24,782

Survey of Annual Fund Performance

und	1991	1990	1989	1988	1987	1986	1985	1984	1983	1982
quity Funds- RRSP-Eligible										
)/20 Cdn Asset Allocation	8.9	5.8	....	....	....	....	....	....	....	....
)/20 Cdn Growth Fund	7.7	1.9	....	....	....	....	....	....	....	....
)/20 RSP Growth Fund	7.2	....	....	....	....	....	....	....	....	....
)/20 Sunset Fund	9.0	2.5	13.7	1.6	10.9	....	....	....	....	....
BC Fully Managed Fund	17.7	5.3	22.5	....	....	....	....	....	....	....
BC Fundamental Value Fund	27.1	6.2	....	....	....	....	....	....	....	....
GF Canadian Equity Fund	-1.2	-9.1	9.2	-7.0	12.0	27.2	35.5	2.6	80.4	-31.5
GF Cdn Resources Fund	-11.8	15.8	-6.1	-15.5	69.4	-15.4	-3.5	-11.3	70.9	-52.4
GF Convertible Income Fund	3.4	-6.2	....	....	....	....	....	....	....	....
GF Growth Equity Fund	2.4	-4.1	4.4	-17.0	20.3	33.2	21.5	-7.6	90.9	-49.8
IC Advantage Fund	14.5	-8.0	11.7	-9.2	16.7	....	....	....	....	....
dmax Canadian Performance	-1.4	....	....	....	....	....	....	....	....	....
l-Canadian Compound Fund	3.3	2.7	7.0	-9.3	15.3	16.8	18.3	3.8	26.9	4.8
l-Canadian Dividend Fund	3.2	2.8	7.0	-9.3	15.3	16.7	17.6	3.0	24.5	4.8
lied Canadian Fund	16.3	-4.6	4.1	-28.6	23.9	....	....	....	....	....
tamira Balanced Fund	-0.9	-5.0	8.6	-14.3	12.5	21.3	....	....	....	....
tamira Capital Growth Fund	3.2	6.3	12.0	-14.6	18.6	10.0	26.2	-8.9	61.3	-11.5
tamira Equity Fund	13.7	18.0	32.7	....	....	....	....	....	....	....
tamira Growth & Income Fund	10.8	3.5	12.2	12.6	12.3	....	....	....	....	....
tamira Resource	8.7	....	....	....	....	....	....	....	....	....
tamira Special Growth Fund	14.3	4.6	8.0	-14.9	12.5	....	....	....	....	....
ssociate Investors	6.0	-3.6	15.0	-0.3	14.9	15.0	33.7	4.2	74.6	-30.6
PI Cdn Equity Fund	-4.5	-1.3	5.3	....	....	....	....	....	....	....
PI One Decision Fund	4.4	0.9	9.4	-4.6	10.3	....	....	....	....	....
arrtor Canadian Fund	10.8	2.3	12.4	0.4	9.5	14.1	....	....	....	....
atirente-Section Action	-1.4	-4.4	13.4	....	....	....	....	....	....	....
atirente-Section Diversifiee	8.7	0.2	13.5	....	....	....	....	....	....	....
ssett Canadian Fund	8.7	-1.3	12.2	-6.8	12.9	25.8	26.9	-1.2	....	....
olton Tremblay Cda Cum Fund	-0.9	-4.6	16.0	-7.7	10.7	19.4	11.7	-2.0	80.0	-32.4
olton Tremblay Cdn Balanced	6.1	-0.3	10.6	....	....	....	....	....	....	....
olton Tremblay Discovery	10.7	-9.8	3.4	....	....	....	....	....	....	....
olton Tremblay Optimal Cdn	5.0	-5.7	16.1	-5.2	10.3	....	....	....	....	....
olton Tremblay Planned Res	7.3	0.5	2.7	-14.0	25.0	5.9	4.0	-3.9	73.3	-33.8
ullock Balanced Fund	5.6	0.7	9.3	....	....	....	....	....	....	....
ullock Growth Fund	5.4	-8.5	7.3	-6.0	4.4	34.0	5.6	-14.2	75.3	-46.1
DA RSP Balanced Fund	8.5	2.7	14.0	0.5	13.0	19.2	24.5	0.4	49.9	-22.7
DA RSP Common Stock Fund	5.1	-1.7	16.2	-4.9	22.4	25.7	31.4	0.6	65.4	-21.5
BC Bal Income & Growth Fund	6.8	5.0	12.0	....	....	....	....	....	....	....
BC Canadian Equity Fund	1.4	2.8	....	....	....	....	....	....	....	....
aisse de Sec du Spectacle	10.5	1.6	9.9	-0.4	7.9	19.4	26.3	-4.1	43.8	1.3
ambridge Balanced Fund	12.7	2.3	8.4	6.9	10.3	29.4	26.7	0.1	26.5	8.3
ambridge Growth Fund	6.3	4.4	12.2	-0.4	26.3	40.7	31.5	-0.3	47.9	-16.9
ambridge Pacific Fund	1.4	12.1	-50.3	-15.9	1.9	19.5	16.9	7.5	....	....
ambridge Resource Fund	-8.4	-7.8	-2.4	-7.7	27.5	17.9	10.6	-0.3	48.6	-13.5
ambridge Special Equity	-19.3	-1.7	17.7	-7.1	....	....	....	....	....	....
anadian Investment Fund	-1.4	0.4	15.4	-7.8	11.1	15.1	27.3	-5.1	66.4	-22.7
anadian Protected Fund	7.0	6.4	5.8	8.8	5.9	22.3	....	....	....	....
apstone Investment Trust	10.3	5.5	9.8	-10.6	10.1	24.6	26.9	-3.8	36.4	1.1
da Life Bal Eqty Income E-2	2.4	-4.8	15.4	0.3	14.3	26.9	33.9	-0.6	65.7	-25.7

Fund	1991	1990	1989	1988	1987	1986	1985	1984	1983	198
Cda Life Cdn & Intl Equity S-9	0.7	-5.2	16.5	1.7	14.0	23.0	31.1	-1.0	64.3	-26
Cda Life Managed Fund S-35	6.1	-0.7	13.0	3.5	11.4	20.0	27.4	....	....	
Cda Trust Inv Fund Equity	1.5	-0.1	12.7	-9.3	19.2	19.5	25.3	-9.5	67.3	-27
Cda Trust RRSP Equity	3.4	-0.1	11.2	-9.8	16.8	18.4	27.3	-8.1	70.2	-31
Cdn Anaesthetists Mutual Accum	1.7	0.6	11.9	-3.7	20.4	21.7	27.2	-2.6	59.5	-25
Central Guaranty Equity	1.4	-2.9	16.5	-8.0	11.9	19.8	31.0	0.7	65.5	-19
Central Guaranty Property Fd	2.3	8.3	15.6	11.4	6.8					
Citadel Premier Fund	4.8	0.2	12.0	-6.2	25.0	12.5	22.4	-6.4	54.5	-11
Colonia Growth Fund	2.6	-3.9	3.2							
Confed Growth Fund	-0.4	-7.0	14.6	-3.4	16.3	25.0	33.9	-2.6	74.6	-31
Corporate Investors Fund	1.7	-2.6	10.3	-2.0	22.3	2.4	27.7	3.3	63.0	-21
Corporate Investors Stock Fund	5.1	-8.0	-9.8	-31.4	13.9	43.0	26.4	-1.5	81.2	-45
Counsel Real Estate Fund	8.4	12.4	14.5	13.7	14.6	21.0	12.6	10.6	....	
Crown Life Commitment Fund	2.6	-2.6	11.1	-4.7						
Crown Life Pen Foreign Equity	0.7	2.9	16.6	-6.0	19.2	26.7	31.1	-5.9	30.9	4
Crown Life Pensions Balanced	8.0	3.0	12.0	2.4	11.0					
Crown Life Pensions Equity	3.8	1.6	15.5	-3.6	18.2	26.9	36.0	-12.1	53.6	-28
Cundill Security Fund	-1.8	-4.5	9.7	2.1	22.6	10.3	23.9	3.4	56.7	-24
Dynamic Fund of Canada	2.4	1.2	12.5	-1.9	25.3	15.2	23.0	-6.5	65.2	-31
Dynamic Managed Portfolio	1.9	1.3	9.2	-2.3	30.0	....	....	....	....	
Dynamic Partners Fund	5.9	4.1								
Dynamic Precious Metals Fund	-3.6	3.1	-12.7	-7.2	73.2	-7.9	1.1	....	....	
EIF Canadian Fund	12.9	-39.4	18.1							
Elliott & Page Balanced Fund	9.0	-0.9	12.5	....	....					
Elliott & Page Equity Fund	8.6	-6.4	20.7	....	....					
Empire Balanced Fund #8	8.1	3.3	....							
Empire Equity Growth Fund #1	3.0	-1.8	14.6	3.5	16.9	23.5	31.9	-9.4	85.9	-26
Empire Equity Growth Fund #3	6.1	-4.1	18.3	0.8	7.2	44.2	27.5	-9.0	86.0	-22
Empire Equity Growth Fund #5	1.2	-2.0	10.3	-13.7	17.0	24.2	43.9	0.7	66.0	-27
Endurance Cdn Balanced Fund	7.7	2.9	....							
Endurance Cdn Equity	3.4		....							
Ethical Growth Fund	7.3	4.0	16.0	13.9	9.1					
Everest Balanced Fund	7.8	2.3	18.2	....						
Everest North American	1.2	-2.0	11.9	-13.6	10.9	26.7	25.0	-5.7	85.3	-28
Everest Special Equity Fund	5.4	-2.4	15.7	-19.5	....					
Everest Stock Fund	2.7	-0.2	....							
F.M.O.Q. Omnibus	12.0	3.9	10.4	2.9	17.5	15.6	25.1	0.7	42.4	4
Fd Des Prof Du Que-Balanced	14.0	3.6	10.8	....						
Fd Des Prof Du Que-Equity	4.7	-4.0	14.7	....						
Fidelity Cap Balanced Fund	6.7	0.4	11.0	....						
Fidelity Capital Builder Fund	13.9	1.3	14.3	....						
First Canadian Balanced Fund	8.4	-0.6	10.1	....						
First Canadian Equity Index	-0.5	-3.7	11.0	....						
First City Growth Fund	3.3	-8.5	13.1	-9.7	....					
First City Realfund	3.7	7.9	11.6	16.2	11.4	14.6	13.2	7.8		
Fonds Desjardins Actions	3.2	-4.7	15.3	-11.0	8.7	16.2	24.9	-10.4	76.2	-29
Fonds Desjardins Equilibre	8.6	0.9	12.2	-0.6	....					
Fonds Ficadre Actions	0.6	0.9	10.7	-23.7	13.0	31.0	....			
Fonds Ficadre Equilibree	4.8	2.4	12.5	-10.0	11.3	....				
Fonds SNF actions	-2.9	-15.0	-3.6	-20.5	....					
Fonds SNF equilibre	5.4	0.9	9.2	-9.5	14.8	23.6	26.6	1.8	40.9	-3
FuturLink Cdn Growth	1.8	-1.0	15.2	....	....					
FuturLink Select Fund	5.2	-0.3	12.6	....						
GBC Canadian Growth	15.2	10.4	....							
Global Strategy Americas	1.0	6.9	10.0	-18.0	....					
Global Strategy Canadian	4.2	-0.2	13.0	....						
Global Strategy Corp	13.5	7.5	4.3	-17.2	24.9	....				
Goldtrust	-3.2	3.1	-18.3	-20.9	56.8	17.4	-7.1	-4.1	94.1	-34
Great-West Life Diversified RS	6.0	2.7	10.6	0.4	12.1	14.6	....			
Great-West Life Eqt/Bond	8.8	1.9	10.8	....						
Great-West Life Equity	3.7	1.8	9.9	-12.5	....					
Great-West Life Equity Index	0.0	-3.9	11.2	-6.8	22.5	14.0	-18.4	40.5	....	
Great-West Life Real Estate	-4.3	11.5	9.9	10.4	7.3	10.7	9.2	10.2	5.0	13.
Green Line Cdn Balanced	6.6	-1.6	14.1	....						
Green Line Cdn Equity	1.3	-5.6	19.0	....						
Green Line Cdn Index	0.5	-3.5	11.6	-6.2	23.3	....				
Guardian Balanced Fund	12.2	5.8	9.7	5.9	14.7	11.5	24.4	0.2	50.5	-8.
Guardian Cdn Equity Fund	-2.4	-4.2	7.0	-7.6	14.5	34.5	23.6	-7.7	59.7	-24.

nd	1991	1990	1989	1988	1987	1986	1985	1984	1983	1982
uardian Diversified Fund	6.9	8.9	....	....	....	....	....	....	....	....
uardian Enterprise Fund	1.5	5.7	2.5	-1.9	8.9	24.4	24.4	0.2	86.9	-24.6
uardian Growth Equity	4.2	6.5	....	....	....	....	....	....	....	....
yro Equity	-3.4	-0.7	9.0	-1.0	28.4	....	....	....	....	....
ongkong Bank Balanced	5.0	....								
ongkong Bank Eqt Index	2.7	....								
yperion Managed Trust	8.5	4.8								
perial Growth Cdn Equity	3.0	-5.9	27.4	17.3	31.3	23.1	28.9	-5.0	71.3	-27.4
perial Growth Diversified	7.4	2.5	....							
dustrial Dividend Fund	-8.7	-5.8	2.7	6.1	27.4	16.5	33.2	6.5	69.7	-21.4
dustrial Equity Fund	-12.5	-13.0	-2.9	-0.5	31.4	18.1	16.8	0.3	88.1	-25.4
dustrial Future Fund	-0.9	-2.6	11.0	....						
dustrial Growth Fund	-1.5	-2.5	8.4	4.5	27.7	16.4	27.1	2.8	77.7	-17.1
dustrial Horizon Fund	0.4	-1.7	10.1	15.2						
dustrial Pension Fund	-9.8	-7.9	3.5	4.3	23.4	20.8	30.6	0.6	84.0	-21.2
tegra Balanced Fund	8.6	-2.5	8.8	....						
vesNAT Balanced Fund	10.1	-0.8	....							
vesNAT Equity Fund	3.4	1.4	....							
vestors Cdn Equity Fund	6.6	2.1	9.1	-6.9	10.1	27.9	25.5	....		
vestors Income Plus Port	10.9	3.5	....							
vestors Income Portfolio	14.2	4.5	....							
vestors Pooled Equity	4.3	-1.1	12.2	-3.0	15.7	15.4	27.0	-4.8	64.9	-27.0
vestors Real Property Fund	5.3	7.3	11.7	9.4	10.0	10.0	9.8	....		
vestors Retire Plus Port	6.7	3.4	....							
vestors Retirement Mutual	1.9	-2.7	12.7	4.6	20.4	13.6	26.7	-3.9	58.3	-27.0
vestors Summa Fund	1.9	-3.3	12.5	-3.1	....					
rislowsky Finsco Balanced	6.5	....								
rislowsky Finsco Cdn Eqt	3.6	-0.8	13.5	-9.2	13.3	....				
nes Heward Cdn Balanced	7.8	0.2	8.1	-2.3	6.4	22.0	18.4	....		
nes Heward Fund	4.5	-9.7	10.7	-3.9	11.8	29.4	31.6	-5.7	73.8	-34.7
ndmark Canadian	7.5	-0.1	....							
ndon Life Diversified Fund	5.7	1.0	12.4	....						
ndon Life Equity Fund	1.1	-8.1	15.0	-0.3	21.0	19.0	28.7	-3.8	65.3	-21.3
tus Fund	7.6	0.4	9.0	-6.1	10.4	19.6	25.7	....		
D Equity Fund	0.9	0.1	10.6	6.1	20.5	20.5	33.9	2.3	62.0	-12.1
D Realty Fund A	-0.1	14.4	14.8	7.7	19.9	5.4	10.1	8.3	....	....
ackenzie Equity Fund	-8.6	-7.1	6.5	4.8	20.8	23.1	29.6	3.0	67.9	-26.8
ackenzie Sentinel Cda Eqt	-6.1	-4.4	6.1	-13.0	22.4	....				
anulife 1 Capital Gains	2.3	0.3	11.8	-8.0	24.3	14.4	28.6	....		
anulife 1 Diversified	6.4	0.5	10.7	-1.2	18.3	13.1	21.6	-2.9	46.5	-3.2
anulife 1 Equity	3.7	-1.9	10.5	-6.1	20.3	9.8	22.5	-7.3	63.4	-19.1
anulife 2 Capital Gains	1.5	-0.4	11.0	-8.7	23.4	13.6	27.7	....		
anulife 2 Diversified	5.6	-0.3	9.9	-2.0	17.5	12.3	20.7	-3.6	45.5	-3.9
anulife 2 Equity	2.9	-2.7	9.7	-6.8	19.4	9.0	21.6	-8.0	62.3	-19.7
argin of Safety Canadian	3.7	....	....	....						
aritime Life Balanced Fund	8.7	0.7	11.2	1.9	....					
aritime Life Growth Fund	-1.0	-4.0	13.5	-11.1	15.2	24.7	34.8	-2.8	73.2	-30.9
arlborough Fund	-6.5	-6.9	11.6	-16.0	13.7	23.0	25.5	-10.4	74.0	-32.3
cLean Budden Balanced Fund	5.9	1.6	13.4	-5.3	10.8	23.1	27.3	-0.7	45.7	-4.9
cLean Budden Balanced Growth	9.3	2.8	....							
cLean Budden Equity Growth	1.1	-2.7	....							
etLife MVP Balanced	5.5	2.2	11.0	-4.1	....					
etLife MVP Equity	-1.5	-0.5	12.9	-11.8	....					
etfin Real Estate Growth Fd	10.3	-6.1	9.0	10.3	24.9	11.5	7.0	....		
etropolitan Balanced Growth	6.4	0.1	9.1	-17.1	7.0	24.7	18.9	-4.1	54.7	-31.6
etropolitan Cdn Mutual Fund	-0.8	-3.2	10.4	-13.6	10.5	26.4	....			
ontreal Trust Balanced	9.0	8.4	....							
ontreal Trust Equity Fund	5.8	-2.0	10.1	-3.9	22.3	14.6	24.5	-9.6	66.1	-30.2
ontreal Trust RRSP-Balanced	8.6	6.7	....							
ontreal Trust RRSP-Equity	4.4	-2.0	11.7	-6.1	20.9	17.7	25.0	-9.7	69.3	-29.5
ontreal Trust RRSP-Tot Ret	10.4	1.0	....							
ontreal Trust Total Return	11.4	1.7	....							
ultiple Opportunities Fund	-3.9	27.3	-35.9	-27.2	93.5	....				
utual Canadian Index Fund	1.0	-0.4	10.4	....						
utual Diversifund 25	9.0	1.5	11.1	3.0	7.0	15.9	....			
utual Diversifund 40	6.3	-2.9	14.1	0.6	6.9	19.7	....			
utual Diversifund 55	3.9	-4.2	16.0	-1.0	7.8	20.9	....			
utual Equifund	-1.9	-8.3	20.4	-6.2	7.9	26.7	....			

Fund	1991	1990	1989	1988	1987	1986	1985	1984	1983	198
NN Balanced Fund	5.8	0.3	8.1	-0.9	....	....	....	....	....	
NN Canadian 35 Index Fund	1.2	-2.3	....	....	....	....	....	....	....	
NN Canadian Growth Fund	4.7	-6.5	9.9	-16.6	20.3	14.6	34.9	-5.6	85.3	-17
NN Gold Bullion Fund	2.5	-10.6	-17.7	....	....	....	....	....	....	
NW Canadian Fund	7.2	3.3	12.1	-8.0	18.4	35.0	32.0	-7.4	83.8	-29
National Trust Equity Fund	6.7	0.8	10.9	-9.7	14.6	24.9	31.0	-5.9	50.9	-20
Natural Resources Growth Fund	-8.9	-15.4	-2.7	-12.4	50.3	-8.1	0.1	-11.1	41.6	-10
O.I.Q. Fonds d'Actions	6.5	-0.3	13.1	-2.8	23.7	17.0	30.8	-7.6	85.3	-37
O.I.Q. Fonds d'Equilibre	12.3	3.6	10.2	2.8	17.2	16.1	25.8	-0.5	51.6	-14
Ont Teachers Grp Balanced	7.5	3.5	12.1	1.8	13.3	....	....	....	....	
Ont Teachers Grp Diversified	-1.4	-0.4	16.9	-4.7	17.3	21.3	34.7	-4.8	68.2	-26
Ont Teachers Grp Growth	-0.6	1.2	18.9	-4.5	18.4	24.8	38.4	-5.4	75.3	-28
PH&N Balanced Fund	9.5	5.7	....	....	....	....	....	....	....	
PH&N Canadian Fund	1.3	4.1	18.2	-2.9	16.1	29.7	28.1	-5.5	88.7	-40
PH&N Pooled Pension Trust	1.9	3.6	14.9	-4.7	18.7	23.8	28.6	-3.5	85.8	-34
PH&N RRSP Fund	1.1	5.2	17.9	-6.3	16.5	29.0	29.3	-7.2	95.3	-38
Protected American Fd	9.1	6.3	5.4	7.2	3.1	....	....	....	....	
Prudential Diversified Inv	9.6	-2.3	13.7	....	....	....	....	....	....	
Prudential Growth Fund	-1.0	-4.0	12.1	-15.6	27.9	23.7	27.9	-5.8	74.7	-35
Prudential Natural Resource	-6.5	14.4	18.7	....	....	....	....	....	....	
Prudential Precious Metals	-15.8	12.2	2.1	....	....	....	....	....	....	
Pursuit Cdn Equity Fund	11.1	-9.6	-2.2	-13.9	5.9	66.4	22.8	-4.7	....	
RoyFund Balanced Fund	4.3	3.8	9.8	....	....	....	....	....	....	
RoyFund Equity Ltd	-6.3	0.1	10.2	-8.3	12.1	34.9	35.2	-0.9	82.1	-40
Royal Life Balanced Fund	11.8	....	....	....	....	....	....	....	....	
Royal Life Equity Fund	11.6	....	....	....	....	....	....	....	....	
Royal Trust Adv Balanced Fd	8.4	3.3	17.1	0.2	....	....	....	....	....	
Royal Trust Cdn Stock Fund	2.6	-4.3	15.1	-5.7	17.8	11.3	24.6	-8.6	79.0	-34
Royal Trust Energy Fund	-7.4	9.4	5.3	-11.4	66.6	-23.7	0.1	-10.3	39.2	-41
Royal Trust Precious Metals	-3.1	-7.7	....	....	....	....	....	....	....	
Roycom-Summit Realty Fund	7.7	12.1	10.7	....	....	....	....	....	....	
Roycom-Summit TDF Fund	7.2	9.9	12.5	14.6	....	....	....	....	....	
Saxon Balanced Fund	3.9	-8.0	3.9	-13.1	4.5	....	....	....	....	
Saxon Small Cap	-2.0	-13.4	9.0	-9.1	11.8	....	....	....	....	
Saxon Stock Fund	1.5	-5.4	2.0	-12.9	5.5	....	....	....	....	
Sceptre Balanced Fund	8.7	0.9	11.7	3.4	13.4	....	....	....	....	
Sceptre Equity Fund	3.2	-0.1	13.4	4.4	....	....	....	....	....	
Scotia Canadian Balance Fd	3.6	1.3	9.2	-5.0	....	....	....	....	....	
Scotia Canadian Eqt Growth Fd	7.6	-2.4	9.9	-10.9	....	....	....	....	....	
Scotia Stock & Bond Fund	4.3	0.6	12.5	-0.9	....	....	....	....	....	
Sovereign Growth Equity Fund	-0.5	1.6	9.3	-7.9	....	....	....	....	....	
Sovereign Revenue Growth Fund	7.3	-0.1	11.3	4.4	....	....	....	....	....	
Sovereign Save & Prosper	8.3	3.7	5.6	8.9	8.2	-5.8	4.7	5.2	9.1	
Special Opportunities Fund	5.9	-15.6	3.5	....	....	....	....	....	....	
Spectrum Canadian Equity Fd	2.6	-4.3	10.1	-3.3	....	....	....	....	....	
Spectrum Diversified Fund	7.2	-0.1	10.2	1.6	....	....	....	....	....	
St-Laurent Fonds d'Actions	0.4	-4.0	12.2	-13.6	16.4	....	....	....	....	
St-Laurent Fonds de Retraite	8.5	0.0	12.3	5.0	8.1	....	....	....	....	
Standard Life Bal 2000	11.7	3.1	10.2	1.0	....	....	....	....	....	
Standard Life Equity 2000	6.7	2.5	9.4	-7.5	....	....	....	....	....	
Strata Fund 60	7.4	-1.9	....	....	....	....	....	....	....	
Strata Growth Fund	2.8	-5.1	....	....	....	....	....	....	....	
StrataFund 40	10.2	-0.6	....	....	....	....	....	....	....	
Talvest Diversified Fund	8.4	3.2	9.1	6.3	13.9	....	....	....	....	
Talvest Growth Fund	10.6	-1.3	8.8	-0.6	25.7	15.4	27.5	-2.8	52.8	-29.
Templeton Heritage Retirement	-3.4	-1.0	....	....	....	....	....	....	....	
Top Fifty Equity Fund	2.2	-5.3	....	....	....	....	....	....	....	
Tradex Investment Fund Ltd	1.1	0.4	12.1	-3.2	20.4	20.8	26.1	-2.4	67.1	-26.
Trans-Canada Equity Fund	1.4	-1.0	10.9	-1.0	26.1	47.0	34.2	-0.3	54.0	-25.
Trans-Canada Income	5.0	-1.9	10.8	3.5	16.9	30.3	32.4	2.7	27.7	-3.
Trans-Canada Pension Fund	6.4	1.4	10.2	-6.0	15.4	23.2	25.6	7.7	....	
Trimark Canadian Fund	5.1	3.1	16.9	1.6	19.6	18.1	31.5	-0.9	85.1	
Trimark Income Growth Fund	7.2	2.7	13.2	....	....	....	....	....	....	
Trimark Select Balanced	10.2	....	....	....	....	....	....	....	....	
Trimark Select Canada Fund	7.9	2.4	....	....	....	....	....	....	....	
Trust General Balanced Fund	7.6	-1.3	12.0	-0.2	....	....	....	....	....	
Trust General Canadian Equity	2.3	-5.8	10.9	-8.2	14.8	19.7	26.1	-4.9	63.5	-36.
Trust General Growth Fund	2.7	-10.5	25.2	....	....	....	....	....	....	

205 SURVEY OF ANNUAL FUND PERFORMANCE

nd	1991	1990	1989	1988	1987	1986	1985	1984	1983	1982
ust La Laurentienne Action	3.0	-5.8	17.0	-6.0	13.4	....	....	....	....	....
ust La Laurentienne Equilibr	9.8	....	....	....	....	....	....	....	....	....
ust Pret Revenu Canadien	3.0	-3.2	12.5	-14.8	17.8	11.1	12.2	-3.8	78.4	-35.6
ust Pret Revenu Retraite	8.9	3.7	10.0	-1.4	11.1	16.0	17.2	3.6	44.5	-7.9
nited Accumulative Retirement	9.5	-4.3	16.0	-2.2	4.8	22.3	42.9	2.4	54.4	-29.0
nited Portfolio of RSP Fds	12.4	-0.1	....							
nited Venture Retirement Fund	3.3	-11.9	13.1	-9.8	13.7	28.9	31.9	-4.5	66.9	-40.5
niversal Canadian Equity	-6.5	-7.0	7.6	11.0	17.1	24.3	31.1	1.3	54.4	-13.4
niversal Canadian Resource	-14.0	-3.6	-8.8	-4.1	51.2	-11.7	4.3	-3.6	81.6	-39.2
king Canadian Fund Ltd	1.6	-11.2	16.9	-2.6	11.1	20.6	25.9	-2.4	66.8	-29.8
ntage Fund	10.5	12.9	17.7	-10.2	25.1	....				
altaine Balanced Fund	9.8	1.5	12.0	1.0	13.3	16.0	21.9	1.5	37.1	1.6
altaine Dividend Growth Fd	5.7	-0.2	13.2	-2.6	....					
orking Ventures Cdn Fund	8.5	....								
HIGHEST IN GROUP	27.1	27.3	32.7	17.3	93.5	66.4	43.9	40.5	95.3	13.0
LOWEST IN GROUP	-19.3	-39.4	-50.3	-31.4	1.9	-23.7	-18.4	-14.2	5.0	-52.4
AVERAGE IN GROUP	4.3	-0.2	10.3	-4.2	18.0	19.6	23.8	-2.1	63.2	-23.2

uity Funds Not RRSP-Eligible

nd	1991	1990	1989	1988	1987	1986	1985	1984	1983	1982
)/20 Amer Tact Asset Allocati	4.7	4.2	....	....						
)/20 US Growth Fund	5.1	10.8	....							
)/20 World Fund	-11.6	10.5	4.3	....						
JF American Growth Fund	-2.6	5.0	21.2	-15.0	8.4	27.0	33.3	-6.0	62.9	-5.3
JF Japan Fund	-16.3	16.1	-6.8	4.6	31.8	92.9	15.9	22.6	32.4	-21.0
JF Special Fund	4.7	8.2	15.3	-8.2	10.5	31.2	23.4	-10.3	96.1	-12.6
C Value Fund	3.7	....								
dmax American Performance	-2.5	....								
lied International Fund	10.9	-9.6	-2.6	-27.7	47.0	....				
tamira Diversified Fund	-10.2	-9.3	5.7	-23.0	3.2	42.5	....			
PI American Equity Growth	6.6	13.1	-17.9	....						
PI Europe & Far East Fund	-25.3	4.0	-9.6	....						
PI Global Equity Fund	-2.5	17.8	11.8	....						
PI Option Equity Fund	-7.4	-6.0	10.2	....						
rrtor American Fund	2.5	28.0	24.9	-14.8	11.9	51.2	36.4	-28.9	96.8	....
rrtor Intl Fund	-19.5	16.9	-2.5	-24.5	15.6	....				
ssett Special Fund	6.8	4.0	....							
lton Tremblay International	-5.5	13.0	11.2	-15.2	19.5	41.1	25.4	1.1	67.6	-9.2
lton Tremblay Taurus Fund	2.1	5.3	14.0	-22.7	1.1	23.8	11.9	-4.3	58.2	-9.9
llock American Fund	22.4	32.1	15.8	-20.7	21.2	56.0	16.8	-16.2	62.6	-16.0
Global Fund	-6.8	....								
BC Global Equity Fund	-10.7	13.4	5.4	....						
mbridge American Fund	-0.2	10.0	2.9	-14.7	....					
mbridge Diversified Fd	-6.9	-2.7	6.4	8.9	19.8	30.9	28.1	3.6	36.2	-12.0
apstone International	4.4	14.5	10.4	-6.2	....					
da Life U.S. & Intl Eqty S-34	3.0	13.3	17.1	-7.4	13.3	31.7	27.8	....		
entury DJ Mutual Fund	3.3	17.7	5.1	-25.6	14.3	....				
andill Value Fund	-5.8	1.7	10.4	10.4	16.5	22.4	13.5	5.5	67.2	-0.3
veloping Growth Stock Fd	-0.9	8.1	....							
ynamic American Fund	-4.0	7.5	16.4	-8.1	22.7	22.3	31.1	2.9	58.5	-11.1
ynamic Europe 1992 Fund	-17.4	....								
F International Fund	9.6	-21.3	8.9	....						
npire Group Equity Growth #6	9.8	-2.8	13.0	-3.2	12.1	....				
npire International Fund #9	3.2	13.2	....							
durance Global Equity	-2.6	....								
erest International Fund	-8.1	26.0	30.0	....						
tro International	-13.2	17.4	-1.6	....						
tro Tiger Fund	-8.9	....								
M.O.Q. Fonds de Placement	13.3	7.7	7.8	-0.8	23.3	12.7	21.4	....		
delity Intl Portfolio Fund	-7.4	22.8	11.6	....						
nds Desjardins International	-2.1	15.8	17.1	-17.0	9.5	43.4	19.9	-7.4	37.4	-4.4
BC International Growth	-12.5	....								
BC North American Growth	-5.5	-1.8	14.2	-7.2	11.2	29.0	23.6	-14.1	88.5	-28.7
obal Strategy Europe	-13.0	14.4	11.5	-25.7	....					
obal Strategy Far East	-10.0	19.7	12.1	-8.8	....					
obal Strategy Fund	-7.3	12.1	11.3	-17.3	24.7	....				
obal Strategy Intl Real Est	-14.3	....								
oldFund	-1.1	3.4	-20.4	-20.0	63.8	7.8	-10.6	-3.4	96.2	-28.1

Fund	1991	1990	1989	1988	1987	1986	1985	1984	1983	19
Green Line U.S. Index	5.4	14.0	17.8	-7.8	....	....				
Guardian American Equity	4.2	11.3	12.3	-13.1	12.8	22.1	10.5	-12.7	41.1	-7
Guardian Global Equity Fd	-12.1	10.0	8.8	-13.9	13.3	51.3	20.2	-7.6	39.1	-20
Guardian North American Fund	0.3	5.7	14.5	-24.0	3.1	24.7	13.1	-12.3	45.1	-1
Guardian Pacific Rim Corp	-6.2	1.9	-2.1	....						
Guardian Vantage International	-9.6	-5.0		....						
Guardian Vantage U.S. Equity	6.7	12.1		....						
Hyperion Asian Trust	-11.7	....								
Imperial Growth N.A. Equity	-12.1	-5.7	12.1	-6.8	24.2	24.3	28.0	-8.9	75.8	-28
Industrial American Fund	-1.1	7.7	8.3	-6.3	18.4	26.3	29.9	-1.3	55.9	-5
Industrial Global Fund	-14.1	8.6	2.8	-1.4	32.1	....				
Investors Global Fund Ltd	-6.4	20.5	3.2	-14.9		....				
Investors Growth Plus Port	5.2	4.9		....						
Investors Growth Portfolio	-1.2	7.1		....						
Investors Japanese Growth	-9.5	-1.7	-2.6	4.5	31.8	87.9	7.2	14.4	34.3	-15
Investors Mutual of Canada	8.1	-0.7	11.6	-1.9	18.4	12.7	21.6	-5.9	68.6	-19
Investors N.A. Growth Fund	7.3	7.9	21.8	-9.8	18.8	25.5	28.5	-7.4	69.2	-23
Investors Retire Growth Port	2.7	0.9		....						
Investors Special Fund	9.4	11.9	18.3	-10.0	16.6	21.3	17.7	-17.9	89.6	-30
Investors U.S. Growth Fund	8.0	7.7	15.8	-14.4	18.5	25.3	27.2	-12.2	66.5	-14
Jarislowsky Finsco Amer Eqt	6.0	9.1	5.6	-14.8	11.9	....				
Jones Heward American Fund	3.6	5.1	20.9	-17.5	14.6	39.0	20.2	2.2	....	
Landmark American	7.4	7.0		....						
Landmark International	0.1	16.7		....						
London Life U.S. Equity Fund	-2.9	-7.4	18.6	....						
MD Growth Investment	-9.5	10.1	8.7	-5.2	25.8	36.9	37.2	0.7	74.3	-16
MD Realty Fund B	-0.7	14.4	14.8	7.5	19.1	4.1	8.7	7.9	....	
Mackenzie Sentinel Amer Eqt	-3.7	10.2	19.7	....						
Mackenzie Sentinel Global	-15.3	10.0	4.7	-21.3		....				
Margin of Safety Fund	16.3	5.2		....						
McLean Budden Amer Growth	15.2	18.0		....						
Metropolitan Collective Mutual	0.5	15.1	11.3	-27.7	6.1	28.9	14.9	-1.0	60.0	-5
Metropolitan Speculators	1.4	16.0	7.8	-20.6	29.1	....				
Metropolitan Venture Fund	-0.9	14.8	8.8	-21.6	17.8	35.1	11.9	-12.0	45.7	-5
Montreal Trust Intl Fund	-1.3	12.9	7.1	-15.7	18.7	37.8	36.1	-4.1	42.6	-1
Mutual Amerifund	-2.6	3.4	10.4	-3.6	9.3	....				
NN Global Fund	-16.8	9.9	6.1	-18.5		....				
NW Equity Fund Ltd	8.7	20.4	14.6	-15.1	6.3	26.1	26.6	-7.4	55.0	-5
PH&N U.S. Fund	9.7	17.6	13.1	-10.6	8.1	28.8	32.4	-15.8	86.2	-4
PH&N U.S. Pooled Pension Fund	10.5	19.4	13.8	-8.8	8.7	28.7	33.4	-8.4	82.0	-3
Pursuit American Fund	21.9	12.1	6.9	-18.1		....				
Royal Trust Adv Growth Fund	5.8	2.9	10.7	-4.4						
Royal Trust American Stock	1.8	18.2	16.1	-15.6	16.8	31.8	21.9	-11.9	45.4	-5
Royal Trust European Growth	-11.8	0.3	3.4	....						
Royal Trust Japanese Stock	-8.5	-4.7	-6.9	-4.7	42.4	87.7	....			
Saxon World Growth	-5.3	-5.1	29.0	-10.8	31.6	....				
Sceptre International Fund	-4.7	19.1	19.5	-4.6		....				
Scotia Amer Eqt Growth Fd	6.8	11.4	-5.9	-22.8		....				
Spectrum Intl Equity Fund	-5.1	11.2	6.9	-17.7		....				
Talvest American Fund	-8.8	9.5	7.8	-14.3	15.9	....				
Talvest Global Diversified	-8.0	14.9	6.1	....						
Templeton Growth Fund	-4.0	11.0	15.4	-10.4	19.3	31.8	28.1	6.7	56.2	-14
Templeton Heritage Fd	-5.7	7.9		....						
Trimark Fund	0.7	8.6	14.9	-0.5	17.5	31.2	26.5	-1.6	82.8	....
Trimark Select Growth Fd	0.0	11.4		....						
Trust General International	-10.2	21.5		....						
Trust General U.S. Equity	-0.3	10.5	19.2	-20.9	18.3	39.9	29.6	-14.1	....	
Trust Pret Revenu American	3.1	13.6	11.2	-22.3	15.0	34.4	24.3	-3.5	37.0	-7
United Accumulative Fund	8.4	3.4	25.7	-14.9	11.7	34.3	32.7	10.6	39.8	-17
United American Fund Ltd	12.6	2.2	19.9	-17.3	6.3	32.3	29.2	9.3	38.7	-10
United Portfolio of Funds	9.8	2.2		....						
United Venture Fund Ltd	-2.5	-14.5	11.2	-18.5	4.3	27.4	30.3	-3.1	55.5	-31
Universal American	0.0	9.4	8.8	-5.8	18.9	26.8	27.6	2.5	37.4	4
Universal Global	2.2	10.8	2.9	-11.4	19.0	....				
Universal Pacific	-7.0	21.4	2.0	-8.0	34.8	110.0	12.0	10.1	23.4	....
Universal Sector American	-1.3	8.5	8.1	....						
Universal Sector Canadian	-6.5	-7.4	7.4	....						
Universal Sector Global	2.3	10.4	2.2	....						

Fund	1991	1990	1989	1988	1987	1986	1985	1984	1983	1982
Universal Sector Pacific	-7.0	20.6	1.8	....	....	....	....	....	....	....
Universal Sector Resource	-12.7	-4.3	-9.0	....	....	....	....	....	....	....
Viking Commonwealth Fund	-1.7	6.5	14.4	-3.4	21.2	30.4	24.3	0.7	55.0	-7.7
Viking Growth Fund	-4.3	1.4	15.6	-8.5	15.2	42.3	27.6	-2.6	50.7	-17.3
Viking International Fund	-4.8	9.3	9.9	-5.2	10.4	32.4	21.1	6.0	54.2	-14.5
HIGHEST IN GROUP	22.4	32.1	30.0	10.4	63.8	110.0	37.2	22.6	96.8	4.2
LOWEST IN GROUP	-25.3	-21.3	-20.4	-27.7	1.1	4.1	-10.6	-28.9	23.4	-31.5
AVERAGE IN GROUP	-1.6	8.7	9.5	-11.9	18.1	35.6	22.9	-3.5	58.8	-12.6

Bond and Mortgage Funds

Fund	1991	1990	1989	1988	1987	1986	1985	1984	1983	1982
10/20 Income Fund	10.3	1.7	8.9	1.3	12.0	....	....	....	....	....
AGF Canadian Bond Fund	10.0	1.4	12.2	7.5	5.8	20.4	31.6	3.5	31.2	18.4
AGF Global Govt Bond*	4.4	11.2	2.6	1.6	....	....	....	....	....	....
Admax Canadian Income	10.3	3.1	....	....	....	....	....	....	....	....
All-Canadian Revenue Growth	9.6	9.3	8.9	6.6	9.0	6.1	20.0	5.5	22.5	11.3
Allied Income Fund	11.4	5.9	10.2	5.9	16.2	....	....	....	....	....
Altamira Bond Fund	11.7	3.6	11.9	....	....	....	....	....	....	....
Altamira Income Fund	14.9	5.8	13.6	10.4	7.5	11.8	21.8	3.2	26.8	13.8
BPI Canadian Bond Fund	9.4	3.8	8.2	....	....	....	....	....	....	....
BPI Global Income Fund*	1.0	-0.2	0.7	....	....	....	....	....	....	....
Batirente-Section Obligations	12.8	-0.1	11.1	....	....	....	....	....	....	....
Bissett Fiduciary Fund	14.4	2.6	11.8	8.1	....	....	....	....	....	....
Bolton Tremblay Bond	14.6	2.5	12.0	....	....	....	....	....	....	....
Bullock Bond Fund	12.7	1.4	8.0	6.1	4.0	9.2	11.0	9.3	10.7	6.8
CDA RSP Bond & Mortgage	14.1	6.2	10.6	8.2	8.1	14.0	21.2	4.8	32.2	15.3
CIBC Fixed Income Fund	12.8	2.6	11.3	....	....	....	....	....	....	....
CIBC Mortgage Income	17.1	7.2	9.4	7.5	8.8	10.3	15.3	8.6	21.6	15.4
Cda Life Fixed Income S-19	12.3	3.4	9.4	6.9	6.4	14.8	24.7	2.5	37.0	12.8
Cda Trust Income Investments	13.8	2.1	10.4	7.5	6.0	13.4	22.9	4.9	25.1	16.1
Cda Trust Inv Fund Income	8.2	4.4	9.5	6.6	6.8	17.1	26.7	4.6	27.6	14.3
Cda Trust RRSP Income	12.4	2.0	9.9	6.9	6.8	16.8	25.8	7.3	26.7	14.2
Cda Trust RRSP Mortgage	15.4	8.4	9.2	9.1	8.4	11.0	17.0	7.9	20.4	17.7
Central Guaranty Income	12.5	0.1	12.9	1.8	4.9	16.9	23.0	2.8	35.1	12.9
Central Guaranty Mortgage	14.2	6.7	7.9	8.8	7.3	9.2	15.1	6.8	19.5	18.5
Church Street Income	13.6	2.5	10.3	....	....	....	....	....	....	....
Confed Mortgage Fund	14.5	9.5	9.1	8.8	8.4	10.4	17.1	8.8	25.4	15.4
Crown Life Pensions Bond Fund	13.0	4.1	10.7	7.7	3.9	15.7	20.1	-6.0	33.6	7.5
Crown Life Pensions Mortgage	16.5	6.2	10.4	8.6	8.6	13.2	21.7	7.8	38.4	15.8
Dynamic Global Bond Fund	-0.7	5.4	2.3	....	....	....	....	....	....	....
Dynamic Income Fund	11.6	4.8	13.9	6.6	8.2	14.1	30.3	1.5	36.3	6.4
Elliot & Page Bond Fund	11.7	6.1	11.8	....	....	....	....	....	....	....
Empire Bond Fund #2	14.0	2.6	11.4	3.0	6.5	....	....	....	....	....
Empire Fixed Income Fund #4	15.6	2.5	12.9	9.1	6.1	....	....	....	....	....
Endurance Government Bond	13.8	4.6	....	....	....	....	....	....	....	....
Everest Bond Fund	12.0	2.9	13.3	10.8	....	....	....	....	....	....
Everest US Bond Fund*	-1.5	....	....	....	....	....	....	....	....	....
Fd Des Prof Du Que-Bonds	15.5	3.7	10.3	....	....	....	....	....	....	....
Fidelity Cap Conservation Fd	6.5	4.6	7.0	....	....	....	....	....	....	....
Finsco Bond Fund	11.4	1.6	9.5	7.8	5.0	14.9	....	....	....	....
First Canadian Bond Fund	13.6	0.9	10.1	....	....	....	....	....	....	....
First Canadian Mortgage Fund	19.2	7.8	9.0	9.2	9.2	11.5	18.4	8.5	21.4	18.4
First City Income Fund	13.1	7.9	10.3	6.5	....	....	....	....	....	....
Fonds Desjardins Hypotheques	14.8	8.6	9.1	9.5	8.8	11.2	18.9	5.8	25.1	17.3
Fonds Desjardins Obligations	13.9	1.1	10.8	7.1	5.4	15.9	29.8	-3.2	37.6	13.7
Fonds Ficadre Obligations	12.3	....	....	....	....	....	....	....	....	....
Fonds SNF obligations	14.1	2.3	10.4	....	....	....	....	....	....	....
FuturLink Government Bond	11.4	-0.8	12.8	....	....	....	....	....	....	....
FuturLink Mortgage Fund	15.0	11.8	....	....	....	....	....	....	....	....
GBC Canadian Bond	14.0	1.4	13.1	8.9	7.0	16.1	....	....	....	....
Global Strategy World Bond*	7.0	1.4	6.3	....	....	....	....	....	....	....
Great-West Life Bond Invest	13.3	0.0	10.6	7.4	5.9	14.7	26.0	1.9	29.0	10.1
Great-West Life Mortgage	13.3	3.5	10.8	7.8	6.7	12.5	18.8	5.3	24.9	15.7
Green Line Canadian Bond	12.2	2.5	7.4	....	....	....	....	....	....	....
Green Line Mortgage	16.2	7.0	11.6	9.7	8.5	10.5	13.7	8.7	22.1	18.3
Guardian Canada Bond Fund	11.4	10.8	10.3	7.0	....	....	....	....	....	....
Guardian Intl Income Fund	3.9	3.4	2.1	-1.4	....	....	....	....	....	....
Guardian Vantage Bond	10.9	10.8	....	....	....	....	....	....	....	....

Fund	1991	1990	1989	1988	1987	1986	1985	1984	1983	198
Gyro Bond	12.5	....	....	....	....	....	....	....	....	..
Hyperion Fixed Income	12.3	....	....	....	....	....	....	....	....	..
Industrial Bond Fund	12.6	1.2	....	....	....	....	....	....	....	..
Industrial Income Fund	8.8	-1.4	12.6	13.2	12.3	18.6	38.0	-0.5	39.0	5.
InvesNAT Income Fund	14.1	2.6	....	....	....	....	....	....	....	..
Investors Bond Fund	13.3	3.3	11.5	7.4	6.4	16.3	28.5	0.0	28.3	13.
Investors Mortgage Fund	15.7	7.1	9.0	8.8	8.4	11.4	18.5	7.0	23.8	16.
Investors Pooled Bond	15.3	3.8	12.7	9.4	8.3	17.4	29.5	0.6	30.8	14.
Investors Pooled Mortgage	16.8	8.7	9.9	9.5	9.3	12.4	20.4	7.1	27.4	15.
Jones Heward Bond	12.4	2.4	11.5	7.7	....	....	....	....	....	..
Landmark Bond	12.9	2.3	....	....	....	....	....	....	....	..
London Life Bond Fund	5.2	3.2	13.2	5.3	4.2	21.2	41.3	2.0	31.6	13.
London Life Mortgage Fund	16.4	7.5	8.9	8.7	9.3	13.7	22.9	5.3	41.9	15.
Mackenzie Income Fund	9.6	-0.9	12.9	13.0	12.5	17.6	30.3	4.3	27.6	14.
Mackenzie Sentinel Cda Bond	12.3	0.6	10.8	6.5	8.0	....	....	....	....	..
Manulife 1 Bond	14.2	3.0	11.8	8.5	7.3	14.8	22.9	2.7	35.5	13.
Manulife 2 Bond	13.4	2.2	11.0	7.7	6.6	14.0	22.0	1.9	34.5	12.
Maritime Life Bond	13.4	....	....	....	....	....	....	....	....	..
McLean Budden Fixed Income	14.4	5.2	....	....	....	....	....	....	....	..
MetLife MVP Bond	12.3	3.8	11.2	2.1	....	....	....	....	....	..
Metropolitan Bond Fund	13.3	2.8	9.6	-3.2	7.9	13.3	27.1	-4.8	31.4	2.
Montreal Trust Income Fund	13.2	0.9	11.8	6.6	7.7	19.5	25.1	-0.8	35.0	11.
Montreal Trust Mortgage Fund	14.5	8.9	8.9	8.9	8.2	10.7	16.6	7.7	20.2	17.
Montreal Trust RRSP-Income	12.6	0.2	11.2	6.7	8.2	17.9	23.1	2.8	43.6	9.
Montreal Trust RRSP-Mortgage	14.6	7.9	8.7	8.5	8.2	10.5	16.4	7.6	19.9	17.
NN Bond Fund	12.5	3.5	9.6	4.9	....	....	....	....	....	..
National Trust Income Fund	13.0	0.7	10.7	7.8	7.3	16.3	30.0	-2.3	43.0	9.
O.I.Q. Fonds d'Obligations	11.1	4.7	11.2	6.3	8.4	15.3	26.2	1.8	45.7	13.
PH&N Bond Fund	14.2	3.2	13.2	9.5	9.4	18.6	34.0	-3.2	44.8	9.
Prudential Income Fund	12.5	1.7	13.2	9.3	7.3	13.3	22.6	4.9	32.1	11.
Pursuit Income Fund	13.6	0.0	1.1	2.2	....	....	....	....	....	..
RoyFund Bond Fund	13.4	3.0	9.4	7.8	6.8	15.7	23.9	1.0	23.4	8.
Royal Life Income Fund	10.0	....	....	....	....	....	....	....	....	..
Royal Trust Adv Income Fd	10.3	4.3	11.4	3.1	....	....	....	....	....	..
Royal Trust Bond Fund	13.6	1.9	11.0	7.3	6.2	16.5	30.0	1.3	35.5	11.
Royal Trust Mortgage Fund	15.7	8.6	8.5	9.2	8.7	11.3	16.8	8.6	20.8	18.
Sceptre Bond Fund	16.1	5.8	8.4	8.5	7.4	....	....	....	....	..
Scotia Defensive Income Fd	12.3	3.7	8.3	....	....	....	....	....	....	..
Scotia Income Fund	11.4	4.5	10.0	6.9	....	....	....	....	....	..
Sovereign Capital Sec Bond	11.9	4.3	9.8	7.1	....	....	....	....	....	..
Spectrum Government Bond	10.7	....	....	....	....	....	....	....	....	..
Spectrum Interest Fund	12.1	3.7	9.8	6.0	....	....	....	....	....	..
St-Laurent Fonds d'Obligation	12.1	0.4	12.8	7.9	7.4	....	....	....	....	..
Standard Life Bond 2000	15.1	3.4	10.7	10.3	....	....	....	....	....	..
Strata Income Fund	14.0	2.4	....	....	....	....	....	....	....	..
Talvest Bond Fund	12.9	2.3	11.6	8.0	9.3	15.9	30.2	2.5	40.7	12.
Talvest Income Fund	13.5	5.6	9.1	8.3	8.6	10.3	19.1	5.8	22.3	16.
Templeton Global Income*	10.0	9.7	....	....	....	....	....	....	....	..
Templeton Heritage Bond	8.6	....	....	....	....	....	....	....	....	..
Top 50 T-Bill/Bond Fund	11.7	10.4	....	....	....	....	....	....	....	..
Tradex Security Fund	11.3	....	....	....	....	....	....	....	....	..
Trans-Canada Bond Fund	11.8	3.9	6.2	9.0	....	....	....	....	....	..
Trust General Bond Fund	13.6	0.6	11.6	7.3	5.4	17.8	32.9	1.6	31.9	14.
Trust General Mortgage Fund	15.2	8.0	8.0	7.9	9.1	12.7	21.7	7.7	23.9	17.
Trust La Laurentienne Obligati	10.6	7.6	6.8	6.4	9.5	....	....	....	....	..
Trust Pret Revenu Fonds H	15.9	7.7	9.3	8.6	9.6	10.9	17.6	7.6	24.2	16.
Trust Pret Revenu Obligat	12.6	4.4	8.6	....	....	....	....	....	....	..
United Mortgage	14.7	6.5	6.2	7.9	7.6	8.9	15.0	9.2	14.8	17.
United Security Fund	16.3	8.4	2.5	5.2	8.1	15.0	27.0	-0.1	21.9	11.
Universal Canadian Bond	12.0	0.9	13.6	12.1	7.0	15.7	36.4	-3.7	50.8	7.
Viking Income Fund	13.0	2.5	10.4	7.7	7.3	16.5	30.9	0.5	37.9	10.
Waltaine Income Fund	9.7	2.9	11.1	2.8	....	....	....	....	....	..
HIGHEST IN GROUP	19.2	11.8	13.9	13.2	16.2	21.2	41.3	9.3	50.8	18.
LOWEST IN GROUP	-1.5	-1.4	0.7	-3.2	3.9	6.1	11.0	-6.0	10.7	2.
AVERAGE IN GROUP	12.4	4.1	9.9	7.2	7.8	14.1	23.8	3.6	29.9	13.

und	1991	1990	1989	1988	1987	1986	1985	1984	1983	1982
referred Dividend Funds										
0/20 Dividend Fund	6.4	2.9	13.9	1.2	14.3	....	....	....	....	....
GF High Income Fund	7.9	....	....	....	....	....	....	....		
llied Dividend Fund	-2.7	0.8	9.1	0.5	5.5	....	....	....	....	....
PI High Yield Fund	2.6	2.1	6.3	....	....	....	....	....		
olton Tremblay Income Fund	9.8	0.1	9.3	3.1	9.7	7.7	13.4	4.4	30.2	14.3
ullock Dividend Fund	6.8	2.2	12.9	0.0	6.2	10.7	....	....	....	....
ynamic Dividend Fund	7.2	2.0	10.1	5.9	11.1	....	....	....	....	....
uturLink Income Fund	13.4	-0.1	13.3	....	....	....	....	....		
uardian Pref Dividend Fund	5.7	1.6	8.4	3.9	8.7	....	....	....		
vestors Dividend Fund	10.6	1.5	12.9	3.6	9.9	9.8	24.2	2.5	55.3	-14.9
lontreal Trust Dividend Fund	9.3	0.4	10.1	-4.7	....	....	....	....		
H&N Dividend Income Fund	5.3	3.5	14.6	2.0	18.8	10.2	20.3	0.8	56.7	-11.1
rudential Dividend Fund	5.5	-11.8	8.0	6.4	....	....	....	....		
oyal Trust Pref Blue Chip	5.5	-0.6	11.0	0.7	7.2	....	....	....		
pectrum Dividend Fund	8.9	1.9	12.7	3.4	....	....	....	....		
iking Dividend Fund Ltd	6.2	2.2	13.5	3.5	11.5	15.3	23.5	6.2	55.4	-14.3
HIGHEST IN GROUP	13.4	3.5	14.6	6.4	18.8	15.3	24.2	6.2	56.7	14.3
LOWEST IN GROUP	-2.7	-11.8	6.3	-4.7	5.5	7.7	13.4	0.8	30.2	-14.9
AVERAGE IN GROUP	6.8	0.6	11.1	2.3	10.3	10.7	20.4	3.5	49.4	-6.5
oney Market Funds										
0/20 Money Market	10.9	....								
GF Money Market Account	11.3	12.1	10.4	8.4	7.8	9.3	10.8	9.4	12.0	18.2
lied Money Fund	10.3	11.4	9.2	8.1	7.9	....	....	....	....	
PI Money Market Fund	10.9	12.1	8.8	....	....	....	....			
tirente-Section MMK	12.8	9.7	9.7	....	....	....				
olton Tremblay Money Fund	11.5	12.3	10.5	8.7	8.2	9.4	11.0	9.1	11.7	....
ullock Money Market Fund	10.2	11.3	9.9	....	....	....				
OA Money Market Fund	11.8	12.2	10.5	8.2	7.5	9.6	11.0	9.5	11.5	16.1
BC Money Market Fund	11.2	12.4	....	....	....	....				
apstone Cash Management	11.9	12.3	10.0	....	....	....				
da Life Money Market S-29	11.7	11.1	9.7	7.3	6.0	7.7	10.0	9.3	12.4	17.2
hurch Street Money Market	11.4	11.4	9.6	....	....	....				
own Life Pen Short Term	11.8	12.6	9.3	9.3	7.4	10.0	10.8	9.0	11.3	17.1
ynamic Money Market Fund	12.2	11.8	8.9	8.1	7.2	8.9	10.3	....	....	
iott & Page Money Fund	12.4	12.6	10.8	8.6	8.5	10.1	....	....	....	
npire Money Market Fund #7	11.6	10.0	....	....	....	....				
erest Money Market Fund	11.8	12.6	11.5	8.1	....	....	....			
M.O.Q. Monetaire	11.3	11.8	....	....	....	....				
Des Prof Du Que-Money Mkt	12.8	9.6	9.9	....	....	....				
sco Cdn Money Mkt	11.3	12.2	9.8	8.4	7.9	9.5	....	....	....	
sco Cdn T-Bill Fund	10.8	11.9	9.9	....	....	....				
sco U.S. Dollar MMK*	6.5	7.9	7.2	6.3	....	....	....			
st Canadian Money Market	11.0	11.1	9.2	....	....	....				
st City Govt Money	11.5	....	....	....	....					
nds Desjardins Marche Moneta	10.9	11.6	....	....	....					
nds Ficadre Monetaire	9.6	11.7	9.6	7.0	7.5	9.0	....	....	....	
turLink Money Market	11.3	12.2	....	....	....	....				
BC Money Market Fund	11.6	12.4	....	....	....	....				
obal Strategy T-Bill Savings	9.6	11.4	9.7	....	....	....				
obal Strategy US Money*	5.7	7.3	7.2	....	....	....				
obal Strategy World Money	5.9	9.3	5.8	....	....	....				
eat-West Life Money Market	10.9	12.0	9.9	7.8	7.0	8.9	10.7	8.6	11.3	17.7
een Line Cdn Money Mkt	11.9	12.7	10.4	....	....	....	....			
een Line U.S. Money Mkt	6.6	7.8	....	....	....	....				
uardian Short Term Money Fund	11.8	13.0	10.9	8.7	7.7	9.3	10.7	9.3	11.4	17.7
uardian US Money Market*	6.7	8.4	8.6	....	....	....				
ongkong Bank Money Mkt	10.7	....	....	....	....					
perial Growth MMK Fund	10.9	10.1	....	....	....	....				
dustrial Cash Management Fd	11.5	12.5	10.7	8.1	7.8	9.4	....	....	....	
vestors Money Market Fund	11.1	11.6	10.1	8.3	7.2	8.9	....	....	....	
ndmark Short Term Interest	9.5	10.4	....	....	....	....				
ndon Life Money Market	11.6	....	....	....	....	....				
D Money Fund	11.4	11.6	9.3	7.6	7.1	9.0	10.5	9.3	11.6	17.5

Fund	1991	1990	1989	1988	1987	1986	1985	1984	1983	198
McLean Budden MMK Fund	11.1	10.8	....	....	....	....	....	....	....	
Metropolitan Protection	10.2	10.7	7.1	....	....	....	....	....	....	
Montreal Trust Money Market	11.3	12.0	10.4	....	....	....	....	....	....	.
Montreal Trust RRSP-MMK	11.5	11.6	10.1	....	....	....	....	....	....	.
Mutual Money Market Fund	10.7	11.3	9.9	7.7	6.8	8.1	....	....	....	
O.I.Q. Fonds Monetaire	11.9	11.8	9.8	8.1	8.4	9.3	11.6	9.3	14.3	17
PH&N Money Market Fund	11.7	12.7	10.4	8.3	....	....	....	....	....	.
Prudential Money Market Fund	11.9	12.2	10.0	8.8	....	....	....	....	....	.
Pursuit Money Market Fund	11.4	11.6	8.7	....	....	....	....	....	....	
RoyFund Money Market Fd	11.4	12.2	10.0	7.8	....	....	....	....	....	
Royal Trust Cdn Money Mkt	11.4	11.4	9.7	....	....	....	....	....	....	.
Sceptre Money Market Fund	11.5	12.1	10.1	....	....	....	....	....	....	
Spectrum Cash Reserve Fund	11.4	12.1	10.5	7.9	....	....	....	....	....	
Spectrum Savings Fund*	11.5	12.5	10.8	....	....	....	....	....	....	
St-Laurent Fonds d'Epargne	13.2	9.6	10.0	8.3	9.0	....	....	....	....	
Strata Money Market Fd	10.7	11.1	....	....	....	....	....	....	....	
Talvest Money Fund	12.0	12.2	10.8	7.9	4.6	....	....	....	....	
Templeton Treasury Bill	11.6	12.3	10.3	....	....	....	....	....	....	
Trans-Cda Money Market Fd	11.2	9.1	3.7	4.0	6.7	9.0	10.6	7.8	....	
Trimark Interest Fund	11.5	12.7	9.6	8.6	....	....	....	....	....	.
Trust General Money Market	12.1	10.7	8.2	11.2	....	....	....	....	....	
Trust Pret Revenu Money Mkt	11.4	11.1	....	....	....	....	....	....	....	.
United Cdn Money Market Fund	11.5	12.9	11.6	....	....	....	....	....	....	
United US$ Money Market*	4.6	7.2	8.7	....	....	....	....	....	....	
Universal Sector Currency*	6.8	7.1	5.1	....	....	....	....	....	....	.
Viking Money Market Fund	11.1	11.9	10.7	8.4	8.3	10.1	....	....	....	.
Waltaine Instant MMF	11.6	12.1	10.5	....	....	....	....	....	....	
HIGHEST IN GROUP	13.2	13.0	11.6	11.2	9.0	10.1	11.6	9.5	14.3	18.
LOWEST IN GROUP	4.6	7.1	3.7	4.0	4.6	7.7	9.6	7.8	11.3	16.
AVERAGE IN GROUP	10.8	11.3	9.5	8.1	7.4	9.1	10.6	9.0	11.9	17.

Market Indexes

	1991	1990	1989	1988	1987	1986	1985	1984	1983	198
91-Day Canada T-Bill	10.9	12.8	11.1	8.7	8.0	9.3	10.7	10.0	10.7	16.
Consumer Price Index	6.1	4.5	4.9	4.1	4.6	4.1	4.0	4.8	5.4	11.
ScotiaMcLeod Universe Bond Ind	15.3	2.8	12.3	8.7	8.4	18.2	31.9	1.1	40.8	11.
Standard & Poor's 500 Index	3.7	11.9	18.9	-15.2	20.6	38.2	34.9	2.2	53.3	-5.
TSE Total Return Index	1.9	-2.4	13.5	-5.2	24.6	17.4	26.7	-5.7	86.9	-39.

Survey of Fund Volatility and Compound Performance

his survey shows the average compound rate of return over three years, five years and ten years. he column labelled "Assets" is the net assets of the fund in millions of dollars. The column labelled %" shows the percentile ranking by volatility within the grouping. For example, a percentile ranking 5 for the fund means that 95% of the funds in the group are more volatile while 4% are less latile. The column labelled "St. D" shows the standard deviation. This measure indicates the nount by which a fund's rate of return is likely to diverge from its average monthly rate of return. A nd with a standard deviation of 6 is twice as volatile as a fund with the same rate of return with a andard deviation of 3.

nd	1yr	3yr	5yr	10yr	Assets	%	St.D.
uity Funds – RRSP-eligible							
)/20 Cdn Asset Allocation	8.9	....	....	....	132	N/A	....
)/20 Cdn Growth Fund	7.7	....	....	....	20	N/A	....
)/20 RSP Growth Fund	7.2	....	....	....	15	N/A	....
)/20 Sunset Fund	9.0	8.3	7.4	....	94	16	2.06
3C Fully Managed Fund	17.7	14.9	....	....	7	13	2.01
3C Fundamental Value Fund	27.1	....	....	....	2	N/A	....
3F Canadian Equity Fund	-1.2	-0.6	0.4	8.4	293	57	4.17
3F Cdn Resources Fund	-11.8	-1.4	6.6	-2.1	35	98	5.85
3F Convertible Income Fund	3.4	....	....	....	17	N/A	....
3F Growth Equity Fund	2.4	0.8	0.5	3.9	89	92	5.20
C Advantage Fund	14.5	5.5	4.5	....	10	97	5.57
1max Canadian Performance	-1.4	....	....	....	6	N/A	....
-Canadian Compound Fund	3.3	4.3	3.5	8.5	12	33	2.83
-Canadian Dividend Fund	3.2	4.3	3.5	8.2	14	33	2.84
ied Canadian Fund	16.3	4.9	0.4	....	!	86	5.04
taFund	....	....	....	....	87	N/A	....
tamira Balanced Fund	-0.9	0.7	-0.3	....	33	48	3.82
tamira Capital Growth Fund	3.2	7.1	4.4	8.4	7	53	4.04
tamira Equity Fund	13.7	21.2	....	....	65	44	3.47
tamira Growth & Income Fund	10.8	8.8	10.2	....	22	11	1.96
tamira Resource	8.7	....	....	....	4	N/A	....
tamira Special Growth Fund	14.3	8.9	4.3	....	9	69	4.48
sociate Investors	6.0	5.5	6.1	10.1	8	41	3.26
Cdn Equity Fund	-4.5	-0.2	....	....	3	54	4.05
1 One Decision Fund	4.4	4.8	3.9	....	17	34	2.96
rrtor Canadian Fund	10.8	8.4	7.0	....	4	15	2.03
tirente-Section Action	-1.4	2.2	....	....	5	33	2.89
tirente-Section Diversifiee	8.7	7.3	....	....	13	6	1.72
sett Canadian Fund	8.7	6.4	4.9	....	2	77	4.72
ton Tremblay Cda Cum Fund	-0.9	3.1	2.3	5.9	66	61	4.24
ton Tremblay Cdn Balanced	6.1	5.4	....	....	4	20	2.23
ton Tremblay Discovery	10.7	1.1	....	....	4	43	3.45
ton Tremblay Optimal Cdn	5.0	4.8	3.7	....	5	54	4.05
ton Tremblay Planned Res	7.3	3.5	3.6	3.8	18	99	5.99
lock Balanced Fund	5.6	5.2	....	....	1	6	1.68
lock Growth Fund	5.4	1.2	0.3	1.5	5	82	4.90
*A RSP Balanced Fund	8.5	8.3	7.6	9.6	10	19	2.19
*A RSP Common Stock Fund	5.1	6.3	6.9	11.7	34	59	4.19
3C Bal Income & Growth Fund	6.8	7.9	....	....	67	11	1.94

Fund	1yr	3yr	5yr	10yr	Assets	%	St.D
CIBC Canadian Equity Fund	1.4	....	....	....	36	N/A	..
Caisse de Sec du Spectacle	10.5	7.3	5.8	10.8	19	22	2.2
Caldwell Securities Associate	....	....	....	....	5	N/A	..
Cambridge Balanced Fund	12.7	7.7	8.1	12.7	6	4	1.4
Cambridge Growth Fund	6.3	7.6	9.4	13.5	27	43	3.4
Cambridge Pacific Fund	1.4	-17.3	-13.5	....	5	99	7.2
Cambridge Resource Fund	-8.4	-6.2	-0.6	5.0	2	89	5.1
Cambridge Special Equity	-19.3	-2.3	....	....	3	96	5.5
Canadian Investment Fund	-1.4	4.5	3.2	7.7	66	69	4.4
Canadian Protected Fund	7.0	6.4	6.7	....	2	2	0.9
Capstone Investment Trust	10.3	8.5	4.7	10.2	7	39	3.1
Cda Life Bal Eqty Income E-2	2.4	4.0	5.2	10.4	28	75	4.7
Cda Life Cdn & Intl Equity S-9	0.7	3.6	5.2	9.5	194	67	4.4
Cda Life Managed Fund S-35	6.1	6.0	6.5	....	311	28	2.5
Cda Trust Inv Fund Equity	1.5	4.5	4.3	7.4	28	84	4.9
Cda Trust RRSP Equity	3.4	4.7	3.9	6.9	289	86	5.0
Cdn Anaesthetists Mutual Accum	1.7	4.6	5.8	9.1	57	56	4.1
Central Guaranty Equity	1.4	4.7	3.4	9.5	15	66	4.3
Central Guaranty Property Fd	2.3	8.6	8.8	....	20	2	1.0
Citadel Premier Fund	4.8	5.6	6.6	9.2	6	81	4.8
Colonia Growth Fund	2.6	0.6	....	....	21	30	2.7
Confed Growth Fund	-0.4	2.0	3.6	8.8	7	53	4.0
Corporate Investors Fund	1.7	3.0	5.6	8.5	9	42	3.3
Corporate Investors Stock Fund	5.1	-4.5	-7.4	1.8	10	83	4.9
Counsel Real Estate Fund	8.4	11.7	12.7	....	73	3	1.0
Crown Life Commitment Fund	2.6	3.5	....	....	6	59	4.1
Crown Life Pen Foreign Equity	0.7	6.5	6.2	11.2	26	65	4.3
Crown Life Pensions Balanced	8.0	7.6	7.2	....	53	10	1.9
Crown Life Pensions Equity	3.8	6.8	6.8	8.8	84	56	4.1
Cundill Security Fund	-1.8	1.0	5.2	8.0	16	41	3.3
Dynamic Fund of Canada	2.4	5.2	7.5	8.0	158	45	3.6
Dynamic Managed Portfolio	1.9	4.1	7.5	....	87	29	2.6
Dynamic Partners Fund	5.9	....	....	....	43	N/A	..
Dynamic Precious Metals Fund	-3.6	-4.7	6.9	....	25	96	5.5
EIF Canadian Fund	12.9	-6.8	....	....	1	100	7.4
Elliott & Page Balanced Fund	9.0	6.7	....	....	3	17	2.1
Elliott & Page Equity Fund	8.6	7.0	....	....	6	49	3.9
Empire Fund #8	8.1	....	....	....	2	N/A	..
Empire Equity Growth Fund #1	3.0	5.0	7.0	11.0	185	64	4.3
Empire Equity Growth Fund #3	6.1	6.4	5.4	12.1	23	60	4.2
Empire Equity Growth Fund #5	1.2	3.0	2.0	9.1	20	79	4.7
Endurance Cdn Balanced Fund	7.7	....	....	....	43	N/A	..
Endurance Cdn Equity	3.4	....	....	....	11	N/A	..
Ethical Growth Fund	7.3	9.0	10.0	....	60	31	2.7
Everest Balanced Fund	7.8	9.2	....	....	6	21	2.2
Everest North American	1.2	3.5	1.2	7.8	13	73	4.6
Everest Special Equity Fund	5.4	6.0	....	....	2	88	5.0
Everest Stock Fund	2.7	....	....	....	9	N/A	..
F.M.O.Q. Omnibus	12.0	8.7	9.2	12.9	49	19	2.2
Fd Des Prof Du Que-Balanced	14.0	9.4	....	....	131	3	1.1
Fd Des Prof Du Que-Equity	4.7	4.9	....	....	18	30	2.6
Fidelity Cap Balanced Fund	6.7	5.9	....	....	18	28	2.5
Fidelity Capital Builder Fund	13.9	9.7	....	....	99	40	3.2
First Canadian Balanced Fund	8.4	5.9	....	....	23	16	2.0
First Canadian Equity Index	-0.5	2.1	....	....	36	44	3.5
First City Growth Fund	3.3	2.3	....	....	10	85	5.0
First City Realfund	3.7	7.7	10.1	....	211	4	1.1
Fonds Desjardins Actions	3.2	4.3	1.9	6.0	27	61	4.2
Fonds Desjardins Environ	....	....	....	....	5	N/A	..
Fonds Desjardins Equilibre	8.6	7.1	....	....	24	12	1.9
Fonds Ficadre Actions	0.6	4.0	-0.6	....	3	62	4.2
Fonds Ficadre Equilibree	4.8	6.5	3.9	....	4	32	2.7
Fonds SNF actions	-2.9	-7.3	....	....	!	83	4.9
Fonds SNF equilibree	5.4	5.1	3.8	10.1	9	35	3.0
FuturLink Cdn Growth	1.8	5.1	....	....	125	39	3.1
FuturLink Select Fund	5.2	5.7	....	....	12	21	2.2
GBC Canadian Growth	15.2	....	....	....	9	N/A	..
Global Strategy Americas	1.0	5.9	....	....	7	85	5.0

und	1yr	3yr	5yr	10yr	Assets	%	St.D.
lobal Strategy Canadian	4.2	5.5	....	....	93	18	2.18
lobal Strategy Corp	13.5	8.3	5.6	....	1	58	4.18
oldtrust	-3.2	-6.6	0.2	3.1	20	94	5.37
reat-West Life Diversified RS	6.0	6.4	6.2	....	50	14	2.02
reat-West Life Eqt/Bond	8.8	7.1	....	....	3	8	1.78
reat-West Life Equity	3.7	5.1	....	....	127	63	4.33
reat-West Life Equity Index	0.0	2.3	4.1	....	200	76	4.72
reat-West Life Real Estate	-4.3	5.4	6.8	8.2	323	1	0.81
reen Line Cdn Balanced	6.6	6.2	....	....	15	24	2.33
reen Line Cdn Equity	1.3	4.4	....	....	27	42	3.40
reen Line Cdn Index	0.5	2.7	4.6	....	34	76	4.72
uardian Balanced Fund	12.2	9.2	9.6	11.7	18	7	1.77
uardian Cdn Equity Fund	-2.4	0.0	1.1	7.0	25	75	4.70
uardian Diversified Fund	6.9	....	....	....	4	N/A	....
uardian Enterprise Fund	1.5	3.2	3.3	9.9	14	80	4.79
uardian Growth Equity	4.2	....	....	....	2	N/A	....
yro Equity	-3.4	1.5	5.8	....	45	93	5.22
ongkong Bank Balanced	5.0	....	....	....	2	N/A	....
ongkong Bank Eqt Index	2.7	....	....	....	6	N/A	....
yperion Managed Trust	8.5	....	....	....	63	N/A	....
nperial Growth Cdn Equity	3.0	7.3	13.7	13.5	81	94	5.28
nperial Growth Diversified	7.4	....	....	....	8	N/A	....
dustrial Balanced	....	....	....	....	47	N/A	....
dustrial Dividend Fund	-8.7	-4.1	3.6	10.2	177	92	5.18
dustrial Equity Fund	-12.5	-9.6	-0.7	6.5	64	72	4.59
dustrial Future Fund	-0.9	2.3	....	....	113	37	3.10
dustrial Growth Fund	-1.5	1.3	6.8	12.0	1339	65	4.37
dustrial Horizon Fund	0.4	2.8	....	1511	36	3.06	....
dustrial Pension Fund	-9.8	-4.9	2.0	9.8	73	90	5.13
tegra Balanced Fund	8.6	4.9	....	....	13	11	1.97
vesNAT Balanced Fund	10.1	....	....	....	4	N/A	....
vesNAT Equity Fund	3.4	....	....	....	10	N/A	....
vestors Cdn Equity Fund	6.6	5.9	4.0	....	326	61	4.24
vestors Income Plus Port	10.9	....	....	....	433	N/A	....
vestors Income Portfolio	14.2	....	....	....	315	N/A	....
vestors Pooled Equity	4.3	5.0	5.4	8.1	69	55	4.10
vestors Real Property Fund	5.3	8.1	8.7	....	282	1	0.54
vestors Retire Plus Port	6.7	....	....	....	263	N/A	....
vestors Retirement Mutual	1.9	3.8	7.1	8.5	971	57	4.14
vestors Summa Fund	1.9	3.5	....	....	60	51	3.98
rislowsky Finsco Balanced	6.5	....	....	....	7	N/A	....
rislowsky Finsco Cdn Eqt	3.6	5.2	3.7	....	6	67	4.43
nes Heward Cdn Balanced	7.8	5.3	4.0	....	5	25	2.37
nes Heward Fund	4.5	1.5	2.3	7.4	42	89	5.07
ndmark Canadian	7.5	....	....	....	37	N/A	....
ndon Life Diversified Fund	5.7	6.3	....	....	133	17	2.06
ndon Life Equity Fund	1.1	2.2	5.2	9.5	170	71	4.56
tus Fund	7.6	5.6	4.1	....	38	37	3.09
D Equity Fund	0.9	3.8	7.4	12.9	1071	45	3.66
D Realty Fund A	-0.1	9.5	11.1	....	251	9	1.84
ackenzie Equity Fund	-8.6	-3.3	2.7	8.7	57	80	4.82
ackenzie Sentinel Cda Eqt	-6.1	-1.6	0.3	....	29	87	5.04
anulife 1 Capital Gains	2.3	4.7	5.6	....	40	88	5.06
anulife 1 Diversified	6.4	5.8	6.7	10.1	379	31	2.72
anulife 1 Equity	3.7	4.0	4.9	7.7	228	94	5.31
anulife 2 Capital Gains	1.5	3.9	4.8	....	40	90	5.12
anulife 2 Diversified	5.6	5.0	5.9	9.3	379	40	3.22
anulife 2 Equity	2.9	3.2	4.1	6.8	228	81	4.84
arathon Equity Fund	....	....	....	....	!	N/A	....
argin of Safety Canadian	3.7	....	....	....	!	N/A	....
aritime Life Balanced Fund	8.7	6.8	....	....	70	27	2.47
aritime Life Growth Fund	-1.0	2.6	2.0	8.0	166	72	4.62
arlborough Fund	-6.5	-0.9	-1.5	4.2	2	97	5.75
cLean Budden Balanced Fund	5.9	6.9	5.1	10.7	8	35	3.03
cLean Budden Balanced Growth	9.3	....	....	....	!	N/A	....
cLean Budden Equity Growth	1.1	....	....	....	1	N/A	....
etLife MVP Balanced	5.5	6.2	....	....	4	27	2.51
etLife MVP Equity	-1.5	3.4	....	....	12	83	4.97

Fund	1yr	3yr	5yr	10yr	Assets	%	St.D
Metfin Real Estate Growth Fd	10.3	4.2	9.3	....	9	12	2.0
Metropolitan Balanced Growth	6.4	5.1	0.6	4.5	33	50	3.9
Metropolitan Cdn Mutual Fund	-0.8	2.0	0.2	....	26	70	4.5
Montreal Trust Balanced	9.0	....	....	....	1	N/A	..
Montreal Trust Equity Fund	5.8	4.5	6.0	7.2	17	56	4.1
Montreal Trust RRSP-Balanced	8.6	....	....	....	4	N/A	..
Montreal Trust RRSP-Equity	4.4	4.6	5.3	7.5	63	72	4.6
Montreal Trust RRSP-Tot Ret	10.4	....	....	....	3	N/A	..
Montreal Trust Total Return	11.4	....	....	....	1	N/A	..
Multiple Opportunities Fund	-3.9	-7.7	2.0	....	5	100	8.4
Mutual Canadian Index Fund	1.0	3.6	....	....	5	44	3.5
Mutual Diversifund 25	9.0	7.1	6.3	....	14	6	1.7
Mutual Diversifund 40	6.3	5.6	4.8	....	121	28	2.5
Mutual Diversifund 55	3.9	4.9	4.3	....	67	36	3.0
Mutual Equifund	-1.9	2.7	1.9	....	68	79	4.7
NN Balanced Fund	5.8	4.7	....	....	8	25	2.3
NN Canadian 35 Index Fund	1.2	....	....	....	2	N/A	..
NN Canadian Growth Fund	4.7	2.5	1.5	9.2	46	62	4.2
NN Gold Bullion Fund	2.5	-9.0	....	....	!	49	3.9
NW Canadian Fund	7.2	7.5	6.2	11.2	5	82	4.8
National Trust Balanced	....	....	....	....	8	N/A	..
National Trust Equity Fund	6.7	6.0	4.3	8.6	106	87	5.0
Natural Resources Growth Fund	-8.9	-9.1	-0.2	0.3	5	93	5.2
O.I.Q. Fonds d'Actions	6.5	6.3	7.6	9.0	45	70	4.5
O.I.Q. Fonds d'Equilibre	12.3	8.6	9.1	11.2	48	17	2.1
Ont Teachers Grp Balanced	7.5	7.6	7.5	....	13	23	2.3
Ont Teachers Grp Diversified	-1.4	4.7	5.1	9.5	27	60	4.2
Ont Teachers Grp Growth	-0.6	6.1	6.2	10.7	15	63	4.3
PH&N Balanced Fund	9.5	....	....	....	74	N/A	..
PH&N Canadian Fund	1.3	7.6	7.0	9.4	56	74	4.6
PH&N Pooled Pension Trust	1.9	6.7	6.5	9.9	69	78	4.7
PH&N RRSP Fund	1.1	7.8	6.5	9.7	29	84	4.9
Polymetric Performance	....	....	....	....	51	N/A	..
Protected American Fd	9.1	6.9	6.2	....	5	5	1.5
Prudential Diversified Inv	9.6	6.8	....	....	6	8	1.8
Prudential Growth Fund	-1.0	2.1	2.8	6.8	61	91	5.1
Prudential Natural Resource	-6.5	8.3	....	....	6	52	4.0
Prudential Precious Metals	-15.8	-1.2	....	....	3	78	4.7
Pursuit Cdn Equity Fund	11.1	-0.6	-2.2	....	3	91	5.1
RoyFund Balanced Fund	4.3	6.0	....	....	67	5	1.6
RoyFund Equity Ltd	-6.3	1.1	1.2	7.6	679	52	4.0
Royal Life Balanced Fund	11.8	....	....	....	3	N/A	..
Royal Life Equity Fund	11.6	....	....	....	5	N/A	..
Royal Trust Adv Balanced Fd	8.4	9.4	....	....	133	24	2.3
Royal Trust Cdn Stock Fund	2.6	4.2	4.7	6.5	251	77	4.7
Royal Trust Energy Fund	-7.4	2.2	9.5	-1.3	24	98	5.8
Royal Trust Precious Metals	-3.1	....	....	....	5	N/A	..
Roycom-Summit Realty Fund	7.7	10.1	....	....	12	9	1.8
Roycom-Summit TDF Fund	7.2	9.8	....	....	10	22	2.2
Saxon Balanced Fund	3.9	-0.3	-2.1	....	1	34	2.9
Saxon Small Cap	-2.0	-2.5	-1.2	....	2	48	3.8
Saxon Stock Fund	1.5	-0.7	-2.1	....	!	39	3.1
Sceptre Balanced Fund	8.7	7.0	7.5	....	32	22	2.2
Sceptre Equity Fund	3.2	5.3	....	....	3	66	4.4
Scotia Canadian Balance Fd	3.6	4.7	....	....	9	38	3.1
Scotia Canadian Eqt Growth Fd	7.6	4.9	....	....	34	73	4.6
Scotia Stock & Bond Fund	4.3	5.7	....	....	32	14	2.0
Sovereign Growth Equity Fund	-0.5	3.4	....	....	2	71	4.5
Sovereign Revenue Growth Fund	7.3	6.1	....	....	!	10	1.9
Sovereign Save & Prosper	8.3	5.8	6.9	....	19	0	0.4
Special Opportunities Fund	5.9	-2.6	....	....	5	95	5.4
Spectrum Canadian Equity Fd	2.6	2.6	....	....	36	47	3.7
Spectrum Diversified Fund	7.2	5.7	....	....	55	15	2.0
St-Laurent Fonds d'Actions	0.4	2.6	1.7	....	!	46	3.7
St-Laurent Fonds de Retraite	8.5	6.8	6.7	....	6	7	1.7
Standard Life Bal 2000	11.7	8.3	....	....	8	26	2.4
Standard Life Equity 2000	6.7	6.2	....	....	7	68	4.4
Strata Fund 60	7.4	....	....	....	8	N/A	..

Fund	1yr	3yr	5yr	10yr	Assets	%	St.D.
Strata Growth Fund	2.8	....	....	....	9	N/A	....
StrataFund 40	10.2	....	....	....	8	N/A	....
Talvest Diversified Fund	8.4	6.9	8.1	....	66	23	2.30
Talvest Growth Fund	10.6	5.9	8.2	8.6	64	55	4.08
Templeton Balanced Fund	....	....	....	....	36	N/A	....
Templeton Heritage Retirement	-3.4	....	....	....	5	N/A	....
Top Fifty Equity Fund	2.2	....	....	....	18	N/A	....
Tradex Investment Fund Ltd	1.1	4.4	5.8	9.3	45	50	3.96
Trans-Canada Equity Fund	1.4	3.6	6.8	12.1	16	45	3.59
Trans-Canada Income	5.0	4.5	6.7	11.6	6	29	2.59
Trans-Canada Pension Fund	6.4	5.9	5.2	....	!	67	4.41
Trimark Canadian Fund	5.1	8.2	9.0	....	489	68	4.48
Trimark Income Growth Fund	7.2	7.6	....	....	79	32	2.78
Trimark Select Balanced	10.2	....	....	....	113	N/A	....
Trimark Select Canada Fund	7.9	....	....	....	403	N/A	....
Trust General Balanced Fund	7.6	5.9	....	....	5	20	2.22
Trust General Canadian Equity	2.3	2.2	2.4	5.4	27	74	4.67
Trust General Growth Fund	2.7	4.8	....	....	!	47	3.80
Trust La Laurentienne Action	3.0	4.3	3.9	....	3	51	4.00
Trust La Laurentienne Equilibr	9.8	....	....	....	2	N/A	....
Trust Pret Revenu Canadien	3.0	3.9	2.4	4.5	13	78	4.72
Trust Pret Revenu Retraite	8.9	7.5	6.4	9.8	22	13	2.00
United Accumulative Retirement	9.5	6.7	4.5	9.3	146	38	3.11
United Portfolio of RSP Fds	12.4	....	....	....	24	N/A	....
United Venture Retirement Fund	3.3	1.0	1.1	5.4	41	58	4.18
Universal Canadian Equity	-6.5	-2.2	4.0	10.4	172	64	4.33
Universal Canadian Resource	-14.0	-8.9	1.9	0.7	18	95	5.55
Viking Canadian Fund Ltd	1.6	1.8	2.7	7.1	178	50	3.96
Vintage Fund	10.5	13.6	10.5	....	10	89	5.07
Waltaine Balanced Fund	9.8	7.7	7.4	11.1	46	18	2.18
Waltaine Dividend Growth Fd	5.7	6.1	....	....	5	26	2.43
Working Ventures Cdn Fund	8.5	....	....	....	5	N/A	....
HIGHEST IN GROUP	27.1	21.2	13.7	13.5			
LOWEST IN GROUP	-19.3	-17.3	-13.5	-2.1			
AVERAGE IN GROUP	4.3	4.2	4.6	8.3			

Equity Funds – Not RRSP-Eligible

Fund	1yr	3yr	5yr	10yr	Assets	%	St.D.
20/20 Amer Tact Asset Allocati	4.7	....	....	....	67	N/A	....
20/20 US Growth Fund	5.1	....	....	....	47	N/A	....
20/20 World Fund	-11.6	0.6	....	....	61	22	4.29
AGF American Growth Fund	-2.6	7.4	2.7	10.9	82	41	4.80
AGF Japan Fund	-16.3	-3.3	4.5	13.6	44	98	7.13
AGF Special Fund	4.7	9.3	5.8	12.7	134	62	5.18
AIC Value Fund	3.7	....	....	....	6	N/A	....
Admax American Performance	-2.5	....	....	....	19	N/A	....
Allied International Fund	10.9	-0.8	0.7	....	!	82	5.69
Altamira Diversified Fund	-10.2	-4.9	-7.3	....	15	28	4.41
BPI American Equity Growth	6.6	-0.3	....	....	2	49	5.02
BPI Europe & Far East Fund	-25.3	-11.1	....	....	!	74	5.51
BPI Global Equity Fund	-2.5	8.7	....	....	25	9	3.32
BPI Option Equity Fund	-7.4	-1.4	....	....	!	2	2.09
Barrtor American Fund	2.5	17.9	9.3	....	7	91	6.23
Barrtor Intl Fund	-19.5	-2.8	-4.4	....	5	56	5.08
Bissett Special Fund	6.8	....	....	....	1	N/A	....
Bolton Tremblay International	-5.5	5.9	3.8	12.6	177	30	4.49
Bolton Tremblay Taurus Fund	2.1	7.0	-0.9	6.1	20	51	5.03
Bullock American Fund	22.4	23.3	12.5	14.1	72	100	7.66
CB Global Fund	-6.8	....	....	....	6	N/A	....
CIBC Global Equity Fund	-10.7	2.2	....	....	15	14	3.61
Cambridge American Fund	-0.2	4.2	....	....	7	76	5.53
Cambridge Diversified Fd	-6.9	-1.2	4.7	10.1	8	6	3.21
Capstone International	4.4	9.7	....	....	!	13	3.52
Cda Life U.S. & Intl Eqty S-34	3.0	11.0	7.5	....	34	26	4.37
Century DJ Mutual Fund	3.3	8.5	1.7	....	!	73	5.51
Cundill Value Fund	-5.8	1.9	6.4	12.8	358	3	2.91
Developing Growth Stock Fd	-0.9	....	....	....	32	N/A	....
Dynamic American Fund	-4.0	6.3	6.2	12.2	48	23	4.29

Fund	1yr	3yr	5yr	10yr	Assets	%	St.D.
Dynamic Europe 1992 Fund	-17.4	....	....	....	62	N/A	....
Dynamic Global Green Fd	....	....	....	....	7	N/A	....
EIF International Fund	9.6	-2.1	....	....	!	77	5.55
Empire Group Equity Growth #6	9.8	6.4	5.5	....	47	38	4.64
Empire International Fund #9	3.2	....	....	....	!	N/A	....
Endurance Global Equity	-2.6	....	....	....	12	N/A	....
Everest International Fund	-8.1	14.6	....	....	4	16	4.00
Everest U.S. Equity	....	....	....	....	10	N/A	....
Extro International	-13.2	0.1	....	....	18	20	4.22
Extro Tiger Fund	-8.9	....	....	....	6	N/A	....
F.M.O.Q. Fonds de Placement	13.3	9.6	10.0	....	2	7	3.22
Fidelity Growth America	....	....	....	....	72	N/A	....
Fidelity Intl Portfolio Fund	-7.4	8.2	....	....	88	21	4.26
Fonds Desjardins International	-2.1	9.9	3.8	9.7	5	37	4.63
GBC International Growth	-12.5	....	....	....	5	N/A	....
GBC North American Growth	-5.5	1.9	1.8	7.2	123	80	5.68
Global Strategy Europe	-13.0	3.5	....	....	26	40	4.76
Global Strategy Far East	-10.0	6.5	....	....	20	89	6.02
Global Strategy Fund	-7.3	5.0	3.6	....	134	31	4.54
Global Strategy Intl Real Est	-14.3	....	....	....	7	N/A	....
GoldFund	-1.1	-6.6	1.3	3.4	7	95	6.35
Green Line U.S. Index	5.4	12.3	....	....	37	55	5.08
Guardian American Equity	4.2	9.2	5.0	7.0	18	69	5.30
Guardian Global Equity Fd	-12.1	1.7	0.5	6.7	4	71	5.36
Guardian North American Fund	0.3	6.7	-1.0	5.3	2	87	5.90
Guardian Pacific Rim Corp	-6.2	-2.2	....	....	3	90	6.19
Guardian Vantage International	-9.6	....	....	....	!	N/A	....
Guardian Vantage U.S. Equity	6.7	....	....	....	!	N/A	....
Hyperion Asian Trust	-11.7	....	....	....	32	N/A	....
Hyperion European Trust	....	....	....	....	11	N/A	....
Imperial Growth N.A. Equity	-12.1	-2.4	1.4	6.9	3	53	5.07
Industrial American Fund	-1.1	4.9	5.1	11.9	273	72	5.49
Industrial Global Fund	-14.1	-1.4	4.5	....	154	29	4.42
Investors European Growth	....	....	....	....	28	N/A	....
Investors Global Fund Ltd	-6.4	5.2	....	....	280	34	4.58
Investors Growth Plus Port	5.2	....	....	....	114	N/A	....
Investors Growth Portfolio	-1.2	....	....	....	142	N/A	....
Investors Japanese Growth	-9.5	-4.7	3.6	12.0	227	96	6.70
Investors Mutual of Canada	8.1	6.2	6.8	9.3	321	11	3.44
Investors N.A. Growth Fund	7.3	12.1	8.6	11.3	524	43	4.82
Investors Pacific Intl	....	....	....	....	48	N/A	....
Investors Retire Growth Port	2.7	....	....	....	110	N/A	....
Investors Special Fund	9.4	13.1	8.7	9.0	84	70	5.31
Investors U.S. Growth Fund	8.0	10.4	6.4	10.5	255	60	5.13
Jarislowsky Finsco Amer Eqt	6.0	6.9	3.1	....	7	24	4.32
Jones Heward American Fund	3.6	9.6	4.5	....	7	81	5.68
Landmark American	7.4	....	....	....	31	N/A	....
Landmark International	0.1	....	....	....	26	N/A	....
London Life U.S. Equity Fund	-2.9	2.2	....	....	27	19	4.19
MD Growth Investment	-9.5	2.7	5.3	13.5	786	65	5.22
MD Realty Fund B	-0.7	9.3	10.8	....	160	1	1.85
Mackenzie Sentinel Amer Eqt	-3.7	8.3	....	....	14	64	5.22
Mackenzie Sentinel Global	-15.3	-0.8	....	....	20	63	5.21
Margin of Safety Fund	16.3	....	....	....	4	N/A	....
McLean Budden Amer Growth	15.2	....	....	....	6	N/A	....
Metropolitan Collective Mutual	0.5	8.8	-0.2	8.2	26	46	4.92
Metropolitan Speculators	1.4	8.2	5.4	....	2	67	5.23
Metropolitan Venture Fund	-0.9	7.3	2.7	7.6	20	48	5.02
Montreal Trust Intl Fund	-1.3	6.1	3.6	11.6	18	50	5.03
Mutual Amerifund	-2.6	3.6	3.2	....	7	82	5.69
NN Global Fund	-16.8	-1.0	....	....	5	68	5.27
NW Equity Fund Ltd	8.7	14.5	6.2	11.4	2	97	6.70
PH&N U.S. Fund	9.7	13.5	7.1	13.7	88	93	6.28
PH&N U.S. Pooled Pension Fund	10.5	14.5	8.3	15.2	237	94	6.30
Pursuit American Fund	21.9	13.4	....	....	!	78	5.61
Royal Trust Adv Growth Fund	5.8	6.4	....	....	11	4	2.95
Royal Trust American Stock	1.8	11.8	6.6	10.3	59	59	5.13
Royal Trust European Growth	-11.8	-2.9	....	....	13	66	5.22

Fund	1yr	3yr	5yr	10yr	Assets	%	St.D.
Royal Trust Japanese Stock	-8.5	-6.7	2.0	....	11	99	7.48
Saxon World Growth	-5.3	5.0	6.3	....	4	86	5.78
Sceptre International Fund	-4.7	10.7	....	....	7	79	5.64
Scotia Amer Eqt Growth Fd	6.8	3.9	....	....	20	52	5.05
Spectrum Intl Equity Fund	-5.1	4.1	....	....	7	32	4.56
Talvest American Fund	-8.8	2.5	1.3	....	3	45	4.85
Talvest Global Diversified	-8.0	3.9	....	....	28	5	3.08
Templeton Growth Fund	-4.0	7.1	5.6	12.3	1006	44	4.83
Templeton Heritage Fd	-5.7	....	....	....	36	N/A	....
Trimark Fund	0.7	7.9	8.0	....	606	84	5.69
Trimark Select Growth Fd	0.0	....	....	....	203	N/A	....
Trust General International	-10.2	....	....	....	2	N/A	....
Trust General U.S. Equity	-0.3	9.5	4.2	....	10	85	5.71
Trust Pret Revenu American	3.1	9.2	3.1	9.1	3	57	5.12
United Accumulative Fund	8.4	12.1	6.0	11.7	244	36	4.62
United American Fund Ltd	12.6	11.3	3.9	11.0	14	47	4.97
United Global Fund	....	....	....	....	4	N/A	....
United Portfolio of Funds	9.8	....	....	....	12	N/A	....
United Venture Fund Ltd	-2.5	-2.5	-4.7	3.0	14	54	5.07
Universal American	0.0	6.0	5.9	12.2	47	61	5.16
Universal Global	2.2	5.2	4.2	....	54	35	4.59
Universal Pacific	-7.0	4.8	7.4	....	84	88	6.01
Universal Sector American	-1.3	5.0	....	....	13	18	4.04
Universal Sector Canadian	-6.5	-2.4	....	....	7	10	3.39
Universal Sector Global	2.3	4.9	....	....	13	15	3.84
Universal Sector Pacific	-7.0	4.6	....	....	18	39	4.73
Universal Sector Resource	-12.7	-8.7	....	....	1	17	4.03
Viking Commonwealth Fund	-1.7	6.2	7.0	12.6	176	12	3.45
Viking Growth Fund	-4.3	3.9	3.4	10.0	96	27	4.39
Viking International Fund	-4.8	4.6	3.7	10.4	110	33	4.57
HIGHEST IN GROUP	22.4	23.3	12.5	15.2			
LOWEST IN GROUP	-25.3	-11.1	-7.3	3.0			
AVERAGE IN GROUP	-1.6	5.1	4.3	10.2			

Bond And Mortgage Funds

Fund	1yr	3yr	5yr	10yr	Assets	%	St.D.
20/20 Income Fund	10.3	6.9	6.8	....	67	65	1.72
AGF Canadian Bond Fund	10.0	7.8	7.3	13.7	476	91	2.27
AGF Global Govt Bond*	4.4	6.0	....	....	38	100	3.13
Admax Canadian Income	10.3	....	....	....	2	N/A	....
All-Canadian Revenue Growth	9.6	9.3	8.7	10.8	1	1	0.36
Allied Income Fund	11.4	9.1	9.8	....	!	98	2.72
Altamira Bond Fund	11.7	9.0	....	....	5	39	1.41
Altamira Income Fund	14.9	11.3	10.4	12.8	33	47	1.50
BPI Canadian Bond Fund	9.4	7.1	....	....	9	52	1.60
BPI Global Income Fund*	1.0	0.5	....	....	!	28	1.25
Batirente-Section Obligations	12.8	8.6	....	....	9	81	1.91
Bissett Fiduciary Fund	14.4	9.5	....	....	2	72	1.83
Bolton Tremblay Bond	14.6	9.6	....	....	20	44	1.45
Bullock Bond Fund	12.7	7.3	6.4	7.9	!	69	1.79
CDA RSP Bond & Mortgage	14.1	10.3	9.4	13.2	28	56	1.63
CIBC Fixed Income Fund	12.8	8.8	....	....	38	53	1.60
CIBC Mortgage Income	17.1	11.1	9.9	12.0	213	19	1.01
Cda Life Fixed Income S-19	12.3	8.3	7.6	12.6	81	54	1.61
Cda Trust Income Investments	13.8	8.7	7.9	12.0	38	59	1.65
Cda Trust Inv Fund Income	8.2	7.3	7.1	12.3	7	90	2.15
Cda Trust RRSP Income	12.4	8.0	7.6	12.6	125	62	1.70
Cda Trust RRSP Mortgage	15.4	11.0	10.1	12.4	132	14	0.73
Central Guaranty Income	12.5	8.3	6.3	11.8	3	99	2.79
Central Guaranty Mortgage	14.2	9.6	9.0	11.3	5	22	1.09
Church Street Income	13.6	8.7	....	....	2	38	1.41
Concorde Hypotheques	....	....	....	....	!	N/A	....
Confed Mortgage Fund	14.5	11.0	10.0	12.6	4	5	0.48
Crown Life Pensions Bond Fund	13.0	9.2	7.8	10.6	75	57	1.63
Crown Life Pensions Mortgage	16.5	10.9	10.0	14.4	83	20	1.06
Dynamic Global Bond Fund	-0.7	2.3	....	....	9	96	2.55
Dynamic Income Fund	11.6	10.0	9.0	12.9	110	31	1.30
Dynamic Strip Bond Fund	....	....	....	....	6	N/A	....

Fund	1yr	3yr	5yr	10yr	Assets	%	St.D.
Elliot & Page Bond Fund	11.7	9.9	....	....	58	16	0.82
Empire Bond Fund #2	14.0	9.2	7.4	....	4	58	1.64
Empire Fixed Income Fund #4	15.6	10.2	9.1	....	25	33	1.33
Endurance Government Bond	13.8	....	....	....	31	N/A	....
Everest Bond Fund	12.0	9.3	....	....	42	60	1.69
Everest US Bond Fund*	-1.5	....	....	....	!	N/A	....
Fd Des Prof Du Que-Bonds	15.5	9.7	....	....	136	23	1.10
Fidelity Cap Conservation Fd	6.5	6.0	....	....	17	64	1.72
Finsco Bond Fund	11.4	7.4	7.0	....	10	46	1.50
First Canadian Bond Fund	13.6	8.1	....	....	24	55	1.61
First Canadian Mortgage Fund	19.2	11.9	10.8	13.1	659	11	0.67
First City Income Fund	13.1	10.4	....	....	16	93	2.41
Fonds Desjardins Hypotheques	14.8	10.8	10.1	12.8	107	4	0.46
Fonds Desjardins Obligations	13.9	8.5	7.6	12.6	31	86	2.02
Fonds Ficadre Obligations	12.3	....	....	....	1	N/A	....
Fonds SNF obligations	14.1	8.8	....	....	2	35	1.34
FuturLink Government Bond	11.4	7.6	....	....	39	88	2.07
FuturLink Mortgage Fund	15.0	....	....	....	31	N/A	....
GBC Canadian Bond	14.0	9.3	8.8	....	21	84	1.97
Global Strategy Income Fund	....	....	....	....	8	N/A	....
Global Strategy World Bond*	7.0	4.9	....	....	32	63	1.71
Great-West Life Bond Invest	13.3	7.8	7.3	11.5	293	74	1.83
Great-West Life Mortgage	13.3	9.1	8.4	11.8	311	24	1.14
Green Line Canadian Bond	12.2	7.3	....	....	24	78	1.87
Green Line Mortgage	16.2	11.5	10.5	12.5	105	27	1.24
Guardian Canada Bond Fund	11.4	10.8	....	....	24	2	0.40
Guardian Intl Income Fund	3.9	3.1	....	....	8	51	1.57
Guardian Vantage Bond	10.9	....	....	....	2	N/A	....
Gyro Bond	12.5	....	....	....	6	N/A	....
Hyperion Fixed Income	12.3	....	....	....	31	N/A	....
Industrial Bond Fund	12.6	....	....	....	946	N/A	....
Industrial Income Fund	8.8	6.5	8.9	13.9	234	89	2.07
InvesNAT Income Fund	14.1	....	....	....	6	N/A	....
Investors Bond Fund	13.3	9.3	8.3	12.5	1104	76	1.86
Investors Mortgage Fund	15.7	10.5	9.8	12.5	1613	10	0.64
Investors Pooled Bond	15.3	10.5	9.8	13.8	75	79	1.89
Investors Pooled Mortgage	16.8	11.8	10.8	13.5	170	8	0.60
Jones Heward Bond	12.4	8.7	....	....	4	30	1.27
Landmark Bond	12.9	....	....	....	71	N/A	....
London Life Bond Fund	5.2	7.1	6.2	13.4	196	97	2.66
London Life Mortgage Fund	16.4	10.8	10.1	14.6	115	7	0.60
Mackenzie Income Fund	9.6	7.0	9.3	13.7	324	87	2.05
Mackenzie Sentinel Cda Bond	12.3	7.8	7.5	....	23	92	2.34
Manulife 1 Bond	14.2	9.5	8.9	13.0	32	73	1.83
Manulife 2 Bond	13.4	8.7	8.1	12.2	32	75	1.84
Maritime Life Bond	13.4	....	....	....	28	N/A	....
McLean Budden Fixed Income	14.4	....	....	....	!	N/A	....
MetLife MVP Bond	12.3	9.0	....	....	3	26	1.21
Metropolitan Bond Fund	13.3	8.5	5.9	9.4	8	83	1.97
Montreal Trust Income Fund	13.2	8.5	8.0	12.6	15	67	1.73
Montreal Trust Mortgage Fund	14.5	10.7	9.8	12.1	11	15	0.79
Montreal Trust RRSP-Income	12.6	7.9	7.7	13.0	58	66	1.72
Montreal Trust RRSP-Mortgage	14.6	10.4	9.5	11.8	49	3	0.42
Mutual Bond Fund	....	....	....	....	4	N/A	....
NN Bond Fund	12.5	8.5	....	....	9	94	2.47
National Trust Income Fund	13.0	8.0	7.8	12.9	14	48	1.52
O.I.Q. Fonds d'Obligations	11.1	9.0	8.3	13.9	23	43	1.44
PH&N Bond Fund	14.2	10.1	9.9	14.5	177	60	1.69
Prudential Income Fund	12.5	9.0	8.7	12.6	45	42	1.44
Pursuit Income Fund	13.6	4.7	....	....	!	70	1.79
RoyFund Bond Fund	13.4	8.5	8.0	11.1	223	40	1.41
Royal Life Income Fund	10.0	....	....	....	7	N/A	....
Royal Trust Adv Income Fd	10.3	8.6	....	....	74	49	1.56
Royal Trust Bond Fund	13.6	8.7	7.9	13.0	409	80	1.89
Royal Trust Mortgage Fund	15.7	10.9	10.1	12.6	949	9	0.61
Sceptre Bond Fund	16.1	10.0	9.2	....	7	29	1.26
Scotia Defensive Income Fd	12.3	8.0	....	....	17	18	0.91
Scotia Income Fund	11.4	8.6	....	....	23	45	1.49

Fund	1yr	3yr	5yr	10yr	Assets	%	St.D.
Sovereign Capital Sec Bond	11.9	8.6	....	....	!	36	1.36
Spectrum Government Bond	10.7	....	....	....	21	N/A	....
Spectrum Interest Fund	12.1	8.5	....	....	159	41	1.44
St-Laurent Fonds d'Obligation	12.1	8.3	8.0	....	1	77	1.87
Standard Life Bond 2000	15.1	9.6	....	....	4	95	2.50
Strata Income Fund	14.0	....	....	....	4	N/A	....
Talvest Bond Fund	12.9	8.9	8.8	14.1	89	68	1.78
Talvest Income Fund	13.5	9.3	9.0	11.8	12	17	0.85
Templeton Global Income*	10.0	....	....	....	22	N/A	....
Templeton Heritage Bond	8.6	....	....	....	20	N/A	....
Top 50 T-Bill/Bond Fund	11.7	....	....	....	9	N/A	....
Tradex Security Fund	11.3	....	....	....	10	N/A	....
Trans-Canada Bond Fund	11.8	7.3	....	....	10	34	1.33
Trust General Bond Fund	13.6	8.5	7.6	13.2	59	85	2.00
Trust General Mortgage Fund	15.2	10.4	9.6	13.0	32	12	0.70
Trust La Laurentienne Obligati	10.6	8.3	8.2	....	1	37	1.39
Trust Pret Revenu Fonds H	15.9	10.9	10.2	12.6	68	6	0.51
Trust Pret Revenu Obligat	12.6	8.5	....	....	4	25	1.17
United Mortgage	14.7	9.1	8.5	10.8	3	13	0.72
United Security Fund	16.3	9.0	8.0	11.3	23	21	1.09
Universal Canadian Bond	12.0	8.7	9.0	14.3	85	82	1.96
Viking Income Fund	13.0	8.5	8.1	13.2	98	71	1.80
Waltaine Income Fund	9.7	7.8	....	....	9	32	1.31
HIGHEST IN GROUP	19.2	11.9	10.8	14.6			
LOWEST IN GROUP	-1.5	0.5	5.9	7.0			
AVERAGE IN GROUP	12.4	8.7	8.6	12.5			

Preferred Dividend Funds

Fund	1yr	3yr	5yr	10yr	Assets	%	St.D.
20/20 Dividend Fund	6.4	7.6	7.6	....	18	N/A	2.61
AGF High Income Fund	7.9	....	....	....	121	N/A	....
Allied Dividend Fund	-2.7	2.3	2.6	....	1	N/A	1.45
BPI High Yield Fund	2.6	3.6	....	....	2	N/A	2.72
Bolton Tremblay Income Fund	9.8	6.3	6.3	9.9	32	N/A	1.41
Bullock Dividend Fund	6.8	7.2	5.5	....	!	N/A	1.95
Dynamic Dividend Fund	7.2	6.4	7.2	....	9	N/A	1.23
FuturLink Income Fund	13.4	8.7	....	....	4	N/A	2.58
Guardian Pref Dividend Fund	5.7	5.2	5.6	....	7	N/A	1.17
Investors Dividend Fund	10.6	8.2	7.6	10.3	1210	N/A	1.85
Montreal Trust Dividend Fund	9.3	6.5	....	....	6	N/A	2.06
PH&N Dividend Income Fund	5.3	7.7	8.6	10.9	17	N/A	3.23
Prudential Dividend Fund	5.5	0.2	....	....	3	N/A	2.46
Royal Trust Pref Blue Chip	5.5	5.2	4.7	....	12	N/A	1.74
Spectrum Dividend Fund	8.9	7.8	....	....	29	N/A	1.70
Viking Dividend Fund Ltd	6.2	7.2	7.3	11.1	146	N/A	2.32
HIGHEST IN GROUP	13.4	8.7	8.6	11.1			
LOWEST IN GROUP	-2.7	0.2	2.6	9.9			
AVERAGE IN GROUP	6.8	6.0	6.3	10.6			

Money Market Funds

Fund	1yr	3yr	5yr	10yr	Assets	%	St.D.
20/20 Money Market	10.9	....	....	....	52	N/A	....
AGF Money Market Account	11.3	11.3	10.0	10.9	212	N/A	0.15
AGF U.S. Money Market*	....	....	....	....	4	N/A	....
Allied Money Fund	10.3	10.3	9.4	....	1	N/A	0.13
BPI Money Market Fund	10.9	10.6	....	....	7	N/A	0.15
Batirente-Section MMK	12.8	10.7	....	....	1	N/A	0.33
Bolton Tremblay Money Fund	11.5	11.4	10.2	....	134	N/A	0.14
Bullock Money Market Fund	10.2	10.5	....	....	!	N/A	0.09
CDA Money Market Fund	11.8	11.5	10.0	10.8	24	N/A	0.22
CIBC Canadian T-Bill	....	....	....	....	208	N/A	....
CIBC Money Market Fund	11.2	....	....	....	1215	N/A	....
CIBC Premium T-Bill	....	....	....	....	380	N/A	....
Capstone Cash Management	11.9	11.4	....	....	5	N/A	0.23
Cda Life Money Market S-29	11.7	10.8	9.1	10.2	130	N/A	0.22
Church Street Money Fund	11.4	10.8	....	....	2	N/A	0.12
Crown Life Pen Short Term	11.8	11.2	10.1	10.8	16	N/A	0.22
Dynamic Money Market Fund	12.2	10.9	9.6	....	107	N/A	0.17

Fund	1yr	3yr	5yr	10yr	Assets	%	St.D.
Elliott & Page Money Fund	12.4	11.9	10.6	....	181	N/A	0.20
Empire Money Market Fund #7	11.6	....	....	....	5	N/A	....
Everest Money Market Fund	11.8	12.0	....	....	89	N/A	0.21
F.M.O.Q. Monetaire	11.3	....	....	....	3	N/A	....
Fd Des Prof Du Que-Money Mkt	12.8	10.8	....	....	11	N/A	0.23
Fidelity Short-Term Asset	....	....	....	....	11	N/A	....
Finsco Cdn Money Mkt	11.3	11.1	9.9	....	52	N/A	0.15
Finsco Cdn T-Bill Fund	10.8	10.9	....	....	259	N/A	0.12
Finsco U.S. Dollar MMK*	6.5	7.2	....	....	30	N/A	0.07
First Canadian Money Market	11.0	10.4	....	....	411	N/A	0.11
First City Govt Money	11.5	....	....	....	164	N/A	....
Fonds Desjardins Marche Moneta	10.9	....	....	....	9	N/A	....
Fonds Ficadre Monetaire	9.6	10.3	9.1	....	!	N/A	1.01
Fonds SNF Monetaire	....	....	....	....	3	N/A	....
FuturLink Money Market	11.3	....	....	....	325	N/A	....
GBC Money Market Fund	11.6	....	....	....	4	N/A	....
Global Strategy T-Bill Savings	9.6	10.2	....	....	2	N/A	0.20
Global Strategy US Money*	5.7	6.7	....	....	3	N/A	0.14
Global Strategy World Money	5.9	7.0	....	....	13	N/A	1.37
Great-West Life Money Market	10.9	10.9	9.5	10.4	175	N/A	0.19
Green Line Cdn Money Mkt	11.9	11.7	....	....	219	N/A	0.12
Green Line U.S. Money Mkt	6.6	....	....	....	23	N/A	....
Guardian Short Term Money Fund	11.8	11.9	10.4	11.0	26	N/A	0.21
Guardian US Money Market*	6.7	7.9	....	....	9	N/A	0.11
Hongkong Bank Money Mkt	10.7	....	....	....	4	N/A	....
Imperial Growth MMK Fund	10.9	....	....	....	7	N/A	....
Industrial Cash Management Fd	11.5	11.6	10.1	....	213	N/A	0.17
Industrial Short-Term	....	....	....	....	34	N/A	....
InvesNAT Money Market	....	....	....	....	105	N/A	....
InvesNAT T-Bill	....	....	....	....	131	N/A	....
Investors Money Market Fund	11.1	10.9	9.7	....	383	N/A	0.15
Landmark Short Term Interest	9.5	....	....	....	11	N/A	....
London Life Money Market	11.6	....	....	....	6	N/A	....
MD Money Fund	11.4	10.7	9.4	10.4	245	N/A	0.20
Mackenzie Sentinel Cda MMK	11.6	10.6	....	....	7	N/A	0.17
Manulife 1 Short Term	11.6	11.2	9.8	....	45	N/A	0.23
Manulife 2 Short Term	10.7	10.4	9.0	....	45	N/A	0.23
Maritime Life Money Market	10.6	10.4	9.1	....	49	N/A	1.01
McLean Budden MMK Fund	11.1	....	....	....	!	N/A	....
Metropolitan Protection	10.2	9.3	....	....	5	N/A	0.78
Montreal Trust Money Market	11.3	11.2	....	....	44	N/A	0.86
Montreal Trust RRSP-MMK	11.5	11.1	....	....	44	N/A	0.14
Mutual Money Market Fund	10.7	10.6	9.3	....	99	N/A	0.16
National Trust Money Mkt	....	....	....	....	22	N/A	....
O.I.Q. Fonds Monetaire	11.9	11.2	10.0	11.1	19	N/A	0.19
PH&N Money Market Fund	11.7	11.6	....	....	184	N/A	0.17
Prudential Money Market Fund	11.9	11.3	....	....	52	N/A	0.14
Pursuit Money Market Fund	11.4	10.5	....	....	!	N/A	0.51
RoyFund Cdn T-Bill	....	....	....	....	200	N/A	....
RoyFund Money Market Fd	11.4	11.2	....	....	516	N/A	0.17
RoyFund U.S. Money Market	....	....	....	....	39	N/A	....
Royal Trust Cdn Money Mkt	11.4	10.8	....	....	1287	N/A	0.12
Royal Trust US Money Mkt*	....	....	....	....	114	N/A	....
Sceptre Money Market Fund	11.5	11.2	....	....	7	N/A	0.14
Scotia Money Market	....	....	....	....	180	N/A	....
Spectrum Cash Reserve Fund	11.4	11.3	....	....	252	N/A	0.15
Spectrum Savings Fund*	11.5	11.6	....	....	52	N/A	0.15
St-Laurent Fonds d'Epargne	13.2	10.9	10.0	....	!	N/A	0.45
Strata Money Market Fd	10.7	....	....	....	23	N/A	....
Talvest Money Fund	12.0	11.7	9.5	....	15	N/A	0.38
Templeton Treasury Bill	11.6	11.4	....	....	16	N/A	0.13
Trans-Cda Money Market Fd	11.2	7.9	6.9	....	1	N/A	0.34
Trimark Interest Fund	11.5	11.3	....	....	68	N/A	0.16
Trust General Money Market	12.1	10.3	....	....	12	N/A	0.42
Trust Pret Revenu Money Mkt	11.4	....	....	....	12	N/A	....
United Cdn Money Market Fund	11.5	12.0	....	....	44	N/A	0.12
United US$ Money Market*	4.6	6.8	....	....	1	N/A	0.19
Universal Money Market	....	....	....	....	15	N/A	....

Fund	1yr	3yr	5yr	10yr	Assets	%	St.D.
Universal Sector Currency*	6.8	6.3	....	....	3	N/A	0.28
Viking Money Market Fund	11.1	11.2	10.1	....	55	N/A	0.14
Waltaine Instant MMF	11.6	11.4	....	....	100	N/A	0.13
HIGHEST IN GROUP	13.2	12.0	10.6	11.1			
LOWEST IN GROUP	4.6	6.3	6.9	10.2			
AVERAGE IN GROUP	10.8	10.6	9.6	10.7			

Market Indexes

	1yr	3yr	5yr	10yr
91 Day Canada T Bill	10.9	11.6	10.3	10.8
Consumer Price Index	6.1	5.2	4.8	5.4
ScotiaMcLeod Universe Bond Ind	15.3	10.0	9.4	14.5
Standard & Poor's 500 Index	3.7	11.3	7.1	14.6
TSE Total Return Index	1.9	4.1	5.9	7.8

Index